AMERICAN INDIAN FOOD

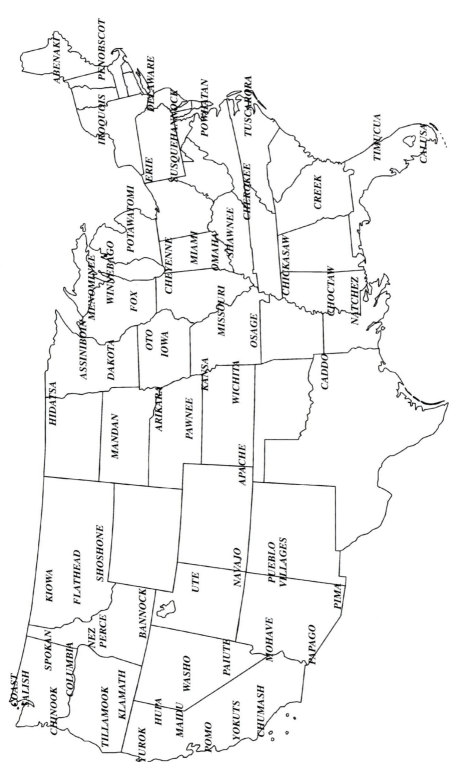

Locations of major tribes in AD 1500, before any significant European contact.

AMERICAN INDIAN FOOD

LINDA MURRAY BERZOK

Food in American History

Greenwood Press
Westport, Connecticut • London

Library of Congress Cataloging-in-Publication Data

Berzok, Linda Murray.
    American Indian food / Linda Murray Berzok.
        p.   cm.—(Food in American history, ISSN 1552-8200)
    Includes bibliographical references and index.
    ISBN 0-313-32989-3 (alk. paper)
    1. Indians of North America—Food.   2. Indians of North America—Eth-
nobotany.   3. Food habits—North America.   4. Plants, Cultivated—North
America.   5. Plants, Useful—North America.   I. Title.   II. Series.
E98.F7B47   2005
394.1'2'08997—dc22   2004027858

British Library Cataloguing in Publication Data is available.

Library of Congress Catalog Card Number: 2004027858
ISBN: 0-313-32989-3
ISSN: 1552-8200

First published in 2005

Greenwood Press, 88 Post Road West, Westport, CT 06881
An imprint of Greenwood Publishing Group, Inc.
www.greenwood.com

Printed in the United States of America

The paper used in this book complies with the
Permanent Paper Standard issued by the National
Information Standards Organization (Z39.48–1984).

10 9 8 7 6 5 4 3 2 1

The publisher has done its best to make sure the instructions and/or recipes in
this book are correct. However, users should apply judgment and experience when
preparing recipes, especially parents and teachers working with young people. The
publisher accepts no responsibility for the outcome of any recipe included in this
volume.

For Bob, husband and best friend,
whose patience, love, support and editorial wisdom
have made this book possible.

CONTENTS

SERIES FOREWORD

This series focuses on food culture as a way to illuminate the societal mores and daily life of Americans throughout our history. These volumes are meant to complement history studies at the high school level on up. In addition, Food Studies is a burgeoning field, and food enthusiasts and food scholars will find much to mine here. The series is comprehensive, with the first volume covering American Indian food and the following volumes each covering an era or eras from Colonial times until today. Regional and group differences are discussed as appropriate.

Each volume is written by a food historian who is an expert on the period. Each volume contains the following:

- Chronology of food-related dates
- Narrative chapters, including
  Introduction (brief overview of period as it relates to food)
  Foodstuffs (staples, agricultural developments, etc.)
  Food Preparation
  Eating Habits (manners, customs, mealtimes, special occasions)
  Concepts of Diet and Nutrition (including religious strictures)
- Recipes
- Period illustrations
- Glossary, if needed
- Bibliography
- Index

PREFACE

Many histories of America are written as if nothing noteworthy happened before the Europeans arrived. Yet North America had existed for thousands of years before 1492, home to hundreds of indigenous cultures. Far from representing a golden beginning, Christopher Columbus' arrival was simply a moment in a long history.

The second misconception that many historians perpetuate is that American Indian ways are relegated to the past. Today, many tribes are hand-harvesting wild rice just as their ancestors had done for thousands of years, making mesquite pudding and baking the sacred blue maize *piki* bread.

I have long been interested in ethnic food, those dishes with distinct cultural markers that come to symbolize specific cultural identities. American Indian food qualifies. Participating in the consumption of daily meals usually served from a communal pot is a process that validates group membership. These are the foods of communities with common social roots. Ethnic foods are most vibrant for their signature flavors and dishes and for the way in which they perpetuate a culture when people no longer live in their homeland. Taste bonds members together, reminds them of home and draws forth deep memories. Most important, ethnic foods survive.

In the case of the American Indians, these foodways have survived the unthinkable—the willful decimation of the native culture by a dominant force with more manpower, horses and guns and, most galling, a conviction of superiority. That there is anything left of Indian foodways is nothing short of a miracle and testament to the power of embedded cultural memory and its transmission.

Native American food holds a unique position in the culinary lexicon as the oldest gastronomy in North America. It is characterized by abundance and variety. Wild plants, fish, meat and cultivated crops were freshly caught, gathered or harvested, and prepared simply. Much was eaten raw, although some was dried or smoked and preserved for the lean winters. Except for trading, American Indians ate only those foods grown, fished or gathered within a relatively small radius of their homes. The cultivation of maize made it possible for the tribes to adopt a less nomadic lifestyle. Settling down to grow crops made for food of place—salmon from the Northwest Coast, blue maize raised by the Hopi in the Southwest, wild rice in Minnesota, black tea made from the yaupon holly bush in the Southeast and clams and mussels from the New England Coast.

To the Indians, the land was sacred; every plant, animal, fish, tree, mountain and river housed a spirit to be revered. This generated an intimate relationship between people and their food sources. Dependence on nature for subsistence gave rise to a rich spiritual tradition with rituals and feasts marking planting and harvesting seasons. The Indians' daily lives revolved around giving thanks for harvests and hunting success and praying for more in the future. First foods celebrations—the ceremonial welcoming of the first ripened fruits and vegetables and caught fish and animals of the season—were almost universal among the tribes.

Over thousands of years, Native Americans evolved their foodways, working out various ways to combine foods, unique processing and preparation methods and effective preservation and storage techniques. Was it cuisine? That depends on definition. The term has been applied on a regional basis, meaning the use of distinct local ingredients that can only be found in a particular place with both geographic and social borders. Beyond that, the cooking methods themselves must also be specific to that locale, and the population must customarily eat the food every day at every meal. The ingredients, methods and formulas must be used on a regular basis to produce both everyday and festival foods. The food represents a creative synthesis of local ingredients, dishes and cooking methods with its own staples. The fare of the Northwest Coast tribes bore little resemblance to that of the Southwest, for example. One region was as different from another as Italian cuisine is from French.

The European invasion of North America forced a radical transformation of American Indian food habits. Foodways were one of the first layers of culture attacked by the invaders. The new arrivals wanted to set strong cultural boundaries between themselves and the Indians. European conviction of superiority over the "savages" (characterized as stupid, lazy and unenlightened), plus the newcomers' desire to re-create their homeland, led them to force the Indians to cultivate European crops such as wheat and grapes, often as slaves. The Europeans did not appreciate the bounty of the new land. Unfamiliar food of a different culture is often considered dangerous, literally so because it might be toxic or poisonous and figuratively because it symbolizes a threat to the social order. For example, in the 1400s the English considered rich French food and wine dangerous because they represented a Catholic culture quite the opposite of English Protestantism. Imagine then the threat posed to Europeans by Native American food.

To gain a sense of the cultural decimation of American Indian culture that took place after the Europeans arrived, suppose that England, Spain, the Netherlands and France had been invaded in the 1500s by a different race of people from an unknown land. Victory came easily to the invaders due to their greater numbers and more advanced technology. To gain a foothold in these vanquished countries, the invaders forced the inhabitants to grow maize, an alien plant, and then insisted they make it into bread baked on an unfamiliar implement, a flat griddle. Furthermore, the invaders required the defeated Europeans to worship maize; perform planting rituals, songs and dances; and celebrate the earliest ripened corn of the season with a Green Corn Feast. Shamans were assigned to convert subjects to the new state religion. Christianity was outlawed.

It is hard to overestimate the impact of European contact on Native American cultures; it was characterized by war, separation of families, arbitrary relocation of tribes from ancestral homelands to totally different environments, religious conversion, introduction of new methods of farming (including livestock and crops) and, of course, a new religion. This policy did not, of course, end when the colonists gained independence from England nor when they formed a new entity, the United States of America. When the federal government decided to evict the tribes of the Southeast in 1830, the Cherokee, who were prospering then as farmers in Georgia, not only refused to move, they also sued in the courts. Although the U.S. Supreme Court backed up the Cherokee, President Andrew Jackson ignored the decision, ordered their crops burned and marched the Cherokee to Oklahoma that winter at gunpoint in the infamous Trail of Tears. Four thousand of the twenty thousand died in the forced march.

Given the crushing power of the European colonizers and the U.S. government against Native Americans, it is all the more remarkable that any semblance of original ethnic food exists today. Some early American cookbooks feature a number of recipes based on Indian formulas, and at least one volume was devoted entirely to maize. Many dishes we still eat today were derived from Native American cooking, including cornbread, clam chowder, New England clambake, succotash, Southern corn pone, hush puppies and grits, western barbecue, hoe cakes and Johnny cake. In the twentieth century efforts were made by a number of scholars to appreciate and understand the cooking and preservation methods developed by the Indians. Native American communities are taking renewed pride in their ethnicity and celebrating their roots through ceremonies, plantings and food. This is the true culinary heritage of America, and it is to these first peoples and first foods that this book is dedicated.

SEMANTICS

Native American or American Indian?

When Columbus landed on a Caribbean island thinking he had arrived in India, he made the colossal blunder of calling the people "Indios." The name stuck. The Spanish created a Council of the Indies to govern the area and the term "Indian" was later adopted by all Europeans. "Indian" is widely used in historical writing and throughout federal Indian law as well as preferred by some tribal members, particularly those in the Southwest.

However, during the 1970s, activists and others considered "Indian" not only inaccurate but derogatory. The term Native American was widely substituted as the politically correct version. It is also flawed. There was no America before the arrival of non-Indians (Europeans), and even then not for about 300 years, so there certainly could not be any natives. Other proposed terms like Amerindians, First Nations Peoples and Indigenous Cultures have never gained wide acceptance.

In recent years, many governmental, cultural and scientific institutions and, most important, tribal peoples themselves, have reverted to American Indian, recognizing its European origins and inaccuracy.

The Smithsonian Institution's National Museum of the American Indian on the Mall in Washington, D.C., opened in September 2004 with the cooperation and support of many tribal people. The *American Indian Culture and Research Journal* at the American Indian Studies Center at the University of California at Los Angeles (one of many American Indian studies programs around the country) is both edited and staffed by American Indians. Those tribes who are comfortable with their cultural identities, specifically most of those in the Southwest, have no objection to "Indian," although they prefer to be known by tribal names such as Navajo, Hopi and Tohono O'odham. On the other hand, the Wampanoag staff at Plimoth Plantation, Plymouth, Massachusetts, prefer to be known as "native peoples" or "First Peoples." I have given "Indian" priority in my writing and used "Native American" for stylistic variety.

Blackfoot or Blackfeet?

Another semantic issue when writing about American Indians is whether tribal names should appear in plural or singular—Pimas or Pima, Navajos or Navajo, and so on. The Smithsonian Institution's classic volume, *Handbook of North American Indians*, is inconsistent on this matter. Because either singular or plural is correct, I have selected singular for simplicity's sake. Besides, as an anthropologist friend pointed out, what is the plural of Blackfoot—Blackfoots or Blackfeet?

Gathering-Hunting

In many contemporary sources, food strategies of the nomadic Indians are described as hunting-gathering, giving primary importance to the tracking and killing of game animals, a male activity. Actually, it was the gathering of wild plants, shellfish, seeds, berries and related foodstuffs—a female activity—that secured most of the calories in the diet. Therefore, I have used "gatherer-hunter" as the term throughout.

Maize and Bison

Maize, the ultimate staple of the Indians, was called by English colonists "Indian corn," "Indian wheat" and "Turkey wheat." Finally, it became simply "corn," a generic English term for any kind of grain or kernel, like wheat, barley and rye. It is the word we use in the

United States today, but everywhere else in the world, with the exception of Britain, the name is some variant of "maize." I have used maize as the preferred term.

Similarly, the wild ox was misnamed "buffalo" by the Europeans, whereas it is properly not a buffalo at all, but a bison. Not only was this the major food animal for tribes that lived between the Mississippi River and Rocky Mountains, it also became the focus of their entire culture. They worshipped the animal, wore its skins and head, and sometimes even ate out of its skull. Aside from quotations from European sources, I have used bison throughout.

Time Period

Most of this book is concerned with the distant past, the time period formerly referred to as "prehistory" or "preliterate," meaning the time before writing is known to have existed. This period is also referred to as pre-Columbian or pre-contact. All of these terms are Eurocentric. The Indians belonged to oral cultures in which information was imprinted on the young by elders through the spoken tradition of myths, stories and legends. For generations, chiefs, elders and (especially where food was concerned) women served as tribal historians, committing to memory a whole body of past experience and traditions. This included which wild plants were edible, where to gather them, how to prepare and preserve them, how to plant maize and guard the fields from predators, how to hunt and fish and how to store food. This folk memory provided the Indians their history.

It is not true, however, that these cultures did not leave readable records. The tribes of the Northern Plains as far back as the 1600s kept what are called "winter counts"—generally tribal histories of catastrophic events like wars and epidemics painted in pictographs and arranged chronologically on bison skin. Each document represented a year's time or a "winter." The count was the responsibility of the band historian, a position passed down from father to son. The Sioux carried notched sticks to commemorate events. The ancient Anasazi of the Southwest left records in the form of petroglyphs scraped into rock and pictographs painted on rock. Most of the images were representational and although scholars disagree on the meaning of these symbols, it is clear that they were an early attempt at "writing." Most tribes also left unintentional archaeological records—human skeletal remains, artifacts including cooking vessels and implements, seeds and jewelry, among other things.

Considering that the term "prehistory" is inaccurate and judgmental, I have placed it in quotes. Similarly, the term "contact" does not seem to reflect reality. It sounds too benign to describe what actually occurred. Therefore, I have referred to this singular event as the Invasion.

HOW DO WE KNOW WHAT THEY ATE?

Anthropologists and ethnologists rely on artifacts, archaeological remains, linguistic and biological evidence plus tribal folklore for information on past foodways. Archaeological excavation has yielded remains in storage pits, refuse, charred faunal and floral remains floated out of soils, seeds stored in baskets and pottery jars, pollen, human and animal skeletons (human bones and teeth give information about diet and cause of death), artifacts such as cooking vessels and utensils, and coprolites (fossilized human feces that can be analyzed for dietary information). This data can be used to confirm or deny historical accounts.

THE FIRST WRITTEN SOURCES

Once the Europeans arrived in North America, they began to keep multiple written records, some of which described Indian culture and food. Traders, explorers, missionaries, artists, ethnologists, pioneers, botanists, captives and adoptees of Indian tribes and political appointees all penned impressions of the people they found. Far from being objective, they were slanted and self-serving, with specific political and social agendas. These were people who, for the most part, looked down on Indians and their habits, believing them to be savage heathens in need of enlightenment. Many things were attributed wrongly to the Indians or mistranslated intentionally for political reasons.

One general source of bias was the fact that the vast majority of these early European accounts were written by men whose primary interest was reporting male activities such as hunting, fishing and war, not foodways. Often, the reporters were sizing up the economic possibilities of the Indian cultures for their sponsors in the Old World. Their disdain might be boldly stated. These observers were likely to describe the Indians as savages who worshipped the devil and ate human flesh (the Europeans were not above using these tracts to attack each other; the Spanish blamed the French for introducing alcohol and vice versa). In these accounts, Indians were given little credit for industriousness and were criticized for eating huge amounts of food and whiling away their between-meal time napping. Much later, between 1804 and 1806, explorers Meriwether Lewis and William Clark were specifically mandated by President Thomas Jefferson to explore the whole of the Louisiana Purchase and bring back information on Indian foodways. This was the exception.

Male writers generally overlooked the primary dietary importance of wild plant gathering, crop cultivation and food preparation—all female activities. Most important, it was women who were the keepers of the culture, transmitting foodways to the next generation.

We are fortunate to have a few references written by women. Mary Jemison's 1755 account of her captivity and later adoption and marriage into the Seneca tribe[1] and Buffalo Bird Woman's 1917 "autobiography,"[2] the best account we have of Hidatsa (Missouri) agriculture, were ironically both recorded by men. Jemison made an interesting observation about the contrast between the burdens of the role of women in her colonial society compared with that in the tribe, concluding that Seneca women had it better. She was not eager to be "rescued."

THE LANGUAGE

Around 1500, there were 600 Native American tribes living in North America, speaking a richness of some 500 languages. None of these were written; they were simply spoken. The Cherokee were the first tribe to develop a written language in 1910 and eventually published their own newspaper. Although they had existed without writing for thousands of years, they quickly became literate. Indian languages were not allowed to be spoken during the boarding school era in the 1800s. Yet, during World War II, members of eighteen tribes played a crucial communications role, speaking their native tongues in what proved to be unbreakable codes.

Many of the earliest English accounts were written in an early form of English that is confusing in its syntax, often substituting "f" for "s" as well as other early spellings. For example, English traveler John Josselyn wrote, "The Natives draw an Oyl, taking the rotteneft Maple Wood, which being burnt to athes, they make a ftrong Lye therewith wherein they boyl their white Oak-Acorns until the Oyl fwim on the top in great quantity; this they fleet off, and put into bladders . . . they eat it likewife with their Meat, it is an excellent clear and fweet Oyl."[3] I have let these quotations stand because with some effort they can be comprehended.

Nineteenth-century American explorers Lewis and Clark were a different case entirely. They wrote their journals with pencil at night by candlelight in their tents after hard, long days, and they were either terrible spellers or simply exhausted, or both. They wrote, for example, that "of the root of this plant the Indians prepare an agreable dish," and also "dryed by being expose to the sun and air or at other times with a slow fire or smoke of the chimnies, it shrinks much in drying."[4] I have also left these quotations alone.

PHOTOGRAPHS

Most of the photographs used in this book are taken from a collection by photographer Edward Curtis that resides in the Library of Congress. In 1900, he began to fear the disappearance of Indian culture and began recording tribal ceremonies. "The passing of every old man or woman means the passing of some tradition," he wrote, "consequently the information that is to be gathered, for the benefit of future generations, respecting the mode of life of one of the great races of mankind, must be collected at once or the opportunity will be lost for all time."[5] His first volume, *The North American Indian*, appeared in 1907, and the twentieth and final in 1930. Although his heart was in the right place, Curtis did not simply record what was happening on reservations at the time, which was that Indians were cooking with government rations and wearing contemporary clothing. In order to portray traditional customs and dress, he removed modern clothes and other signs of early 1900s life from his pictures. Although this was accepted practice for many anthropologists of the time, Curtis has been criticized for his manipulation of reality. However, his collection represents the only comprehensive pictographic attempt to portray Indian life.

A WORD ABOUT INDIAN "RECIPES"

Quite simply, there are no original "recipes." The closest thing are those formulas handed down from one tribal generation to the next and stored in memory. There are some approximations but nothing in writing until the European arrival. As any anthropologist knows, by the time the Europeans/Americans recorded Indian "recipes," the Native culture had already been tainted or irretrievably changed. Some tribes were forced to change climate zones over a few hundred years and lost many memories of recipes as well as ingredients. Settled groups like the Eastern Pueblo, Hopi and Zuni of the Southwest are said by anthropologists to have retained more original formulas because they were not removed from ancestral lands.

Among recipes claiming to be American Indian, it is important to distinguish among three types:

Historical/traditional. Those recipes that cannot readily be duplicated today, such as squirrel soup or blue maize *piki* bread, which requires many years of practiced skill.

Indian-inspired or originated recipes with accommodations to modern ingredients, measurements and techniques. These are closer to original but blueberries may be substituted for salal berries, mixing may include an electric mixer and measurements may be given in terms of cups and spoons.

Modern recipes loosely based on Indian ingredients. These are the least historically accurate. If you read about Navajo lamb ravioli or blue corn bread pudding with mango, you are not in Indian territory at all. At the very least, you are post-European because the Indians had no lamb or mango. These recipes have become seriously Americanized.

In this book, I have used formulas handed down from one generation to another that were then recorded by European colonists, and those recipes later published by contemporary Indians.

NOTES

1. James E. Seaver, *A Narrative of the Life of Mrs. Mary Jemison* (Howden, UK: Printed for R. Parkin, 1826), 48.

2. Gilbert L. Wilson, *Buffalo Bird Woman's Garden: Agriculture of the Hidatsa Indians, an Indian Interpretation* (Minneapolis: Bulletin of the University of Minnesota, 1917), 42.

3. John Josselyn, *New-England's Rarities Discovered* (London: Printed for Giles Widdows at the Green Dragon in St. Paul's Church-yard, 1672), 49.

4. Meriwether Lewis and William Clark, *The Journals of the Lewis and Clark Expedition*, ed. Gary E. Moulton, 13 vols. (Lincoln: University of Nebraska Press, 1983–2001), 2:221.

5. Pedro Ponce, "The Imperfect Eye of Edward Curtis," http://www.neh.gov/news/humanities/2000-05/curtis.html.

ACKNOWLEDGMENTS

Many people have supported me during the research and writing of this book. I thank and acknowledge them all.

To colleagues Ken Albala, Andy Smith and friend and colleague Madge Griswold for their support and advice. I would also like to thank friend and ethnologist Bernard "Bunny" Fontana, formerly with the Arizona State Museum and retired field historian of the University of Arizona Library, for answering my questions, often forwarding references and quotes. All I can say is, what a guy!

There must be a corner in heaven for research librarians. For top haloes, I nominate anthropologist Gregory A. Finnegan, Associate Librarian for Public Services and Head of Reference, Tozzer Library, Harvard University, Cambridge, Massachusetts, and Robert L. Volz, Custodian of the Chapin Rare Book Library at Williams College, Williamstown, Massachusetts. They both gave generously of their time and had great enthusiasm for my project. I am also grateful to Sara Heitshu, reference librarian for the American Indian Studies Program at the University of Arizona; Rebecca Ohm of Sawyer Library at Williams College; and the staffs of the American Indian research collection at Huntington Free Library and Reading Room, Bronx, New York, the Museum of the American Indian, New York City, and the State University of New York at Albany Library. Also deserving of thanks are the wonderfully collegial members of the listserv of the Association for the Study of Food and Society (ASFS), especially Barry Brenton who supplied research material on alkali processing.

To The Culinary Trust (formerly the International Association of

Culinary Professionals Foundation), I am thankful for a Linda D. Russo Travel Grant Award, which made it possible for me to conduct research at Tozzer Library, Harvard; the Museum of the American Indian in New York City and the Huntington Free Library, Bronx, New York.

To my editor, Wendi Schnaufer, Senior Acquisitions Editor at Greenwood Publishing for direction, clarity and support.

One of the best decisions I ever made was to enter the master's program in food studies at New York University's Department of Nutrition, Food and Food Management. Quite simply, I felt like I had come home. For their pioneering efforts in making Food Studies a field of academic inquiry, and for their personal strong support, I will be forever grateful to my advisor, doctoral candidate and director of the Food Studies and Food Management Program, Jennifer Schiff Berg; former department chair Marion Nestle, currently Paulette Goddard Professor of Nutrition, Food Studies and Public Health, New York University and Associate Professor Amy Bentley. Also, to Adjunct Margaret Happel whose wonderful continuing education course clinched my decision to enter the program.

Finally, to Doris Pierson and Billy Rulten, wherever you are.

CHRONOLOGY

18,000– 13,000 BC	Ancient ancestors of American Indians migrate to North America from Asia over the Bering Land Bridge in pursuit of large game animals, including mammoth and mastodon.
11,500 BC	Ice covers most of North America.
10,500 BC	After the Ice Age ends, vegetation appears and descendants of original immigrants migrate over four colonization routes: through the Great Plains south to the Gulf of Mexico; to the Northwest Coast; the Northeast of North America; and down Rocky Mountains into the Southwest, Mexico and Central America.
7000 BC	Some tribes begin domesticating edible seed-producing plants including sunflower, sumpweed, chenopod, knotweed, pigweed, giant ragweed and maygrass.
4500 BC	Huge game animals like mammoth and mastodon become extinct, forcing tribes to look elsewhere for food.
3500 BC	First archaeological evidence of maize in North America from Bat Cave, New Mexico. Its cultivation marks the first cultural transformation of Indian foodways.
2300– 2000 BC	Plant domestication begins in the Southeast.
100 BC	Oldest archaeological evidence of maize from the Northeast Woodlands.

AD 400–700 Beans and squash domesticated in the Southwest.

700   Pueblo Hopi and Zuni cultures in the Southwest initiate intensive cultivation of maize—one of the world's great agricultural revolutions.

1300   Agriculture is well developed among east coast tribes but a severe twenty-three-year drought brings agriculture in the Southwest to a temporary standstill.

1492   Italian explorer Christopher Columbus lands on a Caribbean island and names the indigenous people "Indios" in the belief he has landed in India.

1493   Columbus on second voyage brings horses, sugar and other foods to the island of Hispaniola in the Caribbean.

1500   Maize established as nutritive core of the Native American diet for agricultural tribes, supplemented by squash and beans.

Early 1500s Initial contact between Native Americans and Europeans. Population of Native Americans has consolidated into six geographic cultures, each with its own food staples and traditions.

1513   Spanish expedition lands on coast of Florida, pillaging Indian food stores and burning villages.

1521   Spanish cattle from Mexico migrate northward into the Southwest, where they are captured and raised by Indians. Beef will eventually mean a huge increase in animal protein for Native Americans.

1530   European diseases dramatically reduce the Native American population, decreasing the amount of food they need but leaving fewer and less hardy people to produce it. Introduction of European alcohol undermines Native traditions and weakens social organization.

1540   Spanish conquistador Francisco Vasquez de Coronado and party arrive at cornfields of the Zuni demanding food and eventually conquering eighty pueblos (villages).

1540s   The Spanish force the Navajo, nomadic gatherer-hunters, to farm European crops, completely transforming their diet and way of life. The Navajo will eventually become sheepherders.

The Comanche and Apache of the Southwest acquire horses from Spanish expeditions, enabling them to re-rank bison from a suboptimal food source to a highly desirable staple.

The Spanish introduce sheep, goats, pigs, wheat, peaches, guns and the adobe oven, a major technological step forward in the history of Indian baking, to the Indians of New Mexico.

1600s   Period of war between Native Americans and colonists on the east coast disrupts native hunting territories and Indian planting grounds. Native Americans forced to migrate and adapt to new foods in new territories.

British and French colonists introduce east coast Native Americans to brass and copper kettles, guns and metal traps for hunting and new foods including cows, chickens and eggs. Metal cooking vessels make it possible to cook for a crowd and boil sap into maple sugar. The iron hoe will eventually replace the digging stick.

1620   Pilgrims appropriate the Wampanoag Indian village of Patuxet in Massachusetts, taking over cleared fields and corn bins and robbing storehouses of food.

1625   Abenaki tribe of Maine begins to trade furs to Pilgrims in return for surplus maize, which eventually leads the tribe to give up gathering-hunting lifestyle for settled horticulture.

1630s   Dutch settle New Amsterdam (Manhattan) and allow their livestock to roam, trampling Indian fields and destroying crops. By 1664, the Dutch have wiped out the Algonquin tribe there.

1680   The Pueblo Revolt: The Pueblos in the Southwest unite to drive out the Spanish, the only successful Native American uprising against the Europeans. In the process, the Indians burn every Spanish imported food and, for the first time, the Pueblos share agricultural knowledge and skills.

1700–1780   Horses stolen from the Spanish revolutionize the culture of the Plains Indians. Many formerly sedentary farmers leave villages and become nomads, hunting bison on horseback. Plateau Indians acquire horses from Plains Indians. This marks the end of agriculture for both cultures.

1769–1834   Spanish force California tribes of gatherer-hunters to relocate near missions and cultivate farms and herd animals.

1780   Indians on the Northwest Coast begin trading their furs to the Europeans in return for food.

1800s   United States forces Indians to accept reservations and commitment to farming and European agriculture—which stresses mastery of nature, rather than harmony—in return for guarantees of food, land and water. Government food rations consist of beans, beef or bacon, flour, coffee and sugar, setting in course a dramatic, deleterious dietary change.

1830–1840   Federal Indian Removal Act evicts 60,000 Native Americans east of the Mississippi River to Oklahoma, compelling them to develop totally new foodways. The Chickasaw, Cherokee, Cree, Choctaw and Seminole will become known as the Five Civilized Tribes for adopting "civilization," including European agricultural methods.

1860s   Frontiersman Kit Carson forces Navajo to surrender by destroying their sheep and crops, including peach orchards, obliging them to forego nomadic lifestyle and devote themselves to farming.

1860s–1870s Federal government wages Indian Wars on western tribes to drive them onto reservations.

1861–1862   Gold prospectors' destruction of native game in California forces Yahi Indians into raiding livestock and grain.

1863   Federal troops destroy 400 lodges in Sioux village and 500,000 pounds of dried buffalo meat, a seventy-day supply for these 4,800 people.

1868   Remaining Navajo and Apache Indians incarcerated at Ft. Sumner refuse to farm the poor land anymore; 7,300 survivors are released to return to their homelands.

1872–1874　　Federal government destroys bison (estimated at 60 million) on the Great Plains to solve the "Indian" problem, depriving the Indians of their major resource for food and trade and eradicating the bison culture.

1879　　United States removes tens of thousands of Indian children from their homes and sends them to boarding schools. The girls are taught European cooking techniques, using rations, stoves, yeast, iron griddles and frying pans.

1887　　U.S. General Allotment (Dawes) Act outlaws traditional communal ownership of lands and instead allots each household head 160 acres, selling off "surplus" lands for white settlement.

1890　　U.S. Army is victorious against the Sioux in the Massacre at Wounded Knee, murdering Chief Sitting Bull and signalling the end of the Ghost Dance cult that promised the return of the bison and retreat of the invader.

1924　　Congress grants citizenship to Native Americans.

1934　　Federal government now owns 90 million acres that were originally in Indian hands.
Indian Reorganization (Wheeler-Howard) Act becomes law, permitting Native American communities to form tribal governments and corporations.

1960s–1970s　　Birth of the Pan-Indian movement, in which Native Americans identify with the entire group rather than a particular tribe. Inter-tribal gatherings known as pow-wows become the focus of celebrations of ethnic identity; pow-wow foods include fry bread, buffalo steaks and wild rice.

1973　　Federal District Court in Tacoma, Washington, declares Puget Sound tribes entitled by treaty to 50 percent of area's fish harvest. U.S. Supreme Court upholds decision.

1980s–1990s　　Federal policy shifts toward Native American self-determination. Nations set up their own governing systems to maintain cultural identity and foodways.

1982　　Only 7,000 Indian farmers are left in the United States, compared with more than 48,000 in 1920, half of whom owned the land they farmed.

1990s–
present
Many tribes begin to value their heritage and seek to regenerate traditional agricultural methods, reintroduce heritage crops and animals, lower blood sugar and prevent diabetes through diet, preserve crop diversity and specific varieties by saving seeds, turn traditional foods into cash crops and record oral histories of foodways.

CHAPTER I

INTRODUCTION: FOOD, HISTORY AND CULTURE

If history is defined as a series of narratives, the story of American Indian food begins tens of thousands of years ago when these immigrants first set foot on North America. Broadly speaking, there are two historical periods: the time up to 1500 (before European invasion) and after 1500. This is, of course, simplistic because so many significant events that modified foodways took place in both periods—domestication of crops, development of intensive agriculture, beginning of settled village life rather than nomadism, introduction of European crops, forced relocation to different lands and cultural decimation and renewal. Each ushered in a new historical period marked by significantly altered foodways.

This book deals with cultural evolution and historical developments over many thousands of years. This chapter begins with pre-European invasion, moves on to the radical impact on Native American foodways brought about by the Europeans, and finally discusses the Modern Era, beginning in the twentieth century and continuing to the present.

BEFORE INVASION

The First Immigrants

Some 15,000 to 20,000 years ago, nomadic hunting bands in Asia pursuing large game animals began edging further southeast from

Siberia, crossing the Bering Land Bridge that at the time connected Asia and Alaska. Under severe weather conditions, they traveled no further in a day than was necessary to find fresh game to sustain them for an extended period. The huge mastodons and mammoths supplied so much meat that the hunters could afford to rest. Once in North America, these travelers drifted slowly southward, at first continuing to hunt large game. Once the huge animals became extinct, the immigrants migrated to other parts of the continent, following four colonization routes—one by water to the Northwest coast and three by land from Canada (one to the Northeast of North America, one through the Great Plains south to the Gulf of Mexico and one following the Rocky Mountains down through the Southwest, Mexico and Central America).

Most of what is now the northeast United States was at 11,500 BC under a glacier. At the end of the last Ice Age, the initial penetration and settlement of the Northeast began about 10,500 BC when the first vegetation appeared, mainly tundra plants such as grasses, sedge, alders and willow. As the nomads found their way south of the ice-free corridor, they were confronted with unfamiliar hunting conditions that precipitated food shortages and stress. A process of natural selection favored those able to store calories efficiently as fat. As the big game species disappeared, becoming extinct about 4500 BC, the people went after smaller animals and plants with edible seeds; consequently, they developed greater variety in their diet and encountered cultural shifts. About 11,000 years ago, wild plant foods became important in their diet. Most descendants of the original settlers moved east to the Great Plains, forming the flourishing Plano cultures around 7500 BC.

Beginnings of Agriculture

Around 7000 BC, some tribes began to domesticate a great variety of plants, producing edible seeds including sunflowers, sumpweed, chenopods, knotweed, pigweed, giant ragweed and maygrass. Until about 3,000 years ago, the tribes were primarily gatherer-hunters surviving on edible plants and wild animals. They lived in nomadic bands of no more than several hundred people so they could easily gather their belongings and move from place to place, following the herds and seasons. Where staple food could be collected easily, like wild rice in Minnesota and acorns in parts of California, the Indians often formed seasonal settlements.

The first archaeological evidence of maize dates from around 3500 BC and was found at Bat Cave, New Mexico. This marks the first cultural transformation of Indian foodways. Perhaps maize diffused northward from Mexico, where it has been dated to 5000 BC in the southern state of Puebla, the earliest known cultivation of the crop. Beans and squash were also first domesticated in the Southwest, beans being introduced between AD 400 and 700. The knowledge could have filtered northward from Mexico and Central America or developed independently in the Southwest.

Gradually, some tribes began to live a more settled existence, all made possible by agriculture primarily based on the Indian Triad (maize, beans and squash). Plant domestication may have developed in the Southeast independent of Mexico between 2300 and 2000 BC. The Mogollon and Hohokam cultures in the Southwest began maize cultivation sometime between 1500 BC to AD 1500, whereas the Eastern Woodlands did not begin until between AD 800 to 1500, and corn was not widespread on the central Plains until AD 1000. Cultivated plants were present by 1000 BC in the southern part of the Northeast and slowly spread northward afterward. The oldest directly dated maize from the Northeast Woodlands comes from a site in Illinois from the first century BC, but it was no more than a minor crop before AD 800 to 900.[1] Cultivation of maize and beans is thought to have begun sometime after 700 BC in southern New England.

Domestication of plants gave the Indians a food source over which they had some control. Agriculture meant generally a greater yield, better nutrition and lower infant mortality. As a result, the population increased and tribal members developed feelings of territoriality and attachment to their land. The settled lifestyle made possible permanent places of worship and development of ceremonies and dances. This helped reinforce feelings about the sacred and symbolic importance of food for which gratitude should be expressed. The life-giving plants became the subjects of many ceremonies, ritual plantings, harvest festivals and feasts.

Relying on the vigor of a handful of crops (rather than the diversity of items gathered and hunted) made the people vulnerable to vagaries such as drought, crop failure and raids from other tribes. Although there was some malnutrition, disease, starvation and famine, sometimes leading to death, on the whole agriculture was a giant step forward. It set the foundation for more sophisticated cultures because the basic question of what to eat was no longer a full-time preoccupation.

As groups became larger—and particularly when a surplus was generated—a more elaborate social system developed, with a leader or chief and his attendants at the top. The ruling elite consumed food rather than producing it, a task left to farmers, who occupied a lower status.

By AD 1000, a number of different food cultures were operating in North America; some were gatherer-hunters, others farmer-hunters and some primarily agriculturalists supplemented by gathering-hunting. Some authorities believe that the yield of agricultural crops did not equal that of nonagricultural and game sources and represented only between 30 and 50 percent of subsistence for some tribes. By AD 1300, agriculture was well developed among East Coast tribes, while a severe twenty-three-year drought had brought agriculture in the Southwest to a temporary standstill.

SIX REGIONS, SIX FOODWAYS

When Christopher Columbus came ashore in the Caribbean in 1492, there were an estimated 8 million Indians living in six culture (geographic) areas in North America. The foodways, beliefs and customs of each zone were markedly different from the others. Moreover, many practices were peculiar to single tribes. Although some anthropologists identify as many as seventeen culture areas, most narrow this down to six: Southwest, Northwest Coast, Great Plains, California/Great Basin/Plateau, Northeast and Southeast. In all but one zone, some tribe(s) practiced gathering-hunting exclusively, even when the majority of the neighboring tribes were practicing some farming. Two areas—the Northwest Coast and the California/Great Basin/Plateau—were devoted to foraging, fishing and hunting with no agriculture. As there were 600 tribes when the Europeans arrived, it is not possible to list every one here. Major tribes for each area are identified.

Southwest

Geography. The Southwest extends over Arizona, New Mexico and parts of Colorado and Utah.

Environment. Arid desert, mountains, canyons, mesas, buttes and cliffs, forests of pine and juniper as well as saguaro cactus and some rivers punctuate this land. The climate ranges from extreme dry heat alternating with below-freezing temperatures at night in the desert with little rain for much of the year. However, there are heavy spring and summer monsoons and there is snow in the northern part.

Major Tribes. Apache, Hopi, Navajo (call themselves the Dine— "The People"), Paiute, Pascua Yaqui, Pima, Tewa, Tohono O'odham (known as Papago "Bean Eaters" until the 1980s), Ute, Yuma (Cocopa, Havasupai, Maricopa, Mojave), Zuni.

Cultural History. The Southwest has been inhabited for at least 6,000 years. The Hopi pueblo at Oaribi, Arizona, is one of two oldest continuously occupied settlements on the continent north of Mexico. From AD 700 to 1350, four cultures thrived: Anasazi in the area where Utah, Colorado, New Mexico and Arizona meet (called The Four Corners); Mogollon in the Mogollon Mountains stretching from present central Arizona into southern New Mexico, Hohokam in the southern Arizona desert, where they designed a far-reaching system of irrigation canals, made the most diverse plantings of any tribe and created one of the largest canal systems, 1,750 miles; and the Patayan in northwest Arizona and along the Colorado River.

The villages of these four cultures grew in size and sophistication until some became cities. However, a series of invasions and severe drought caused the Mogollon to disappear and the other three cultures to be transformed. When the Spanish arrived, the conquistadors encountered descendants of these four original cultures. In the mountainous northwest, they found the Havasupais, the Yavapais and the Walapais, whose culture was descended from the Patayan. To the south, near the Arizona-California border were the Tohono O'odham and Pima, whose culture was descended from the Hohokam. Each family lived in a dome-shaped brush house with a cooking enclosure. The Zuni in west-central New Mexico, the Hopi in northeast Arizona and the Rio Grande people along the valley of the Rio Grande River were descended from the Anasazi (now called Ancestral Puebloans) and lived in cliff dwellings, called *pueblos* by the Spanish. Constructed of stone in the west and clay along the Rio Grande, some were three to four stories high and accommodated nearly 200 people. Outside these perimeters lived the hunting-gathering Apache and Navajo who often attacked the settled tribes.

Culture: Farming supplemented by Gathering-Hunting. Staples were farmed maize, squash and beans, supplemented by gathering seeds and pods, wild fruits and greens and hunted small game. Each tribe viewed farming somewhat differently depending on its importance to their way of life. Some authorities believe that the yield from agricultural crops amounted to only between 30 and 50 percent of subsistence with the remainder made up by gathering-hunting. Soft-grained flour maize adapted well to dry regions of the west and could be ground on milling stones designed for wild seeds.

In the pueblos, where intensive agriculture was practiced, wild plants were less important than cultivated ones. In these communities, some scholars believe that agricultural products accounted for 85 to 90 percent of the calories consumed. Famine was a real threat due to drought. Large game was scarce (deer, antelope and mountain sheep were taken by spear only occasionally) and small game furnished more meat; rabbit killed with a throwing stick was the most common single species. The Hopi and Zuni traded their textiles and maize to the Plains Indians for bison meat.

There were few large game animals anywhere in the Southwest; Native Americans in this area were mostly vegetarian. They were able to obtain adequate nutrition from grasses, nuts, fruits, roots and especially seeds. "Desert plants produce great quantities of seeds, and thus manage to propagate themselves in an area of uncertain growing conditions."[2] With the help of milling stones and stone rollers used for grinding (called *manos* by the Spanish) that characterized these cultures, maize, nuts and seeds could be made into flour for bread or mush. These tools represented a revolution in food processing techniques during this period.

The women picked squawberries, gathered prickly pear fruit and cleaned stickers off cholla buds before grinding them. All of this was tedious work. Except for the fruit of the saguaro cactus, all these foods were consumed over a wide geographic range from California to Texas, from Mexico to Colorado, Utah and Nevada.

The Apache, on the other hand, relied on game and wild plants equally. For the River Yuman and the Mojave, farm crops formed about half of the total diet; they supplied 40 percent for the Yuma, 30 percent for the Cocopa, and less for the Maricopa. Wild plants ranked first for these last two tribes, game second and farming third.

Some Southwest cultures used irrigated agriculture that made possible more intensive farming. The Pima and Maricopa developed elaborate irrigation systems. Although the Pima lived near the Gila River, every fifth year, on average, the river failed in midwinter so they had to eat supplementary gathered wild foods. If they could not find enough, they were forced to make long trips to the mountains in search of animal foods, roots, berries and agave. These journeys inevitably took them into enemy territory belonging to the Apache. At other times, flooding destroyed the crops. Because the Tohono O'odham further to the south did not live near a major river, they had much less agriculture. When they did farm, they located their plantings at the mouth of a wash after the seasonal downpour. Digging holes with a planting stick, the Tohono O'odham dropped four kernels into each and spoke to the seeds while kneeling. They had fresh foods for only short periods of the year. Otherwise, their diet consisted of dried foods, dehydrated vegetables and sun-dried meat.

Northwest Coast

Geography. This area extends along the Pacific coastline from the panhandle of southeastern Alaska through British Columbia, Washington and Oregon to the northwest corner of California.

Environment. The Northwest Coast is characterized by thickly wooded, dense forests, temperate climate, heavy rainfall, many islands, mountains, coast, sounds, fjords and rivers.

Major Tribes. Bella Bella, Chinook, Haida, Hupa, Kalapuya, Kwakiutl, Makah, Nootka, Quileute, Tolowa, Tsimshian, Wiyot, Yurok.

Culture: Fishing/Gathering-Hunting. The staple of these tribes was salmon; other fish ranked second. Female salmon migrated annually from the ocean up rivers and streams to lay eggs. They made easy prey, as they could be trapped or speared by the thousands. Many were then dried. Ceremonies were held every year to ensure their return. The tribes also caught at least a dozen species of saltwater fish, including halibut and cod. The most important, culturally speaking, was the candlefish—so oily that it burned like a candle when a wick was inserted. The highly prized oil also was used as sauce for both meat and fish. Fish were baked in shallow pits using the direct-fire method, or roasted and dried (often eaten for breakfast). Fins, tails and bones were boiled and the heads steamed. Heat smoking and drying were the major forms of preservation. At least a dozen species of shellfish and sea mammals including seals, sea lions, dolphins, porpoises and whales were also taken. Seal, porpoise and sea lion were hunted by canoe and harpoon. Sea lion was captured with a spear with a detachable head and attached rope. The hunters left the canoe in shallow water and swam toward their prey, rushing at the mammal when they were close enough. The coastal people gathered sea plants and then dried and pressed them into cakes for future use. These Indians also foraged for about sixty species of wild land plants, berries and camas roots. In the interior they hunted for deer, elk and bear.

In some areas mountain goat was hunted and made into a kind of brisket or steamed on red-hot stones. After the frost in spring, many wild plants and roots such as clover, eelgrass, fern and skunk cabbage roots, camas, lupine, carrots, lily bulbs and berries were dug and gathered. Salal and huckleberries were dried and drizzled with the ubiquitous fish oil. *Wappato*, a water plant with a bulb that grows in the bottom of shallow lakes and pools, was gathered by wading in, locating plants with toes and prying them loose to float to the surface. The interior Indians ate the most roots, particularly the plentiful camas that became brittle when dried, smashed and pressed into cakes.

The isolation of the Northwest Coast helped to develop a culture peculiar to these tribes. They lived in plank houses (supported by a framework of logs to which planks were attached) occupied by several families. These cultures enjoyed great food wealth, which gave way to the emergence of social classes. There was an emphasis on material goods and public display that culminated in the idiosyncratic feast known as potlatch, where rank and status were accrued depending on how much food and other material goods could be given away.

Great Plains

Geography. This area extends from central Alberta, Canada, just north of the border, south to Texas. Bounded by the Rocky Mountains on the west and the Missouri River on the east, the zone covers a vast swath of the continent's midsection. It includes parts of Montana, North Dakota, South Dakota, Nebraska, Kansas, Oklahoma, Colorado, New Mexico, Texas and Wyoming.

Environment. Most of the land is rolling grasslands between the Mississippi River and foothills of the Rocky Mountains.

Major Tribes. Arapahoe, Arikara, Assiniboin, Blackfoot, Cheyenne, Comanche, Crow, Dakota, Hidatsa, Iowa, Kansa, Kiowa, Lakota, Mandan, Missouri, Nez Perce, Oglala Sioux, Omaha, Osage, Pawnee, Plains Cree, Salish, Shoshone, Wichita.

Two Coexisting Cultures: Settled and Gathering-Hunting. The sedentary culture was made up of farmers who migrated from neighboring regions and initially settled along the great river valleys, where they raised maize, squash, beans and sunflowers. These tribes lived in fortified villages and traded surplus cornmeal and beans to the nomadic tribes for bison meat. Dwellings took three forms: earth lodges in the Missouri River drainage (round with a tunnel-like entrance; the whole covered with earth, housing a number of families), grass-thatched houses in the south and tipis like those used by the nomadic tribes for the Dakota.

The nomadic people were gatherer-hunters who depended more than any other culture on one game species—bison. The hunters used mass-kill techniques, driving a small herd over a cliff to its death in a blind trap. As hundreds were killed at once in this method, the Indians typically butchered only the uppermost layers and left the rest to predators or to rot. Bison was supplemented by elk, antelope, bear and occasionally smaller game. Bison meat was turned into *pemmican* by pounding, drying and adding berries, which were the only plant food collected in any quantity. It was a precarious existence. Some meat was exchanged with members of the sedentary culture for maize. The Indians of the High Plains (semi-arid area) had more plant resources and ate less raw meat and fewer internal organs than those of the far north, so plants were important for vitamin C. The Omaha Indians from Nebraska determined the route of their summer bison hunt by the location of prairie turnips and other wild foods rather than likely bison areas. They made camp where both vegetable and animal foods could be obtained. The nomads lived in conical portable tipis made of bison hide.

California, Great Basin and Plateau

These three regions in the West and Northwest are usually considered together.

Geography. The area extends from above the Canadian border through the plateau and mountain area of the Sierra Nevada Mountains in California on the west, the Wasatch Mountains in Utah on the east and the northern edge of the Mojave Desert and watershed of the Virgin River on the south. It includes about two-thirds of California, Colorado Nevada, parts of Utah, Oregon, Montana, Idaho, Washington and Wyoming.

Environment. This was an inhospitable environment of desert, sparse rainfall and salt flats intersected by mountains. The latitude and

9

elevation produced a "cold-desert" environment. The Great Basin is one of the driest regions in the United States. The Plateau includes the semi-desert environment of the southern portion.

Major Tribes. Bannock, Chumash, Klamath, Paiute, Pomo, Shoshone Paiute, Spokane, Ute, Yokuts, Yurok.

Culture: Gathering-Hunting. The tribes of California, the Great Basin and the Plateau were all forager-hunters.

California. In the interior, acorns were the staple. They were ground into meal, leached out with water to remove the tannic acid, then boiled to make mush or baked into unleavened bread. Second in importance were wild plants used as greens and for their seeds; the smaller seeds were parched and then ground into meal. Also vital for sustenance was small game, rodents and birds, plus invertebrates such as worms, grasshoppers and caterpillars. These sources probably furnished more year-round food than deer and other large game. On the coast, seafood was the staple; fish from streams were of secondary importance in the interior. The California tribes were relatively free of famine and lived in domed, thatched houses made of a framework of bent and tied poles.

Great Basin. The number one wild plant food was pinyon nuts— really seeds from the pinyon pine. The pinyon crop failed too often to be called a staple. Many other seeds were harvested, along with a few roots dug with digging sticks in the north. The Paiute, Ute and Shoshone lived on wild plants and animals from the deserts and mountains. Deer was the most common hunted large game animal, along with mountain sheep and some antelope to the north. These prey were scarce and furnished a smaller part of the diet than rodents, rabbits, reptiles and insects. The Indians of the Great Basin were master foragers and were not dependent on any single source of food. It was possible to travel from desert to the juniper-pinyon, oak–ponderosa pine and even aspen-fir forests by foot in one day, so these peoples had access to a greater range of food resources.

Their diet depended on the season. In spring, they camped at the edge of the marsh and captured water fowl and gathered plants. On the rivers they netted newly hatched fish. By full summer, they moved into the hills to gather plants, berries and rice grass. In autumn, they harvested pinyon nuts and hunted jackrabbits and other small animals. The winter was harsh, but they could still hunt some small burrowing animals. Famines were common and people were hungry much of time. The tribes in the Great Basin lived in tipis covered most often with an underlayer of thatch topped with hide or bark.

To the south during the summer harvest the Indians of northern California and southern Oregon harvested lily *wokas*, yellow water lilies gathered by the women with ten-foot-long poles from shovel-nosed dugouts. The pods were full of seeds and a jelly-like substance that contained protein.

Plateau. On the coast, fish—particularly salmon—was the staple. In the north the Indians depended on moose and other large game; in the west and east, large animals such as moose, elk and deer were staples. However, wild plant foods dominated in the corridor running from Oregon to California. In Washington and Idaho, tribes ate considerable quantities of wild plants, especially camas roots and bulbs—one of the most important roots and a good source of starch. The culture showed influences from both the Northwest Coast and Plains areas.

Many of those who lived near the Columbia and Fraser Rivers and tributaries planned their lives around the spring running of the salmon, camping near the rivers from May to September. They either netted or speared the fish or caught them in weirs; some were speared from small light canoes. The salmon were smoked or sun dried; some were crushed into powder and cooked as cakes or added to stews. During the rest of the year these Indians migrated to hunt game such as deer, elk and caribou; mule or blacktailed deer were hunted at lower altitudes.

Northeast Woodlands and Great Lakes

Geography. This area extends over the eastern part of the United States, roughly from the Atlantic Ocean to the Mississippi River, including the Great Lakes. It includes present-day Connecticut, Illinois, Indiana, Maine, Maryland, Massachusetts, Michigan, Minnesota, New Hampshire, New Jersey, New York, Ohio, Pennsylvania, Rhode Island, Vermont and Wisconsin.

Environment. This zone is covered with fertile woodlands, eastern prairies, coastline, lakes and rivers.

Major Tribes. Abenaki, Algonquin, Cayuga, Chippewa, Delaware, Erie, Huron, Illinois, Iroquois, Kickapoo, Massachuset, Menomini, Miami, Mohawk, Mohican (Mohegan), Montauk, Narragansett,

Ojibwa (Chippewa), Onondaga, Oneida, Ottawa, Penobscot, Pequot, Powhatan, Seneca, Shawnee, Wampanoag, Winnebago.

Cultural History. The Northeast is distinct as a culture area because its people organized into the most advanced civilizations in North America and the largest political units north of the Aztec and Mayan cultures in Mexico. All of this depended on their ability to generate large food surpluses.

Iroquois Confederacy/League of the Iroquois/League of Five Nations. A unique entity in the Northeast was the Iroquois Confederacy, a powerful political alliance consisting of the Mohawk, Onandaga, Cayuga, Oneida and Seneca (the Five Nations), established by 1500 to pacify infighting and unite these tribes against the Huron and Algonquin. In lean times, these tribes pledged to help each other out with stores of food.

The Moundbuilders. From AD 750 to 1350, an advanced society known as the Mississippians or Moundbuildlers began to emerge in what is known as the American Bottom, a wide area of the Mississippi River Valley near St. Louis. On this fertile floodplain, there was a major change in food production around AD 750, when people began to grow and eat more maize. From that point on, the staples were maize, maygrass, chenopod, knotweed, a little barley and squash/gourds. Storage methods evolved from household pits of the sixth century, to central-communal pits during the late ninth century, to above-ground granaries a century later. The Indians here also started making large pottery bowls. These developments signaled a significant shift that gradually led to the development of Cahokia, a huge urban center that flourished between 800 and 1350 near what is now East St. Louis. Possibly the largest city north of Mexico before the eighteenth century, Cahokia housed 20,000 people. Chiefs oversaw networks of agricultural hamlets that produced food for the urban center. Other associated mounds have been found at Coosa and Etowah in Georgia, Moundsville in Alabama and Natchez, Mississippi. By about 1350, however, these societies declined, partly because of decreased agricultural productivity due to climactic change. In Cahokia, severe deforestation from overexploitation caused erosion and unpredictable flooding.

Culture: Farming Supplemented by Gathering-Hunting. The people in the Northeast were for the most part maize farmers (the hard-grained flint variety that kept better in the humid areas of the northeast), supplemented by gathering and hunting. Next to maize, beans and squash were the most important cultivated crops (together called The Three Sisters by the Iroquois). The groundnut, a starchy tuber prepared and eaten like a potato, was the most important gathered plant and became a staple. Deer, the most important single hunted animal, was as crucial to survival in the northeast as bison was to the Plains Indians. Deer was supplemented by bear, geese and turkey. Wild plant foods, especially nuts, were somewhat important. The Iroquois lived in longhouses, structures of sixty feet in length consisting of a frame covered with bark, most often elm. In winter, moose, caribou, beaver, muskrat and otter were hunted using bow and arrow or long lance and knife. In spring, the sap of the sugar maple was collected, and berries, nuts such as hickory, walnut, butternut, hazlenut, acorns, seeds and wild fruits including cherries and grapes supplemented the diet. Fish was only about as important as wild plant foods, except on the coast where shellfish made up a significant part of subsistence. Clams were a staple when in season, and during the winter were taken along with eels from tidal flats as emergency rations. Famines were rare. The Abenaki tribe of Maine continued hunting, fishing and gathering into the seventeenth century.

In the Wisconsin area, wild rice was more important as a staple than maize; it was the first-ranking food of the Menomini tribe. Around the Great Lakes, fishing rivaled hunting.

Southeast

Geography. This area extends westward from the Atlantic Ocean to the lower Mississippi River, southward from Virginia and Kentucky to the Gulf of Mexico, and northward to the colder regions of the Mississippi and Ohio Valleys. It includes Alabama, Arkansas, Florida, Kentucky, Louisiana, Mississippi and Tennessee.

Environment. The land contains forests and fertile soil and is fortunate in having mild winters and abundant rainfall. Along the east coast, there is a low plain of sand dunes, saltwater marshes and grasses crossed by numerous sluggish streams. To the west, a plateau of more than 1,000 miles by 150 miles wide backs up against the southern reaches of the Appalachian Mountains. South of the Appalachians and stretching to the Mississippi is an area of deep, fertile soil known as the Black Belt.

Florida Indians planting seeds and cultivating a field. Courtesy of Library of Congress, Prints & Photographs Division (reproduction number: LC-DIG-ppmsca-02937).

Major Tribes. Apalachee, Cherokee, Chickasaw, Choctaw, Creek, Guale, Muskogean, Natchez, Seminole, Timucuan.

Culture: Farming Supplemented by Gathering-Hunting. Domesticated maize became an important resource between AD 800 and 1350. There were three subsistence areas in the Southeast—one coastal and two types of "shifting" maize agriculture (requiring periodic shifts of residence to cultivable land), supplemented by hunting and collection of wild plant foods. Maize agriculture took a different form among the most sedentary interior Apalachee tribe than with the Guale Indians and other coastal groups. For the Apalachee, in the interior east of the Mississippi River, the areas of cultivable land were large enough to allow for fields to be almost continuously worked with little fallowing. This meant they could live in the area year-round. Production was high, probably accounting for more than 50 percent of total subsistence. Crops were supplemented by gathering black walnuts, chestnuts, acorns and hickory nuts. Among the Guale on the coast, however, arable land was found in small and widely scat-

14

tered patches in sandy soils with low water capacity. This meant that these Indians had to shift residence each time a new field was opened to cultivation and an old one allowed to fallow. Coastal people relied on fish, while others combined wild plants with cultivation without the intensive farming practiced in the interior. The seasonal availability of sea turtle was a vital beach resource both for its flesh and its eggs. Fall collecting followed the maize harvest. The most important coastal tribes in the South Florida region lacked agriculture (which was completely absent from the area west of the Apalachicola River) and depended on plant and animal resources. Plant collecting went on year-round and became intensive in the fall with acorns, hickory nuts, persimmons, wild grapes, saw palmetto berries, yucca, cocoa plums, sea grapes, china brier, Spanish bayonet, live oak acorns, cabbage palm, and prickly pear. In spring, there was a second collecting time when blueberries and blackberries ripened in May and early June. Spring was probably a time of famine on the coast, when greens such as pokeweed became important and hickory nuts and acorns were sources of vegetable oil; animal sources were secondary. The hunters used bow-and-arrow and blowgun, and some caught fish by poisoning streams. Shellfish, particularly oysters, were an important winter food. Guale families moved to the marsh for shellfish gathering after the maize harvest. The Gulf coastal groups had more permanently established villages in the southwestern and western parts of the region. Sharks, sting rays and whales were important food sources.

THE INVASION: 1500 AND BEYOND

Into these relatively stable Native American societies with their established foodways came groups of aliens speaking different languages, dressed in strange clothes, eating odd foods and carrying deadly weapons. The first contact between Native Americans and Europeans took place in the early 1500s. Major players were the Spanish, English, Dutch and French. These people came as religious refugees, soldiers of fortune, gold-diggers, adventurers and political aggrandizers, motivated to undertake the long, dangerous sea passage from Europe for freedom of worship, profit and proselytizing. Each group had its own culture and foodways that they hoped to establish in what was ironically referred to as the "new" world. These invaders cared not a whit about Indian food or about the Indians themselves, who they considered ignorant savages in need of civilizing. A Dutch attorney wrote in 1649, "Their fare, or food, is poor and gross, for they drink water, having no other beverage; they eat the flesh of all sorts of game that the country supplies, even badgers, dogs, eagles and similar trash, which Christians in no way regard; these they cook uncleansed and undressed. . . . Moreover, all sorts of fish, likewise snakes, frogs and such like, which they usually cook with the offals and entrails."[3] However, when the Europeans first arrived and were hungry, they were happy to accept gifts of native food or raid Indian stores.

The Indians were equally unimpressed by European food. They thought wheat vastly inferior to maize and were horrified when they saw the newcomers feeding corn, as they called it, to their pigs and cattle. When a French ship docked in the St. Lawrence River in Canada and the crew offered shore Indians some ship's biscuits and what was apparently wine, the natives were appalled that these visitors "drank blood and ate wood." They promptly threw the biscuits in the water.[4]

"New World" foodstuffs held little attraction for Europeans as they were establishing their colonies, looking for gold, pursuing the fountain of youth and trading for furs. They sought to impose their own cultures on the continent, complete with their foods, preparation and utensils, so they would feel at home. Indian slaves taken by the Spanish and English were forced to try to grow European crops or were shipped to the Caribbean to work the sugar plantations so they could not run home. Forced conversions to Christianity disrupted the native ceremonial cycle and, consequently, the foodways.

Conflicts and all-out war erupted as English settlers in the northeast coveted more Indian land. Some tribes sold land for minimal compensation, but much was just taken outright. Settlement disrupted the native hunting territories and claimed fallow Indian planting grounds. Native Americans were forced to migrate and adapt to new foods in new territories.

The Spanish

Florida. Florida's Apalachee, Guale and Timucua tribes are thought to be the first Indians on the North American continent proper to encounter Europeans. The event occurred in 1513 when a Spanish expedition landed on the coast. The Indians were immediately taken into slavery, their food stores pillaged and villages burned.

As early as 1530, European diseases including smallpox were being transmitted to these Southeast natives and rapidly reduced the population. Although this decreased the amount of food production required by the Indians, there were fewer people left to farm and those who survived the disease were in a weakened state.

Other Spanish adventurers extended north and west into the interior. Well-known explorer Hernando de Soto and his forces in their first expedition in 1539 made contact either directly or indirectly with nearly all Indian societies living in the area. The second year of de Soto's expedition, 1540, is used as a marker of the end of the aboriginal period in North America. Lifestyles would be forever altered by obligatory labor demands, missionization and forced farming.

Southwest. In 1539, a Spanish party made its way north from Mexico to what is today Arizona and New Mexico, finally reaching the Zuni pueblo of Halona where they demanded food, among other things. A more elaborate expedition was mounted by the famed Francisco Vásquez de Coronado in 1540. Upon his group's arrival, the Zuni sprinkled a dividing line of cornmeal that the Europeans were told not to cross. They did nevertheless, shooting some Indians and helping themselves to stores of maize. Although the Spanish pushed on to the Hopi and Rio Grande Pueblos on this expedition, they became discouraged, perhaps by lack of treasure, and retreated south for forty years. When they returned in 1580 with missionaries, they requisitioned corn, let their horses feed in the fields and forced Pueblo men into slavery. This time the Spanish were there to stay and set about transforming foodways and saving souls.

The arrival of the Spanish was an initial nutritional disaster for the Navajo, who were strictly nomadic hunters and gatherers but were now forced into farming Spanish crops. Their diet and way of life were completely transformed. By stealing sheep from the invaders, the Navajo launched their long tribal tradition of raising this animal, which gave them a steady supply of meat.

The Pueblo Revolt of 1680. The Spanish set about to dominate the Pueblo Indians, demanding high quotas of corn as tribute for the governor in Santa Fe and the local priest. As more Spanish kept arriving, the requisitioned amounts increased. To make matters worse, during periods of drought, nomadic tribes raided the pueblos. The year 1660 was one of severe drought and starvation as the Puebloans endeavored unsuccessfully to cultivate Spanish crops such as wheat, olives, watermelon and grapes. Having suffered eighty years of frustration and often hunger at the hands of the Spanish, the Pueblo leaders met secretly and decided to rebel. During the violent Pueblo Revolt, the Indians burned every object of Spanish origin, including the crops, and slaughtered 400 Spaniards. This event was the only successful native uprising against the Europeans anywhere on the continent. The Puebloans continued to hold off the invaders successfully for the next twelve years. In the process, members of the various pueblos shared their agricultural knowledge and skills for the first time. However, the Spanish did return in 1692, and this time there would be no revolt.

California. In 1542, Spanish galleons still seeking a passage to Asia, made a stop in the Santa Barbara Channel, surprising the coastal Indians. These "natives" seemed an ideal labor force. During the Mission Period in California, which lasted sixty-five years beginning with San Diego de Alcala in 1769, Native Americans who had been gatherer-hunters were forced to give up their lifestyles, cultivate mission farms and herd animals. Families from scattered villages were rounded up and relocated near the twenty-one missions.

The English

Virginia. The first permanent English settlement in North America was established at Jamestown in 1607. Captain John Smith who was appointed to govern by the Virginia Company traded metal objects to the Kecoughtan Indians for food. On one occasion, by convincing them he was not desperate, he was able to acquire sixteen bushels of maize at a very good price. A second version of the story relates that he used gunshots to scare the Indians into running while he and his men grabbed a sacred idol and held it in ransom for wild game and bread.[5]

Massachusetts. The tale of the Pilgrims' settlement of Plymouth Rock, lesser known as the Indian village of Patuxet (also the name of a tribe), has become an American origin myth. Like all new arrivals, a primary concern of the Pilgrims was food. Almost the first entry by Governor William Bradford in his journal on November 11, 1620, was a note of the discovery of a cache of Indian maize, which the newcomers promptly stole.[6] This tendency complicated later negotiations with the Indians. In 1622, when the English tried to make a peace settlement with the Narragansett tribe, they were refused for having stolen maize. Rather than avenging themselves, the Indians, accustomed to sharing food, offered what they could. Without this help, the Pilgrims would not have survived the first winter. One early observer noted, "At the most critical stages in colonial history corn played an important part. Our Pilgrim fathers and the less hardy cavaliers of Jamestown and Maryland were rescued from starvation more than once when it was hard upon them by foods made from the corn given them by the Indians who had cultivated and harvested it."[7]

The Pilgrims quickly appropriated the village of Patuxet, taking over cleared fields, appropriating corn bins and stealing from storehouses. In the spring of 1621, Squanto (the lone survivor of the Patuxet tribe) and Chief Massasoit of the Wampanoag taught the Pilgrims how to plant the strange new foods, particularly maize. A European traveler commented, "Afterwards, they, as many as were able, began to plant their corne, in which servise Squanto stood them in great stead, showing them both ye manner how to set it, and after how to dress and tend it. He also told them excepte they gott fish and set with it in these cold grounds it would come to nothing."[8] Although using a dead fish as a source of fertilizing nitrogen was supposedly an Indian tradition, it was actually a European technique that Squanto had learned when he was taken to England to be displayed as a curiousity. The Indians also taught the Pilgrims how to hunt and fish in the new land. Governor Bradford recorded, "And besids water foule, ther was great store of wild Turkies, of which they tooke many, besids venison, &c. Besids they had aboute a peck of meale a weeke to a person, or now since harvest, Indian corne to the proportion."[9]

The First Thanksgiving. The iconic American holiday is supposedly based on an actual event in which the Pilgrims and the Indians sat together harmoniously to share a meal. As the most celebrated holiday in America, it is meant to commemorate a kind of nirvana of Indian-European relations. The "first Thanksgiving" is supposed to have taken place in Plymouth after the first harvest. Did it really happen, and what is meant by "first"? Harvest festivals offering gratitude to the spirits for bountiful harvest had been celebrated for thousands of years in almost every Native American tribe. As for the English, settlers in Jamestown, Virginia, had celebrated many days of thanksgiving before the settlement in New England. The Puritans themselves had long observed religious days of thanksgiving throughout the year without any specific day on an annual basis. In Plymouth, the first harvest took place in 1621. A letter written in that year describes a three-day celebratory event, which occurred sometime in October. Only one document, a church record from 1636, suggests that the event included a feast. When the earlier letter was published in 1841, some sources seized on it retrospectively (over 200 years later) as evidence of the "first" Thanksgiving. As many as ninety Indians were said to have attended, including Chief Massasoit, and they were credited with having brought five deer. As one culinary historian summed up, "The Pilgrims and their proverbial First Thanksgiving are origin myths, tracing America to its beginnings."[10] It is a nice story, but not to many modern Indians, who have designated Thanksgiving as a national day of mourning.[11]

Maine. By 1625, the Pilgrims were producing enough corn to generate a surplus that they traded to the Abenaki Indians in Maine for furs. This influx of maize made it possible for the tribe to change its gathering-hunting lifestyle to settled horticulture because they were finally able to establish winter residence in the large villages, generate a surplus themselves, and exchange items like furs for food in the years of crop failure.

Southeast. As they pushed southward from their Virginia base, the British began to trade with the Indians for deer pelts and slaves. This induced the tribes to hunt deer only for their pelts rather than meat and to raid neighboring tribal villages for slaves. These they sold to traders who took them to British headquarters at Charleston, South Carolina, where they were sold again. To pay off advances extended by white slave traders, the Indians began signing away their sacred land.

The French

Northeast. French fur traders were the first to reach the Great Lakes and beyond. In 1605–1606, French explorer Samuel de Champlain made two voyages to the new continent, reaching as far south as Cape Cod. French Jesuits tried to establish missions in the northeast woodlands area, but the Mohawk destroyed the main one in 1658. In retaliation, the French sent a special military force, which burned many Native American villages. In the 1670s, French Jesuits Jacques Marquette and Louis Jolliet were among the first whites to explore the Mississippi River Valley.

Southeast. Explorer René-Robert Cavelier La Salle descended all the way to the Gulf of Mexico in 1682 and claimed the entire Mississippi Valley for France, calling it Louisiana. He built outposts along the lower river, and in 1718, New Orleans was founded. By the late seventeenth century, there was intense and competitive occupation of the Southeast by the French and English. The Seven Years War, known to the colonists as the French and Indian War (1754–1766), was fought for control of eastern North America and mostly pitted the French and their Indian allies against the British and their allies among the Iroquois. The English won and the victory marked the end of French power on the North American continent. The treaty gave New France to the English and split Louisiana between England and Spain.

The Dutch

Hudson River Valley and New Amsterdam (Manhattan). After Henry Hudson explored the Hudson River Valley in 1609, the Dutch laid claim to the area, which they saw as an approach to the fur trade, specifically beaver. Pelts from these animals were made into very fashionable and expensive felt hats in Europe. Beaver had been used by the Indians as a prized source of grease and fat, especially for winter. The Dutch developed a good relationship with the Mohawk, giving them iron cooking pots, axes, hoes, guns and liquor. They settled at New Amsterdam in the 1630s, allowing their livestock to roam, trampling Indian fields and destroying crops. By the time the Dutch were forced to sell New Amsterdam to the British in 1664, they had wiped out the Algonquin tribe there.

EUROPEAN CULINARY INTRODUCTIONS

Determined to recreate their own foodways on the newly discovered continent, the newcomers imported seeds, cuttings and livestock from home. The Spanish wanted wheat and grapes for sacred as well as secular purposes. They also brought chickpeas, melons, onions, radishes, salad greens, fruit stones, figs, hazelnuts, cucumbers, cabbage, lettuce, pomegranates, herbs, garlic, barley, greens, quince, mulberry, pear, bergamot, potatoes (actually discovered in Peru), peas, turnips, carrots, lima beans, oats, honey, dill, sage, bay leaf and parsley. Some items like the sweet potato were brought by the Spanish from the Caribbean to Florida. Some of the European introductions improved the nutrition of the Indians even as they eroded their traditional foodways.

Crops

Wheat. Wheat, ground into flour for yeast-raised bread, was as central to European culture as maize was to Native American Society. The corn goddess was the central deity, worshipped and assuaged. Both were regarded as defining staples in their respective cultures. They were tied to religion integrally. In the Catholic part of Europe, flour was used to make communion wafers. In the 1700s in the Southwest, Father Eusebio Francisco Kino, a Jesuit missionary, dis-

After European contact: a Tohono O'odham woman winnowing wheat. Courtesy of Library of Congress, Prints & Photographs Division, Edward S. Curtis Collection (reproduction number: LC-USZ62-123312).

tributed much wheat seed to the Pima and Tohono O'odham, and the new food soon replaced maize as the leading crop. In other areas like the Southeast, however, wheat did not thrive.

Citrus, Apples, Melons (Cantaloupe and Watermelon), Peaches, Grapes. All of these items were introduced by the Spanish with the exception of apples, which came from the English. Watermelon and peaches were some of the first Old World plants adopted by Native Americans. Their cultivation rapidly dispersed throughout the Southeast. Watermelon, originally from Africa, was introduced to the New World by the Spanish as early as the seventeenth century. Eventually it was cultivated by tribes in Arizona, North and South Dakota, Minnesota, Nebraska, New York and Wisconsin. Among the Hopi in New Mexico, watermelon even became a seasonal staple. The variety grown there produced fruit into February. The peach was so successful in the Southeast that later naturalists believed it was native to the area. The Iroquois cultivated large apple orchards.

Native Americans were not universally enthusiastic about the new crops. It was not just that these foods were unfamiliar; it was also that they expressed nothing of Indian culture and identity. A member of the Tohono O'odham nation, remarked, "All the year round we were watching where the wild things grew so we could pick them. Elder Brother planted those things for us. He told us where they are and how to cook them. You would not know if it had not been Given. You would not know you could eat cactus stems and shake the seeds out of the weeds. Elder Brother did not tell the whites that. To them he gave peaches and grapes and wheat, but to us he gave the wild seeds and the cactus. Those are the good foods."[12]

Animals

Livestock. Native Americans had no domesticated animals when the newcomers arrived except for some dogs and turkeys. The Europeans quickly imported their pigs, goats, sheep, cattle, cows and chickens. This made available a host of new foodstuffs—lard, pork, mutton, lamb, beef and milk. Cheese-making was taught the Navajo by the Spanish. Of all the livestock imported to the New World, pigs adapted the most readily—almost too well. When Spanish explorer Hernando De Soto arrived in Florida in 1539, he brought thirteen pigs along. Three years later, those pigs had multiplied to 700. Sheep were introduced by the Spanish in the Southwest in the 1500s and quickly became a valued dietary staple. Cattle were brought to Mexico by the conquistadors in 1521; soon many were running wild in Texas. When they wandered further north, some were captured by the Yaqui Indians in Arizona and the Pueblo natives in New Mexico to start their own stocks. The beef supplied by these cattle produced a huge increase in available animal protein. They also became a threat to the integrity of the land by destroying the network of plants and roots that prevented erosion through trampling and overgrazing. Sheep rarely went wild and were available to the Indians only as a result of raids perpetrated on the Spanish. The Navajo became owners of large herds.

The Horse. On his second voyage to the Americas in 1493, Columbus brought horses to the island of Hispaniola. By the end of the sixteenth century, they were running wild in Durango in north Mexico. When Spanish conquistador Francisco Vásquez de Coronado and his men rode into Zuni territory in the 1540s and left their horses in a stockade, the nomadic Comanche and Apache Indians helped themselves to the animals. Raiding became the fastest way to acquire more horses; in fact, the presence of horses gave rise to an extensive raiding culture. In the wake of the Pueblo Revolt of 1680, still more Spanish horses fell into Indian hands and soon revolutionized the culture. By 1780, most Plains tribesmen were accomplished riders, mounted on specially trained strong and fast horses to hunt bison with bow and arrow. They were able to target the choicest animals. Bison, long a suboptimal food resource, became a highly desirable staple. Many members of the sedentary Plains farming culture abandoned their villages and converted to the nomadic way of life. This marked the end of agriculture on the Plains. Horses also gave Native Americans their first beasts of burden. Because the animals enabled nomads to carry more *pemmican* (pounded and dried bison meat), it was possible to travel further and to hunt longer. With many more bison being killed than the Indians needed for survival, they quickly acquired a surplus for trading. The dominance of the Plains horseman continued for three or four generations until the destruction of the bison herds by the U.S. government.

Horses acquired from the Plains Indians also transformed the lives of the Plateau Indians. Around 1730, they left their settlements and also became nomads who hunted bison, although they also continued to fish for salmon and gather camas bulbs. After the Spanish arrived in California, herds of horses were soon roaming the coastal foothills. The Chaucila tribe quickly captured some, enabling them to make the thirty-mile trip from their villages and back to gather acorns without having to set up temporary residences.

Products

Sugar. Columbus brought sugar in 1493 and its use migrated northward. Sugar reduced the importance of native use of maple syrup, berries and wild honey as sweeteners.

Coffee. Coffee was introduced by the Spanish into the Southwest and became a favorite trading post item. It replaced traditional Indian herbal teas and *atole*, a hot drink made from maize.

Alcohol. Certainly the most destructive European introduction to Native Americans was distilled alcohol. Although Indians traditionally fermented substances such as saguaro cactus fruit, the resulting wine contained only about 2 percent alcohol and was drunk on ritual occasions. In a very short time high-proof liquor, bestowed as gifts or as payment to Indians for land and slaves, wreaked havoc among the native cultures. Although there is ongoing debate about whether nature or nurture plays the primary role in high rates of Indian alcoholism, there is general agreement that genetics play a role. It seems that Native Americans have a faster rate of clearance of ethanol from their bodies than Europeans do, causing them to become inebriated more quickly and develop severe addiction. This did not escape European notice and was used to advantage in negotiations. An American captive of the Seneca tribe in New York State, Mary Jemison, writing in 1823, noted that "the use of ardent spirits amongst the Indians . . . has constantly made them worse and worse; increased their vices, and robbed them of many of their virtues; and will ultimately produce their extermination."[13]

Other less-sympathetic Europeans used the vulnerability to underscore Native inferiority. One said that Indians typically downed a glass of wine in five minutes and would continue at this pace for two hours. "They always took down the glass at a single swallow and poured it brimming full. . . . They are a wild and untamed race."[14] A Tohono O'odham elder speaking in 1979 observed, "Anglos made wine for every day [meaning, not just for ceremonial purposes]. Now the Indian people stay drunk for days. When our god gave the cactus wine, it was for a sacred purpose [the rain-making ritual], not to abuse it."[15]

Culinary Technology

Metal Kettles, Pots, Cooking and Agricultural Implements, Knives and Traps. Although some prehistoric Indian tribes mined copper and lead (the Moundbuilders even made tools of copper), they did not have the technology to fashion it into large pieces. When the Europeans arrived with metal—iron, brass, copper—cooking pots and utensils, they quickly became one of the most common and sought-after trade items by the Indians. Pottery and bark vessels were limited in size, broke easily and could not withstand high temperatures. With metal kettles, it became possible to cook for a crowd as well as make maple sugar, which requires higher temperatures than can be accommodated by bark vessels. Iron frying pans made deep frying possible. Buffalo Bird Woman of the Hidatsa tribe noted, "The first pots, or kettles, of metal that we Hidatsas got were of yellow tin [brass]; the French and the Crees also traded us kettles made of red tin [copper]."[16] The Plains Indians acquired copper kettles, steel knives for skinning bison and metal scrapers that speeded up the fleshing of hides. Metal hunting traps were also a popular item. In the eighteenth century, the iron hoe was introduced to replace the digging stick. Clearly these items made farming, hunting and cooking much more efficient enterprises.

Adobe Oven. Wheat bread needs an enclosed hot-space environment in which to rise; in other words, an enclosed oven as opposed to the Indian earth oven or pit. Spanish explorer Juan de Onate, during his colonizing expedition in the Southwest in 1598, introduced the above-ground, dome-shaped *horno* made of molded adobe bricks. About four feet high, the communal *horno* was built on the roof of each story of the pueblos. The firing process was time-consuming and complex and the heat could not be regulated, but the adobe oven was a major technological step forward in the history of Indian baking. While waiting for the dough to rise, the women built a fire inside the *horno*, adding more wood until the inside turned white. After the fire died down, they swept out the ashes with juniper branches. If drops of water shaken from branches inside the oven boiled and evaporated, the *horno* was ready for baking. Archaeological remains of five *hornos* from the village of San Gabriel del Yunque in New Mexico, the earliest known for the Southwest, have been excavated and described by an archaeologist: "Raised above the ground by a platform a few inches high, simply made of cobbles held in adobe [differ-

Hopi man with a hoe. Courtesy of Library of Congress, Prints & Photographs Division, Detroit Publishing Company Collection (reproduction number: LC-USZ62-104602).

ent from those made of adobe bricks] and topped by a dome of clay with an opening at the base and vent hole above, it was heated by a fire built inside. The ashes and charcoal then swept out and the door opening closed with a slab after the goods to be baked had been set inside."[17] In the pueblos, the *horno* quickly became the standard oven for baking both wheat and maize products.

Guns. Not surprisingly, the introduction of the gun increased the bison-hunting efficiency of the Plains Indians. French fur traders supplied Indians with guns to make them more effective hunters. In some cases, it worked so well that game became scarce. British traders in the Southeast traded firearms to Indians for deerskins. Later, of course, the Europeans would come to regret this introduction when the guns were turned on them.

EVICTION AND RELOCATION: UPROOTED FROM THE SACRED LAND

Nothing was more sacred to American Indians than their ancestral lands. Many tribes called the earth Mother, the giver of all nourishment. Every rock, mountain and stream contained a spirit. The landscape had great cultural meaning. The loss of those lands was devastating. Once the American Revolution was over, the Indians were confronted by a new entity—the United States of America—that would govern where they could live, hunt, fish, farm, and consequently, what they ate. The opening of the western frontier, triggered by the Louisiana Purchase in 1803 (some 900,000 acres gained from the French), encouraged many people to move west into Indian country. This was bound to produce conflict. Congress thought the solution was The Federal Indian Removal Act of 1830, which forced eviction of 100,000 Native Americans east of the Mississippi River to Indian Territory in Oklahoma, further disrupting the ceremonial calendar and foodways. The Choctaw went first, then the Creek. The Cherokee in Georgia were prospering as farmers, even owning slaves to work their fields. They had no intention of leaving, so the tribe sued the new government and won before the U.S. Supreme Court. President Andrew Jackson, however, ignored the decision. In 1838, he ordered federal troops to burn the Cherokee's crops and made 20,000 tribal members walk west at gunpoint during winter in the tragic march known as the Trail of Tears. About 4,000 died along the way of malnutrition, starvation, disease and execution. Only the Florida Seminole in the Southeast resisted eviction and fought from 1835 to 1842 until their population was reduced to 500. In all 60,000 Indians were relocated. Within a decade the eastern states were cleared and the five major tribes of the Southeast (the Chickasaw, Cherokee, Cree, Choctaw and Seminole) became known as the Five Civilized Tribes of Oklahoma—so-called for adopting civilization, including European agricultural methods.

The California Gold Rush of 1848 brought new hordes of Americans to the western Indian lands. Many were driven to frenzy by the prospect of riches and saw the Indians as obstacles. The Yahi Indians of north-central California were forced into raiding livestock and grain by the white man's destruction of game. White vigilante groups retaliated by setting about to exterminate the Yahi.

The Long Walk

In the 1850s, the federal government began to administer Indian affairs for the Southwest tribes. In 1864, the government took control of the area north of the Rio Grande and began settling nomadic tribes on reservations. This, of course, meant deciding what land they should occupy. Frontiersman Kit Carson, often hailed as an early western hero, was charged with relocating the Navajo. First, he forced them into submission by slaughtering their sheep and burning their crops, including fields of maize and peach orchards (a European introduction). As a condition of surrender, the Indians had agreed to abandon their nomadic lifestyle (even though the Navajo were mostly settled), relocate to a reservation and devote themselves to farming. The government decided to move the defeated 8,300 Navajo and Mescalero Apache to Bosque Redondo or Fort Sumner in southeastern New Mexico. Some Indians went into hiding and lived on insects and rodents rather than join the exhausting 350-mile Long Walk. Those who survived arrived sick and starved. The Apache, traditionally gatherer-hunters were forced to farm for the first time. During four years of internment, there was not enough tillable land to grow maize, too little grass for grazing sheep and goats, and inadequate government rations. Consequently, the Indians made frequent raids of government stock. Crops suffered from drought, floods and hail. Flour rations were full of insects. The alkaline water caused constant dysentery. In 1868, the Indians at Fort Sumner refused to farm anymore. They were only interested in ration coupons. Their dependence for sustenance was complete. Finally, the government freed the 7,300 survivors to return to their "homelands."

Transcontinental Railroad

Work on the transcontinental railroad, completed in 1869, created even more conflict for the Indians. As the government built forts along the west-bound wagon roads to protect white settlers and workers, the Indians pushed north and south of the lines of travel, some forced to move repeatedly so there was no time to adjust to new environments. The Great Lakes tribes, used to fishing, hunting and gathering, found themselves on waterless plains, while the Great Plains horsemen were forced to compete with displaced tribes even as the supply of bison was dwindling. Starvation was frequent. The government reacted by issuing food rations, and withheld them to manipulate the Indians, using food as the tool of power. The system fostered more food dependency and population declined.

Destruction of Bison in the Great Plains

Between 1872 and 1874, the government encouraged white professionals and tourists to slaughter hundreds of thousands of bison for hides and sport. Free ammunition was provided to any hunter on request. After the railroad was built, there was even more sanctioned slaughter because herds of bison held up the trains. Finally it became government policy to destroy the bison herd to ensure that the Indians would not ride the Plains. This effectively deprived Indians of their major resource for food and trade and eradicated the bison culture of the Plains. Bison were as important to the Plains Indians for both sustenance and culture as maize was to the agricultural tribes. The slaughter ended the traditional nomadic way of life that most Plains Indians—the formerly sedentary tribes as well—had taken up after the introduction of the horse. Some sources claim that 60 million bison were killed, which reduced their numbers to a few thousand in only thirty years. The Plains were littered with skeletons.

The Sioux

The Sioux held power in the west. In 1874, Colonel George Custer discovered gold on the Sioux Reservation in the Black Hills of South Dakota. He asked tribal members to sell the land to the government. The Indians refused. The Sioux had to go. The following year, Custer and the Seventh Cavalry attacked. The combined forces of the Sioux and Cheyenne defeated them at Little Big Horn, Montana. In retaliation, the government mounted the Great Sioux War, the most decisive military battle on the Great Plains, from 1876 to 1877. At one point, federal troops destroyed 400 lodges in a Sioux village along with 500,000 pounds of dried bison meat, a seventy-day supply for the 4,800 residents. The Army won.

In the late 1880s, the Sioux were faced with an indomitable enemy, substandard rations including moldy beef and rancid flour, and an epidemic killing their cattle. In desperation, they turned to a new spiritualism based on the teachings of a Paiute shaman. The prescribed rites were said to bring back the bison and cause the retreat of the invaders. This cult of resistance was called Ghost Dance by whites. It was a doomed effort.

Two Dakota Sioux Indians cutting meat and drying it on poles. Courtesy of Library of Congress, Prints & Photographs Division, Edward S. Curtis Collection (reproduction number: LC-USZ62-101184).

In 1890, the government suspected that Chief Sitting Bull of the Sioux was fomenting a revolt. He was arrested, and a gunfight took place between the Sioux and Army in which thirteen people including the chief were killed. The Seventh Cavalry pursued the scattering Indians to Wounded Knee where the famed massacre took place, slaughtering, according to various estimates, between 150 and 370 Indians.

RESERVATION FOODWAYS

Since at least 1830, the government possessed legislation that allowed it to force at gunpoint if necessary the relocation of Indians to reservations anywhere else in the country. That absolute power was strengthened in 1871 when the federal body decreed it would no longer treat Native Americans as individual tribal nations but made them wards of the state. In 1875, the government took away the Indians' rights to make treaties, saying it knew what was best for them. The wholesale move to reservations was made easier for the government by the fact that between battles and diseases, the number of tribes had been reduced to 100 from the original pre-contact 600. The reservations were often in barren areas and far from the natural resources the tribes had relied on for traditional subsistence. It was a national tragedy.

The battle was over. The Indians were forced to accept reservations in return for guarantees of land, water and other resources. On reservations, assimilation into white culture was the goal. Agriculture was the means to dispossess Indians of their nomadic habits and make them settle. It was intended to teach them appreciation of private property and the European concept of mastery of nature instead of harmony. This would foster competition and independence, it was thought, which would do away with tribal/communal focus. In Yankton Sioux villages, the people refused to give up such "bad habits" as frequent feasts. The women would learn the skills of farm wives, such as baking bread, while the men would raise crops. However, in Native American culture, tending crops was women's work, not men's. Nevertheless, only those Indians who found some way to adapt to reservation life survived this period without cultural demoralization. The so-called Five Civilized Tribes relocated in the 1830s to Oklahoma proved adept at blending their own traditions with white ways. The Navajo, on the other hand, clung to their cultural heritage with only bits of white culture. They suffered from "cultural neurosis," with one foot in a culture widely scorned (Navajo) and the other in the alien dominant culture.

Government Food Rations

Federal food programs on reservations shunned traditional foods. Beans, beef (or its equivalent in bacon), flour, coffee and sugar were distributed twice a month and lead to one of the most dramatic dietary changes in history. The intention was to supply rations only as an interim solution until Native Americans were raising enough food of their own. Instead, Indians became wholly dependent on rations and there were never enough. Government documents record the urgent request for more from one Indian agent in 1895. He requested that his 1,440 charges receive in all 5,040 pounds of flour, (3½ pounds per person), 14,400 pounds of beef (about 5 pounds each); 480 pounds of sugar (or ⅓ pound each) and 240 pounds of coffee,

(⅙ pound each on weekly basis). If not, he warned, the Indians intended to go hunting during the winter to keep from starving.[18] In 1900, the Bureau of Indian Affairs ordered agents to enforce labor by withholding rations. The Indians were little more than slaves for whom food was used as a weapon. In a rare sympathetic report to Congress in 1900, Commissioner of Indian Affairs W.A. Jones summed up the situation: "To confine a people upon reservations where the natural conditions are such that agriculture is more or less a failure and all other means of making a livelihood limited and uncertain, it follows inevitably that they must be fed wholly or in part from outside sources or drop out of existence."[19] Becoming dependent on rations undermined confidence in traditional wisdom and produced a decline in growing and preparing heritage foods. Many "recipes" and seeds were lost. Commodities set the stage for today's unhealthy Native American diet marked by high-calorie, fat, sugar and cholesterol.

Domestic Science Education

Beginning in 1879, tens of thousands of Indian children were removed from their homes and sent often hundreds of miles away to boarding schools run by government agencies and missionaries. Required to speak English and wear western dress, they were isolated from their families and what little was left of their tribal traditions. The curriculum was little more than forced assimilation. After leaving, those who returned to native ways were ridiculed. As "apprentices to civilization," Indian girls were taught European cooking techniques with rations, stoves, yeast, iron griddles and frying pans.[20] Prohibited from practicing their culture, they did not learn how to collect, process and cook wild foods. The diet at the schools often consisted primarily of starches with little fresh fruit or vegetables.

Actually, the training at these boarding schools was intended to shape these children for a future as members of the lower socioeconomic status as small-scale farmers and domestics. They were not allowed to be Indian in any way. These racist, repressive policies continued until the 1960s.

Taking Sacred Land in Allotments: The Dawes Act

Now confined to reservations away from their ancestral lands, the Indians soon confronted another injustice. The Dawes Act of 1887 was one of the most significant laws in American Indian history because it outlawed traditional communal ownership of lands. Instead, the reservations were divided into lots of 160 acres for each head of household, and smaller plots to individuals. Anything left over was declared "surplus" and sold as bargains to land-hungry or speculating whites. Government policy toward Indians aimed at emphasizing family and self-support in an effort to break up tribal allegiance and to do away with the need for rations and, eventually, with reservations themselves. The allotments were poor lands and speculators were allowed to buy high-yield areas of former reservations. The impact was devastating. The Iowa tribe of Oklahoma, for example, retained only 8,568 acres, with 107,174 declared surplus. By the 1890s the struggle was over and the white populations had won. Also in 1887, Congress opened up for white settlement 2 million acres in Indian Territory (Oklahoma). By 1907, tribal lands in the United States had been reduced by more than half. In all, 90 million acres passed out of Indian ownership to the federal government. Native Americans reached their lowest population after the turn of the twentieth century. The traditions of working the land, gathering wild plants, hunting and fishing communally had been broken forever.

Field Matrons

In 1890, the Office of Indian Affairs introduced "field matrons" to the reservations to promote assimilation through intensive domestic work with Indian women, a program that continued into the 1930s. The matrons taught the women "proper" meal times, food preparation and serving—more training to serve the upper classes. Canning and sanitary food storage were very difficult for Indian women to adopt.

New Agriculture

The government also attempted to change Indian life by providing new seeds and planting instructions. Buffalo Bird Woman of the Hidatsa tribe summed up this experiment:

> The government has changed our old way of cultivating corn and our other vegetables, and has brought us seeds of many new vegetables and grains, and taught us their use. . . .
>
> New kinds of seeds were issued to us, oats and wheat; and we were made to plant them in these newly plowed fields. Another field was plowed for us down in the bottom land along the Missouri; and here we were taught to plant potatoes.

We Hidatsas did not like potatoes, because they smelled so strongly! Then we sometimes dug up our potatoes and took them into our earth lodges; and when cold weather came, the potatoes were frozen, and spoiled. For these reasons we did not take much interest in our potatoes, and often left them in the ground, not bothering to dig them.[21]

MODERN ERA

Federal policy toward Native Americans has vacillated. Once the allotment era ended in 1934, the United States took a different tack and acknowledged the continuing value of tribal existence. The Indian Reorganization Act of 1934 provided for reacquisition of tribal lands. After World War II, the U.S. government created a new policy of terminating federal trust responsibility. Federal services were withdrawn from about 11,500 Native Americans and trust protection removed from 1.5 million acres. The land was often sold and proceeds divided among tribal members. The federal government still holds about 56 million acres in trust for 314 federally recognized tribes and groups. The largest is the Navajo (mostly in Arizona) with 16 million acres and over 140,000 people.

By 1990, the population of Native Americans had been reduced to 2 million. A little more than a third lived on the 278 reservations in 35 states; about half in urban areas.

Status of Foodways

Foodways are particularly resistant to change. They are the earliest-formed layers of culture and the last to erode. In this context, taste is conditioned to like certain foods and continue to seek them; preferences are part of culture.[22]

When foodways have been decimated by a dominant culture that then controls raw ingredients, however, it is almost impossible to resurrect the originals. The reservation rations diet led to high rates of obesity in part due to the forced foregoing of gathering, hunting, fishing and intensive agriculture and adoption of a sedentary lifestyle. After a while, many Indians did not want to go back to growing and eating maize, squash and beans, supplemented by freshly caught meat and fish and gathered wild plants. It was simply too much work. The younger generation wanted to be part of the mainstream and looked down on traditional foods. They wanted culinary assimilation and the status associated with eating white food.

The experience on the Navajo reservation reported by an anthropologist in 1940 is typical: "As other food became available the native foodstuffs and equipment became obsolescent. The women who had not heard of these practices were the younger ones, and those from families where they had no occasion to learn of them through the stories of an older relative."[23] Those women best informed were family members of male ceremonial singers, as it was at a ceremonial that the family would serve both ancient and modern foods. At The Night Chant, for example, twenty-one traditional dishes were eaten as part of the ritual vigil of the fourth night.[24] The anthropologist continued, "The foods which showed no variation are the maize foods prepared with or without juniper bushes [the ashes were used for hulling kernels]. This may have been because they are used ceremonially hence their preparation is prescribed."[25] The original ethnic foods were relegated to feast days and special celebrations. Among the Zuni, *piki*, the wafer-thin bread made of blue maize; blue marbles (a kind of dumpling) and bean stew had become special-occasion dishes.

By the 1970s on both the Navajo and Hopi reservations, pottery vessels had been replaced by aluminum, stainless steel or even pressure cookers, and grinding stones by electric grinders and food mills. Many families owned refrigerators, freezers and electric stoves. Culinary ashes were not being saved in the traditional special building devoted to that purpose. The women shopped at supermarkets for processed foods. Instead of traditional foods, Indians just like other Americans were eating high-fat, -calorie, -salt and -sugar processed foods lacking the micronutrients found in traditional, fresh foods.

Fry Bread: The Making of an Icon

Almost anyone who has set foot on an Indian reservation, and many who have not, knows fry bread or *Ban ik' aha*: puffed circles of white wheat-flour dough, deep-fried in lard, served with powdered sugar or honey. Its reservation origins are obscure. Some say it was a Navajo invention from the four-year incarceration at Fort Sumner after the Long Walk. Unable to grow maize in the new location, it is thought that these Indians began making fry bread from rations. The Lakota tell a similar story, while a Comanche author makes an early reference to the bread as having been made on the Plains in the 1860s or 1870s.

The one sure thing about fry bread is that there is absolutely nothing native about it, not its ingredients, technique or the cooking ves-

sel. It is often attributed to Spanish or Mexican origin (think sopapil-
las and tostados). Fried breads were a Spanish tradition; they brought
wheat, lard (from pigs) and metal fry pans to the Southwest. There
is another theory that it was introduced by French trappers travers-
ing and settling the Mississippi from Canada to New Orleans. The
relocation of tribes brought them into contact with new ones and
could have facilitated the spread of fry bread.

Today, the basic ingredients for making fry bread are flour, baking
powder, salt and water or powdered milk. The dough rests a while
and then is pulled into balls; each ball is patted into a circle. The circles are then deep-fried until puffed, crisp and golden on one side
and turned over to fry on the other. Lard is usually used for the deep-
frying but a member of the Salish tribe commented that her ancestors always used groundhog grease. A further refinement is the
so-called Navajo Taco, a concoction of fry bread, topped with layers
of fried ground beef or lamb, generous dollops of beans, cheddar
cheese, chiles, shredded lettuce, chopped onion and diced tomato,
served as a snack or meal substitute. Fry bread is a staple for feasts,
at powwows or any cultural gathering. It is fast, easy and cheap. In
some places it is made daily and served with almost every meal. It
has become so synonymous with Native Americans that even many
native peoples believe it is an Indian tradition.

The Price of the Westernized Diet

American Indians have indeed become assimilated to the worst of
the white man's modern diet. This process was accelerated in the
1950s when relocation policy offered Indians incentives to leave their
reservations and move to cities to seek employment. They came to
depend not on food produced by their own labor but on that from
larger society. Converting to the Western diet has had profound
health consequences. Over many thousands of years, the physiology
of Native Americans had adapted genetically to their diet. On the
Western diet, genetic predispositions were activated. Obesity, diabetes, heart disease and cancer were the result.

Diabetes occurs more than twice as often among Native American
adults than whites. About 14.5 percent of all adult Indian men and
15.9 percent of all adult women have the condition, a jump of almost
50 percent in only eight years. The highest rate is among the Tohono
O'odham and the Pima of Arizona, with at least 50 percent of those
over thirty-five afflicted. This is the highest rate of diabetes in the

world. Complications include kidney disease, heart disease, stroke, neuropathy and blindness. One in ten on the Tohono O'odham Reservation have to undergo regular kidney dialysis due to complications of diabetes, and life expectancy is ten years less than the national average. Before 1940, diabetes was rare among Native Americans; as recently as the 1960s, no one in the Tohono O'odham Nation was afflicted. The metabolism of these people evolved and adapted to traditional desert foods—like tepary and mesquite beans, cholla buds and chia seeds—that helped regulate sugar absorption and increased insulin production and sensitivity. A study of 165 nondiabetic Pima Indians found that those who ate an Anglo diet were 2.5 times more likely to develop the condition than those eating a traditional diet.

Some experts have argued that the high rate of obesity accounts for the elevated diabetes rates, but even normal-weight Pima have a greater incidence. First, the white man gave the Indians deadly contagious diseases. Now, Native Americans have inherited the health and nutritional consequences of the modern American lifestyle.

Red Power and Pan-Indian Food

During the socially and politically conscious 1960s, Native Americans, like black Americans, began to develop ethnic pride. A generation of activists pitted traditionalism against assimilation. The Red Power movement encouraged tribes to elevate their "Indianness," which, of course, included celebration of traditional foods as symbols of cultural identity. Just as soul food became a rallying point for African American identity, traditional Indian foods, their preparation and sharing became a ritual of the new revival. In 1968, the militant anti-assimilation group American Indian Movement (AIM) was formed. Native Americans began holding inter-tribal gatherings known as powwows where they could celebrate their ethnic identity. A set of "Indian" foods including fry bread, bison steaks and wild rice were often part of this pan-Indian movement. These foods spread along the intertribal pow-wow circuit. Fry bread entered a new era in the twentieth century and became a symbol of intertribal Indian unity. This is ironic considering that it is not at all a traditional dish but rather a testament to the foreign powers that invaded North America.

The Right to Fish. Protests known as fish-ins began to take place in the 1960s particularly in Washington, Oregon and Idaho. In treaties negotiated in 1854 and 1855, the tribes in these states gave up large amounts of land but preserved fishing rights along the waterways. The state and federal government ignored these agreements. Fish-ins covered by the media attracted attention to this issue. The most dramatic conflict came in Washington when the Indians defied the ban and a battle took place on water. This was the first full-scale intertribal action since the Sioux and Cheyenne defeated General Custer at Little Bighorn in 1876. As a result, the Federal District Court in Tacoma, Washington, declared the Puget Sound tribes entitled by treaty to 50 percent of the area's fish harvest. The U.S. Supreme Court upheld the decision.

Wounded Knee. In 1973, 200 members of AIM seized the Sioux village of Wounded Knee, South Dakota, calling for a return to traditional ways and self-government. The seventy-one-day armed conflict turned violent with the killing of two FBI agents (there is still disagreement about the culprit) and an AIM member. The stand-off ended in a cease-fire.

Reclaiming Land. Tribes have increasingly resorted to federal court actions to assert long-ignored treaty rights to land, water and off-reservation hunting and fishing. Some efforts have also led to the return of many religious sites including the sacred Blue Lake of Taos Pueblo. The Alaska Native Land Claims Settlement Act of 1971 awarded the Inuit and Aleut population $962 million and 16 million acres. Many tribes in the eastern United States began land claims in the 1970s, and in 1980 Congress settled with three Maine tribes for 300,000 acres and a $27 million trust fund.

RENEWAL

As a result of raising ethnic consciousness, there emerged a reappraisal of ancient ways by white observers as well as Indians themselves. This was helped along during the 1980s and 1990s by a shift in federal policy toward recognizing tribal nations and granting their own governing systems. (The Indian Reorganization Act passed in 1934 had already allowed Indians living on reservations to organize themselves as nations under federally approved constitutions and by-laws.) This recognition helped place a greater value on cultural identity including foods. In reality, the government was probably motivated by a desire to disengage from responsibility for Native Americans.

Although some predicted the extinction of Native Americans at the opening of the twentieth century, by the year 2000, their numbers had actually increased tenfold to 2.5 million. This was partly because anyone who could claim any Indian heritage came forward to take advantage of special benefits and tax breaks. Most Native Americans now live in Oklahoma, California, Arizona and New Mexico. The image of the Indian has gradually become more positive as other Americans have gained an appreciation for their cultures and greater empathy for their removal from ancestral lands.

Building on the activist awakening generated in the 1960s and 1970s, many Native American assimilationists began to rediscover the positive elements in traditional practices. In the Southwest, Northwest and Great Lakes in particular, tremendous efforts have been made to prevent further economic and environmental assaults on land where traditional foods are gathered or grown. Only in certain cultures in the Southwest, however, did Native Americans succeed in preserving something more than tokens of their culture, and their tribal entities have remained intact. There, most indigenous peoples continue to occupy at least portions of the lands controlled by their ancestors in the sixteenth century. Some foods are still prepared as they have been for hundreds of years. Others incorporate contemporary ingredients and utensils. The Pueblos held onto their way of life with intensive agriculture of maize fields, some of which have been cultivated for thousands of years.

The Hopi in Arizona, for example, still plant blue maize with no artificial irrigation. Many traditional dishes including the wafer-thin blue *piki* bread, the ultimate food of the Hopi, are prepared in the same way used by ancient ancestors. Granted, there are fewer types of crops and varieties grown in the terraced gardens of the Hopi, and the decision of what to plant is based on need for traditional social and religious occasions rather than staples.

Maize is the one product that has no store-bought substitute because its symbolism and meaning would not be the same. Maize is still central to Hopi identity.[26] Maize rituals are still in place. Where its production is concerned, nothing is taken for granted. Offerings are made to maize plants in song and prayer and believed to help them grow and be productive. Among the Apache, maize pollen is still used in every girl's coming-of-age ceremony.

A number of Indian tribes have initiated projects to reinstate traditional foods. These cultural preservation efforts, funded by public and private grants, seek to regenerate traditional agricultural methods, reintroduce heritage crops and animals, lower blood sugar through diet, preserve crop diversity and specific varieties by saving seeds and turn traditional foods into cash crops by marketing them to the public. Here is a sampling.

Combatting Diabetes

Food System Development Project, Tohono O'odham Nation, Arizona. Faced with escalating diabetes rates, the Tohono O'odham in Arizona set about rebuilding their native food system. Community members knew that foods like tepary and mesquite beans, cholla buds and chia seeds are capable of slowing sugar absorption and decreasing the rate and severity of diabetes.

First, the community surveyed attitudes toward traditional foods and found that people were receptive to eating them. However, they were not readily available and took longer to prepare. The connection between the foods and better health was not widely known.

The Tohono O'odham traditionally farmed the desert. Tribal members supplied free seeds and fencing for planting four acres of traditional desert crops using flood-based farming. This is traditional farming, as opposed to European agricultural methods. A fifty-five-acre farm was plowed and planted to increase production to meet the high demand. A farm equipment cooperative and seed bank were organized. The group also initiated a desert foods–collecting program, planted family and village gardens and established community gardens. Locally produced, healthy traditional foods were included in the local food assistance program. To underscore the role of culture in local food systems, the nation members organized the first *Nawait I'l*—the "bringing down the clouds" or rain ceremony that had not been held in one village for thirty years. The community purchased automated equipment for food processing and began training people to process grains and beans. Reservation farmers markets were established and traditional foods were marketed to government food assistance programs. The community even produced recordings of heritage songs and stories associated with desert foods. They are revitalizing their food system along with their cultural traditions.

Indigenous Diabetes Education Project, Rapid City, South Dakota. The Plains Indians in South Dakota realized that bison is a much healthier alternative to beef. A 3.5-ounce serving contains 2.42 grams of fat and 143 calories; the same amount of beef contains 9.28 grams of fat and 211 calories. Fort Belknap Indian Reservation in Rapid City, South Dakota, is working with public health officials to provide Native-raised, grass-fed bison meat for diabetics. They are monitoring the diabetics' health for two years to determine the impact of traditional food sources on ongoing diabetes. This will help restore cultural traditions that respect the centrality of bison to Native cultures of the Northern Plains.

The Mino-Miijim (Good Eating) Program of the White Earth Land Recovery Program (WELRP). This Ojibwe Indian program provides traditional and healthy foods to 172 diabetic people and their families. Each month they receive a bag containing bison meat, hominy maize, chokecherry or plum jelly, maple syrup and wild rice. According to the program's brochure, "Our teachings tell us that traditional foods are medicine; they provide both nourishment and healing for our people. When we harvest and eat these foods, we become connected to the cycle of the seasons and the rhythm of the earth. Our ancestors understood the importance of eating in harmony with the earth. That is why so many stories deal with the sacred nature of our traditional foods. Eating these traditional foods re-connects us with the stories and traditions of our people."[27]

Seed Saving

It was a tradition among Native Americans to save the best seed from each crop to plant the following year. Among the Hopi, household seed stocks were acquired through the family and community networks. When given commercial seed by the government, many American Indians found that these plants could not adapt to local conditions. Other reasons for seed saving were cultural. One Mohawk Indian related, "In seed selection, we look over our crop and select the best looking, uniform cobs. Corn is part of the sacred. We pray and then I try to get the crop in the ground early in the spring. As soon as it is big enough—green corn—we have a thanksgiving ceremony. We give thanks for all food not just for corn. But corn is sacred. It's been with our people forever."[28]

Today, a small Zuni community seedbank makes old-style seeds available to the community. A member of the Tohono O'odham nation explained, "Where an agricultural scientist sees a seed as a capsule of genetic information, a native farmer can hold that same seed and see part of his cultural identity. The crop has been part of our people for thousands of years, and when we plant it, we continue a cycle of planting, tending, harvesting and saving seeds that we hope will last another thousand years."[29]

Native Seeds/SEARCH (NSS), Tucson, Arizona. When Indians on the Tohono O'odham reservation expressed interest in planting the seeds of their elders, some University of Arizona students launched a project called Native Seeds/SEARCH. Volunteers collected, spread and saved the ancient seeds of arid, traditional and arid-adapted crops throughout the Southwest. Currently, there are some 2,000 seed samples in storage. Native Americans living in the Southwest receive seeds from NSS free of charge. Some are sold to the public along with native foods like blue maize meal and saguaro cactus syrup. On the sixty-acre Conservancy Farm owned by NSS, stored seeds are periodically regenerated by growing out a particular crop and saving the new seeds. The Cultural Memory Bank Project preserves cultural and historical data about each crop variety in the seed bank.

Native Seed Project of the Eastern Native Seed Conservancy, Great Barrington, Massachusetts. The Native Seed Project preserves the oldest domesticated plants from the Northeast, such as maize and beans, as living cultural resources. The project sponsors collection, propagation, perpetuation and redistribution of seed to Native people. Some seed is sold to the public. Native crops from the region exhibit significant qualities of vigor, cold hardiness, early ripening and disease and insect resistance. The long-term goal of the program is the development and expansion of native sustainable economies based on traditional activities.

Regenerating Traditional Agriculture

In 1920, there were still more than 48,000 Indian farmers in the United States, and half owned the land they farmed. Today, more than 8,000 such farms operate on reservations, but produce few crops for local consumption. In the process of cultural decimation, almost two generations were discouraged from producing and eating traditional foods. The seeds and methods for specific varieties of crops have been lost and agricultural knowledge sharing between generations severely reduced. Community networks have fallen apart and far fewer people live on reservations.

However, there are also signs of regeneration. The Zuni Organic Farmers Cooperative sponsors a farm equipment rental program to enable poor farmers to cultivate family fields again. The Akiimiel O'odham and Tohono O'odham, both of Arizona, have traditionally planted some of the world's most drought-hardy, heat-tolerant and alkali-adapted crops, including maize, tepary beans and cushaw squash. They are grown by what is called *Ak Chin* farming (or dry farming), which is anything but dry. The people built brush dams at the mouths of arroyos or washes to spread water from summer thunderstorms over adjacent fields. Corn, beans and squash were planted as soon as the fields were wet, usually July or August. The floodwater or runoff irrigated crops. If all went well, there would be a harvest in October or November. As late as the 1920s, the Tohono O'odham were cultivating over 20,000 acres in floodplain; by 1949, this had dropped to 2,500 acres and today, 25. In the 1930s, about 1.8 million pounds of crops were produced annually; in 2001, less than 100 pounds. One member of the Tohono O'odham Nation observed, "To survive on a little bit of water, you use a huge watershed to collect enough water to farm one small area."[30]

Carrying Traditions into the Future. For centuries prior to the American Revolution, the Oneida Nation of upstate New York fished, hunted and cultivated enough croplands to provide food to maintain traditional, healthful lives. Following their forced relocation to Wisconsin, their agricultural prowess declined. Succeeding generations struggled. The Oneida Nation of Wisconsin has now launched one of the most extensive Native food system efforts in the country, targeting and reintroducing youth to agriculture and food systems. The education teaches practical hands-on skills, increases knowledge about health and diet and provides information on natural farming techniques and sharing the harvest.

Expanding Sustainable Agriculture Systems. Accustomed to living on dry lands, the Navajo were expert at managing water resources such as the annual storm and flooding seasons. The Navajo Agricultural Technology Empowerment Center is leading a major agricultural effort to develop gardens based on knowledge while educating community members about traditional growing techniques. It combines both traditional and high-tech approaches. Program elements include construction of forty new family farms with dry-land techniques and a computer network linking 110 Navajo chapters to share information on moisture content, soil conditions, seed sources, pest control and irrigation. Courses on construction of traditional root cellars for winter storage and centuries-old heritage culinary practices, food preservation and organic pest management are conducted, some led by tribal elders who can recall traditional techniques.

Reintroducing Bison to the Great Plains

Bison was the central focus of the culture on the Great Plains. The InterTribal Bison Cooperative (ITBC) was established in 1990 by nineteen Great Plains tribes "to restore bison to Indian Nations in a manner that is compatible with their spiritual and cultural beliefs and practices."[31] Today it includes forty-two tribes and an 8,000-plus bison herd. Fred DuBray, a member of the Cheyenne River Sioux noted, "We recognize the bison is a symbol of our strength and unity, and that as we bring our herds back to health, we will also bring our people back to health."[32] Not all contemporary Indians, however, proved receptive to eating bison. The Intertribal Bison Cooperative had to hire a young Winnebago cook to develop acceptable recipes.

Marketing Traditional Foods

Ojibwe Wild Rice. The White Earth Land Recovery Project (WELRP), founded at the beginning of the 1990s at the Ojibwe Indian Reservation in White Earth, Minnesota, is working to preserve its traditional wild rice staple. This grass is hand-harvested by families from canoes. The rice is poled and brushed into the bed of the canoe, then spread to dry and parched in large metal drums. It is a long, tedious process. Wild rice remains an Ojibwe staple. Now some has been turned into a cash crop, marketed at a reservation store and online.

Iroquois White Corn. For centuries, the Iroquois had grown heirloom Iroquois white corn, which is 50 percent higher in protein than ordinary field corn. The crop practically disappeared, however, over the past 200 years. Efforts to save it began in 1995. They were only possible because Indian farmers had preserved their seed. Now the Iroquois cultivate about 100 acres. The maize is picked by hand, hulled and left whole for hominy, stoneground into tamal flour or roasted.

Restoring Indigenous Food

The Yankton Dakota in southeastern South Dakota found their indigenous food sources increasingly hard to find. This meant a lack of nutritional foods, special foods for ceremonies and typical foods to barter or trade for other goods. Today, the nation is assisting members to preserve traditional practices and foods including chokecherry bushes, wild plums, wild mint and wild turnips, providing indigenous plants to grow on members' land and running workshops to teach how to make traditional food products as well as learning their uses and mastering preservation techniques.

Food Festivals

Native foods festivals have become one way of introducing both young tribal members and outsiders to indigenous foods.

Annual Feast of Green Corn and Dance, Schemitzun. This celebration presented by the Mashantucket Pequot Tribal Nation of southeastern Connecticut takes place in August over a four-day period in Stonington, Connecticut, at the time when the green (immature) corn is ready to pick. It draws 3,000 Native dancers and many food vendors serving Native American cuisine.

Celebration of Basketweaving and Native Foods Festival. This annual event held at the Heard Museum in Phoenix, Arizona in early December includes demonstrations by many tribes of such culinary arts as making *piki* bread and acorn soup, roasting salmon in a fire pit, cleaning pinyon nuts and parching corn. The role of baskets in food production and preparation is highlighted.

Green Corn Dance and Fiesta. This annual feast day is held in July at the Santa Ana Pueblo, sixteen miles north of Albuquerque, New Mexico.

Mescalero Apache Mescal Roast. At the annual mescal (also known as agave and century plant) roast held at Carlsbad, New Mexico, by the Mescalero Apache, twenty to thirty mescal are harvested and roasted by traditional counselors. After the blessing, the mescal are placed in the roasting pit in the ground, which is then covered with damp grass and three feet of soil to seal in heat and moisture for the four-day cooking process. Once cooked, half the mescals are shared among attendees following communal tradition and the other half returned to the reservation for use by the Feast Givers at the annual girls' puberty ceremony in July.

NOTES

1. C. Margaret Scarry, ed., *Foraging and Farming in the Eastern Woodlands* (Gainesville: University Press of Florida, 1993), 10–11.

2. Carolyn Niethammer, *American Indian Food and Lore* (New York: Macmillian, 1974), xxi.

3. Adriaen Van der Donck, qtd. in Reginald Pelham Bolton, *Indian Life of Long Ago in the City of New York* (New York: J. Graham, 1934), 106.

4. James Axtell, *After Columbus: Essays in the Ethnohistory of Colonial North America* (New York: Oxford University Press, 1988), 129.

5. Caleb Crain, "He That Will Not Worke Shall Not Eate," *The New York Times Book Review*, October 19, 2003, 13.

6. William Bradford, *Of Plymouth Plantation, 1620–1657* (New York: Modern Library, 1967), 65.

7. Arthur C. Parker, *Parker on the Iroquois*, ed. William N. Fenton (1910; reprint Syracuse, NY: Syracuse University Press, 1968), 13.

8. Ibid., 14.

9. William Bradford, *History of Plymouth Plantation, 1620–1647* (Boston: Little Brown and Company, 1856), 5.

10. Andrew F. Smith, "The First Thanksgiving," *Gastronomica: The Journal of Food and Culture* 3, no. 4 (Fall 2003): 85.

11. Ibid., 85.

12. Maria Chona, as told to Ruth M. Underhill, *Autobiography of a Papago Woman* (Menasha, WI: American Anthropological Association, 1936), x.

13. James E. Seaver, *A Narrative of the Life of Mrs. Mary Jemison* (Howden, UK: Printed for R. Parkin, 1826), 48.

14. Lewis Henry Morgan, *The Indian Journals, 1859–62*, eds. Leslie A. White and Clyde Walton (Ann Arbor: University of Michigan Press, 1959), 33.

15. Bernard I. Fontana, "Ethnobotany of the Saguaro, an Annotated Bibliography," *Desert Plants* 2, no. 1 (1980): 63.

16. Gilbert L. Wilson, *Buffalo Bird Woman's Garden: Agriculture of the Hidatsa Indians, an Indian Interpretation* (Minneapolis: Bulletin of the University of Minnesota, 1917), 120.

17. Florence Hawley Ellis, "The Long Lost 'City' of San Gabriel del Yunque, Second Oldest European Settlement in the United States," in *When Cultures Meet: Remembering San Gabriel del Yunge Oweenge* (Santa Fe, NM: Sunstone Press, 1987), 30.

18. Wilcomb E. Washburn, comp., *The American Indian and the United States: A Documentary History*, 4 vols. (Westport, CT: Greenwood Press, 1979), 1:644.

19. Ibid., 693.

20. Ibid., 330.

21. Ibid., 119–120.

22. Susan Kalcik, "Ethnic Foodways in America: Symbol and the Performance of Identity," in *Ethnic and Regional Foodways in the United States: The Performance of Group Identity,* eds. Linda Keller Brown and Kay Mussell (Knoxville: University of Tennessee Press, 1984), 40.

23. Flora L. Bailey, "Navajo Foods and Cooking Methods," *American Anthropologist,* New Series, 42, no. 2 (1940): 271.

24. Ibid., 272.

25. Ibid., 273.

26. Barrett P. Brenton, "Fermented Foods in New World Prehistory: North America," in *Diet and Subsistence: Current Archaeological Perspectives: Proceedings of the Nineteenth Annual Conference of the Archaeological Association of the University of Calgary,* eds. Brenda V. Kennedy and Genevieve M. LeMoine (Calgary, AB: University of Calgary Archaeological Association, 1988), 4.

27. Allison Kadecki, "Indian Fry Bread: A True Traditional Food?" *The Snail* 2, 2004.

28. Junior Richard Cook, http://www.bioneers.org.

29. Underhill, 13.

30. Angelo Joacquin, qtd. in Keiton Dahl, *Wild Foods of the Sonora Desert* (Tucson: Arizona-Sonora Desert Museum Press, 1995), 13.

31. Mission statement, InterTribal Bison Cooperative, http://www.intertribalbison.org/main.asp?id=1.

32. Ibid.

CHAPTER 2
FOODSTUFFS

Native Americans lived in environments that offered great abundance and variety of foods. There were wild plants, berries and seeds for gathering, streams and rivers teeming with fish, coastal areas where shellfish abounded, animals to hunt for their meat and, in some areas, domesticated crops, chiefly maize. Particular foods that could be easily obtained or cultivated, and then preserved for lean times, became the primary foods. These often changed by season—there might be one staple during summer and another for winter.

The foods in this chapter are organized by type and importance of each in the diet. Descriptions include, when possible, nutritional value (although Native Americans had no scientific concept of nutrients, only what evolved through trial and error), how the food was obtained, some idea of how it was prepared, as well as its social and symbolic significance.

CULTIVATED CROPS

Maize, Beans and Squash: The Three Sisters or Indian Triad

These three primary crops were usually grown together with beans twining themselves up cornstalks and squash vines trailing down the side of corn mounds, covering the ground and keeping it shady, moist and weed-free, like mulch. The beans provided nitrogen to the soil while the maize provided not only the trellis for the beans to climb up but also shade and water condensation. The three crops were a culinary as well as an agricultural triad. The Iroquois called them the Three Sisters, believing the trio of spirits inseparable, and therefore the core of every meal. English trader James Adair, recorded, "They plant the corn in straight rows, putting five or six grains in one hole, about two inches distant—they cover them with clay in the form of a small hill. Each row is a yard asunder, and in the vacant ground they plant pumpkins . . . sun-flowers and sundry sorts of beans and peas, the last two of which yield a large increase."[1] This efficient, successful system maximized the bounty of these three staples while limiting the energy expended to grow them. Once harvested, they were easily dried and stored; the Wampanoag tied the three together to keep the spirits of the Indian Triad united.

Maize. No food is more identified with American Indian culture than maize, a word created by the Spanish from the Caribbean Arawak tribe, *Mahiz*; Maize was also called Indian corn, Indian wheat, and turkey wheat by the English colonists. Quite simply, this starch known in English as corn, which so well nourished the peoples of the Southwest, Southeast, Northeast and some of the Plains, was synonymous with life. Almighty maize was "the nutritive anchor of an entire culture," a phrase coined by an anthropologist to describe the core carbohydrate present in almost every society over a period of some 10,000 years.[2] He notes, "Its character, names, distinctive tastes and textures, the difficulties associated with its cultivation, its history, mythical or not, are projected on the human affairs of a people who consider what they eat to be the basic food, *the* definition of food."[3]

There are four major groupings of maize distinguished by the amounts and distribution of two types of tissue in the endosperm—one that is hard, corneous and translucent and the other, which is soft, floury and opaque. Flint maize has relatively little floury tissue, stores well and has much resistance to insects. Dent maize, used for roasting, has a floury middle and a corneous outer layer; when the grain dries, the floury tissue shrinks and gets pulled down, creating the telltale dent. Flour corn is almost entirely made up of floury, soft tissue and is used for grinding into cornmeal and flour; Popcorn is almost entirely made up of corneous tissue.

Maize was worshipped, guarded and hoarded, and became the focus of song, dance and chant. The Zuni of New Mexico used the name *Ta'-a*, meaning the Seed of Seeds, while the Iroquois called maize by a name that translates as "our life" or "it sustains us."

Touching Leaves Woman of the Lenape tribe in Delaware recalls, "We had high regard for Corn, and she was called 'Our Mother.'"[4] "Corn Mother" was often used to signify the pinnacle position of maize in the hierarchy of the spirits. Maize was celebrated in creation stories, myths and legends, used in rituals and thanked in ceremonial feasts.

As a food, maize has tremendous versatility: it can be ground into meal, formed into cakes and baked, roasted or boiled; used as milk in its immature stage known as green corn; combined with other foods including meats and vegetables in stews, dried and easily stored and parched for eating as a snack or trail food. Husks were used to wrap cakes and breads; dried silk was a seasoning or thickener and corn smut fungus was gathered and dried. Buffalo Bird Woman of the Hidatsa tribe of Missouri recalled in 1839, "We looked upon the *mape'di* [corn smut fungus] that grew on the corn as a kind of corn, because it was corne on the cob; it was found on the ears the grain of which was growing solid, or was about ready to be eaten as green corn."[5]

Tribes could easily have prepared maize thirty or forty ways, including the ubiquitous gruel, mush and hominy, a word taken from the Algonquian *rockahommie*, referring to maize hulled by soaking in lye created by the mixture of ashes and water. Those people who did not grow their own maize, including the Comanche in Texas and Crow in Montana, traded for this staple with eastern tribes. Buffalo Bird Woman remembered, "The Standing Rock Sioux used to buy corn of us, coming up in mid-summer or autumn. They came not because they were in need of food, but because they liked to eat our corn, and had always meat and skins to trade to us. For one string of braided corn they gave us one tanned buffalo robe."[6]

Maize was domesticated first in Mexico around 5500 BC and gradually spread northward, appearing first in America around 3500 BC, according to archaeological evidence from a cave in New Mexico. In the arid Southwest, Native peoples devised ingenious irrigation methods to ensure that corn would thrive in the desert. Excavation of the ruins of Pueblo Grande outside Phoenix, Arizona, have found that the Hohokam people, who were growing maize by 300 BC, constructed about 600 miles of irrigation canals from AD 50 to 1450 to water their fields. This allowed development of intensive agriculture and a more advanced civilization than in other parts of North America. By AD 400, the Anasazi culture that flourished at the Four Corners region (where Arizona, New Mexico, Colorado and Utah come together), developed what is called today "flood farming"—a method designed to take advantage of the late summer monsoon rains to irrigate the maize planted in canyon clefts. A network of walls and dams distributed water gradually to the crop.

The earliest evidence for cultivation of corn in the Northeast Woodlands/Great Lakes region dates from the first century BC at a site in present-day Illinois. It remained a minor crop until AD 800 to 900. By that time, maize was the underpinning for sophisticated societies in the Mississippi Valley. This culture came under the leadership of chiefs representing elite kin groups, a development related to the need for organization and management of increasing numbers of people. The threat of crop failure may have prompted the need for a permanent supervisor who collected tributes of maize (similar to taxes) during times of abundance and redistributed stored food when crops failed.

Maize was an ideal core carbohydrate. It is easy to grow, takes only 120 days to mature and produces abundant yields ideally suited to drying and long-term storage. Early Europeans marveled at this crop previously unknown to them. Explorer John Fiske remarked that "when Indian corn is sown on tilled land it yields with little labor more than twice as much per acre than any other grain."[7] Major John Burrows, part of an American contingent sent to fight the Iroquois, noted in his diary in 1779, "The land exceeds any I have ever seen. Some corn stalks measured eighteen feet and a cob one foot and a half long."[8] When the French under the command of Jacques-Rene de Brisay, governor of New France, tried to rout the Iroquois, their strategy was to destroy caches of stored maize rather than engage the Indians in battle. In 1687, a raid burned 1,200,000 bushels.[9] Although this figure may have been inflated, it was a substantial amount; still, it did not break the powerful Iroquois Confederacy, a league formed of the Mohawk, Oneida, Onondaga, Cayuga and Seneca tribes.

Maize came in a host of colors. John Josselyn, an early English traveler in New England, observed in 1663 what he called "*Indian* Wheat of which there is three forts, yellow, red and blew; the blew is commonly Ripe before the other a Month."[10] There was also white, black, blue and multi-colored, each taking on a different symbolic significance, often as one of the four cardinal points (north, south, east and west). The color is only contained in the thin outer layer covering the endosperm, so it is literally only skin deep. Maize varieties included soft, also known as bread corn; eight-rowed flint; dent and even popped corn, which came from the tiny ricelike kernels of a small-eared kind, much smaller kernels than what we pop today. This is what Governor John Winthrop of Connecticut referred to as "parched corn" when he saw natives stirring it about in the fire ashes until it "turned almost white inside outward, which will be almost white and flowery."[11] Buffalo Bird Woman claimed that each of the five principal varieties—hard and soft white, hard and soft yellow and gummy—had its own distinctive taste. She could immediately tell even in the dark which variety she was eating. Sweet maize—what we eat today as corn on the cob—was perhaps the least favorite of Native Americans, although the Hopi from Arizona grew some for ceremonial purposes. In late July at the time of the final Kachina dance, the dancers, also called *kachinas* because they represented the spirits of the Kachina cult, gave gifts of this corn to the children, introducing them to the spirit-beings so crucial to Hopi religion.

The Indians were greatly concerned with preserving the purity of color and type of their maize because each had a sacred meaning. Blue was particularly highly prized by the Hopi, who devised ways of

Four young Hopi women grinding corn. Courtesy of Library of Congress, Prints & Photographs Division, Edward S. Curtis Collection (reproduction number: LC-USZ62-094089).

intensifying and setting the color. The flour ground from this maize was the basis for making *piki,* a tissue paper–thin wafer bread, the quintessential food of the Hopi. The reason for the importance of blue maize goes back to the Hopi creation story, in which the Creator presented all colors of maize to the tribes. One by one each color was claimed while the Hopi, showing great restraint and respect, were left with a blue ear. The Creator looked upon this favorably and assured the Hopi that this maize would sustain them. Blue maize came to represent the westerly direction of the winds, which bring the life-giving clouds and rain. These Indians also used blue meal to make boiled dumplings called *mumuozpiki,* pancakes (*saquavikavike*) and fried grits (*huzrusuki*).

Buffalo Bird Woman told her biographer, "We Indians understood perfectly the need of keeping the strains pure, for the different varieties had not all the same uses with us. . . . We Indians knew that corn can travel, as we say; thus, if the seed planted in one field is of white corn, and that in an adjoining field is of some variety of yellow corn, the white will travel to the yellow corn field, and the yellow to the white corn field."[12] To prevent this, the Zuni constructed earthwork barriers between different colors. Only the most perfect ears were saved to become next year's seed. Buffalo Bird Woman observed, "Knowing that seed corn kept good for at least two years, it was my family's custom to gather enough seed for at least two years, in seasons in which our crops were good."[13]

The seasonal planting and harvesting of maize organized village life. New York State archaeologist Arthur C. Parker wrote in 1910, "Maize played an important part in Iroquois culture and history. Its cultivation on the large scale to which they carried it necessitated permanent settlements, and it was, therefore, an influential factor in determining and fixing their special type of culture."[14] Men cleared the fields while the women were charged with planting, tending the young plants and guarding the developing maize from birds, animals and thieves, a task they worked at in shifts from a raised "watchers' stage." To pass the time, they sang traditional songs. Buffalo Bird Woman related, "We cared for our corn in those days as we would care for a child; for we Indian people loved our gardens, just as a mother loves her children; and we thought that our growing corn liked to hear us sing, just as children like to hear their mother sing to them."[15]

Kernels could be eaten at every stage of the plant's growth. Green maize, which refers not to color but to young corn specifically planted to be harvested young, was a tremendous favorite and in many tribes became the focus of specific ceremonies. These cobs were "in the milk," containing a milky liquid in their unripe kernels that could be scraped off cobs with mussel or oyster shells or half a deer's jaw before being pounded into liquid. This was the origin of creamed corn and green-corn pudding.

This recipe for corn-in-the-milk bread from around 1907 is adapted from Touching Leaves Woman of the Lenape tribe. It is obvious that it is not the ancient way of doing things because she talks about metal cake pans and baking in an oven.

Corn-in-the-Milk Bread

Ingredients:
Corn; when in the milk stage
Salt

Grate the corn off the cobs taking care not to cut any of the cob along with the milk and kernels. The best corn to use is flour corn or open-pollinated field corn. Grate enough to half fill a large cake pan, about 60 to 70 ears.

Add about two teaspoons of Salt and stir up well. Pour into a greased pan, and bake in the oven at 375 degrees for about two hours or until golden brown.[16]

After the immature milky stage, maize developed over roughly thirty days to the dough stage, then denting and finally maturity or ripe, sweet.

Beans. Domesticated first in Mexico as early as 6000 BC, beans may have diffused north or been independently domesticated in the Southwest between AD 400 and 700. When Europeans arrived in the Northeast, the Iroquois were already growing many varieties (sixty according to one source) including cranberry, navy, marrow, several types of kidney, "snap" or "string" beans and pole beans. The tribe classified beans according to two functions: "bread beans" (those that were mashed and made into bread) and "soup beans." Cultivation of beans required an even more settled life than maize because legumes require almost constant attention.

Buffalo Bird Woman gave this recipe for "Beans Boiled": "The beans were boiled in a clay pot, with a piece of buffalo fat, or some bone grease. If the beans were dried beans, they were boiled a little longer than squash is boiled—a half hour or more."[17]

Beans in the Southwest were entirely different varieties and occupied a higher niche in the food hierarchy. The diets of the Tohono O'odham (formerly the Papago, meaning "Bean Eaters") and the

River Pima Indians, both of Arizona, were based primarily on legumes rather than maize. The chief wild bean was mesquite—hard, dark beans in a sweet pulp contained in yellow pods about six inches long growing on a shrub. They had a high protein content of 20 to 30 percent. These were more important than cultivated foods, including maize, for centuries. These pods along with their close relative, the screw bean, were the basic food for the Yuma and Mojave of California and the Cocopa, Tohono O'odham and Pima of Arizona. Even among the relatively agricultural River Pima an annual harvest of millions of pounds of mesquite beans was typical. The pods were gathered by the women who shelled, dried and stored the beans in the family granary bin. Those considered not good enough for storage were ground into meal before storing. At some future time, the meal could be sprinkled with water and formed into small, round, hard cakes that were sliced before cooking or used to thicken stews or simply eaten raw. During the winter, the Tohono O'odham often ate two daily meals of mesquite gruel.

Tepary Beans. The key cultivated food in the Southwest was tepary beans (taken from the Tohono O'odham word *t'pawi*). The legume was well adapted to Southwest heat and drought because it required little water. The Pima sometimes ground white teparies, dampened the flour and kneaded it into lumps that were dried and stored, then reconstituted by boiling, parching, grinding and mixing with maize or little bits of meat. Eaten twice a day, the beans supplied the Pima with 49 percent of their protein, 70 percent of iron, 52 percent niacin and 51 percent calcium, even though they made up less than one-third of the typical daily calorie ration.

Squash. Derived from the New England Native American word *askutasquash*, this vegetable included summer varieties like scalloped, yellow straightneck, yellow crookneck and zucchini and fall/winter ones such as acorn and pumpkin. The Hopi were particularly fond of cushaw, a soft-shelled squash, one of the oldest varieties. The flesh, seeds, flowers and leaves of squash were all consumed. Often, the vegetable was baked or roasted whole in the fire, or cut into pieces for boiling. Squash was a familiar ingredient of *eschoinque*, a soup including shredded meat or fish, thickened with dried corn meal. In some tribes, squash gained ceremonial importance as the focus of feasts held in response to dreams. John Heckewelder, a Moravian missionary from England, observed of the Mohican of New York State and the Delaware of Delaware, "They are very particular in their choice of pumpkins and squashes, and in their manner of cooking them. The women say the less water is put to them, the better dish they make, and that it would be still better if they were stewed without any water, merely in the steam of the sap which they contain."[18]

Domesticated independently in Mexico and the eastern United States—in the Southeast possibly as early as 4500 BC—squash were prepared for winter storage by removing their seeds, cutting them into strips and then air-drying on large basket trays. Colonist Peter Kalm wrote in 1749, "The Indians, in order to preserve the pumpkins for a very long time, cut them in long slices which they fasten or twist together and dry either in the sun or by the fire in a room. When they are thus dried, they will keep for years, and when boiled they taste very well. The Indians prepare them thus at home and on their journeys."[19]

Although early Europeans did not generally wax enthusiastic about Native foods, one French traveler among the Iroquois wrote in 1636 that "the squashes last sometimes four and five months, and are so abundant that they are to be had almost for nothing, and so good that, on being cooked in the ashes, they are eaten as apples are in France."[20]

Sunflower

The sunflower was cultivated in the Northeast even earlier than maize. Creation myths of the Mandan who lived in the Dakotas suggest that prior to introduction of maize, the sunflower occupied the key role in ceremonial life not only of the Mandan, but also the neighboring Hidatsa and Arikara. Archaeological evidence from AD 900 to 1000 in the Plains region has yielded many remains of sunflowers, lending support to the theory that they were second only to maize in subsistence importance in this area. The Hidatsa cultivated black, white, red, and striped sunflowers, although they were all prepared in the same way and tasted alike. These giant blossoms also figured prominently in the myths of the Southwest Indians, where sunflowers were the only domesticated food plant before introduction of beans, squash and corn. Hopi women ground the dried petals and mixed the powder with yellow cornmeal to decorate their faces for the Basket Dance.

The sunflower harvest took place in mid-October when the heads were cut off and placed face down on the roofs of the mud-brick dwellings to dry. Next the seeds were threshed out with beating sticks to be stored or parched and pounded in a mortar to make meal. Sometimes, the women squeezed the meal into balls of high-energy trail food for warriors and hunters. Buffalo Bird Woman said, "When worn with fatigue or overcome with sleep and weariness, the warrior took out his sunflower-seed ball, and nibbled at it to refresh himself. It was amazing what effect nibbling at the sunflower-seed ball had. If the warrior was weary, he began to feel fresh again; if sleepy, he grew wakeful."[21] Parched seeds could be ground into flour for bread and thickening soups, and diluted with water for a beverage. In the Southwest, the seeds were winnowed, parched and ground into meal on a grinding trough called a *metate* by the Spanish. The highly esteemed sunflower cooking oil was produced by crushing the seeds in water and skimming oil off the surface.

Sunflower dishes included the "four-in-one-corn ball," for which corn, sunflower seeds, squash and beans were ground together. For "corn ball loaf," corn and sunflower meal were cooked together along with beans and squash to make a thick dough to be formed into a loaf and packed in a hide that could be carried. Buffalo Bird Woman told how she made a winter dish called "four-vegetables mixed" for a family of five: First, she put a clay pot with water on the fire. Then she added a double-handful of beans. Next she cut a piece of dried squash "as long as from my elbow to the tip of my thumb," tying the two ends together so it would fit in the pot. When the squash was cooked, it was removed, chopped and mashed, and returned to the pot. Next she added four or five double handfuls of mixed meal of parched sunflower seeds and corn and boiled the dish for a few minutes.[22]

Sunflowers provided in greater amounts than maize what nutritionists today know are important dietary components: eleven times as much fat (a high ratio of polyunsaturated to saturated), three times the protein (each seed contains 52 percent protein) and twice the fiber at only one-fifth the percentage of carbohydrates.

Sunchoke or Sun Root

A tuber and member of the sunflower family, sunchoke (also known as Jerusalem artichoke), a native of the Midwest prairies, was domesticated by the Northeast Indians and cultivated widely. Growing three to ten feet tall, it produced edible tubers shaped liked knobby potatoes, three to five inches long, that were harvested in late fall. More nutritious than potatoes and lower in starch, the Jerusalem artichoke was prepared by boiling or roasting. Like the sunflower, it was a staple before maize was cultivated. Although the sunchoke produced almost twice as much food as potatoes, the tubers were small and did not store well.

Agave

This huge artichoke-like Southwestern plant, which grows wild throughout the Sonora Desert in Arizona, was a daily staple of the Mescalero Apache of Arizona. It is also known by the names mescal and century plant. German Jesuit missionary Ignaz Pfefferkorn noted in 1794 that "the root of this plant is as thick as the head of a large man and has a skin covered with scales like those of a fish."[23] Archaeological evidence attests to cultivation of agave in "orchards" of hundreds of hectares (the Spanish used the word "plantations" to describe the fields of the California Indians) by the Hohokam of Arizona. It could be planted on otherwise useless rocky hills and mountains where there was little moisture. There might be as many as 102,000 agave growing in one community. Each year, about one-tenth would mature and be ready for harvesting. The Indians dug them out of the ground with long sticks and stripped off the outer leaves.

Although toxic when raw, burning the mouth, mescal (the heart of the agave) was edible when roasted. The Indians dug huge roasting pits in the fields, ten to twelve feet in diameter, three to four feet deep, lined with large flat rocks; a mound of oak or juniper wood was placed in the bottom and the fire ignited before dawn. By noon, it had died down and moist grass was laid on the stones. Between one and three dozen agave crowns were roasted together, each surrounded by a mound of rocks to hold moisture in the ground. The pit was covered with bear grass, a tall western plant used to make baskets, and then a thick layer of earth and allowed to roast for two days. After the crowns cooled, the center portion or heart was eaten or dried in the sun. As agave was harvested before the plant produced its flower, it contained a large store of carbohydrates that converted to a sugary, highly nutritious food. Each heart furnished about 347 calories, 4.5 grams of protein per 100 grams weight and more calcium than a glass of milk.

Missionary Pfefferkorn, who sampled roasted agave wrote, "They are pleasantly sweet, are nourishing, and have the added advantage of keeping for some weeks without spoiling. Hence, they are much liked by the inhabitants and practically constitute the daily fare of the Apaches, in whose country the mescal grows in larger quantities in Sonora."[24]

Cranberry

Another native domesticate, this low trailing vine grew in bogs from New England to the Great Lakes region, and beyond in Oregon, and southward to the coast and mountains of North Carolina. It was not cultivated, however, until the early 1800s in Massachusetts and was known by the name *sassamenesh* in Wampanoag. In the early fall, the Indians gathered the berries, sometimes by hand. Wampanoag Chief Earl Mills Sr. later recalled that "harvesting was a festive time. . . . Relatives who had moved away often came back to town for the harvesting, and there was a sense of community with everyone working together."[25]

The task was made easier once the bogs froze hard enough for walking. Berries were then gathered until the snows arrived. Too bitter to eat raw, cranberries were usually mixed with maple syrup and stored for winter. Traveler John Heckwelder wrote, "They [the Indians] make an excellent preserve from the cranberry and crab-apple, to which, after it has been well stewed, they add a proper quantity of sugar or molasses."[26] His account clearly reflects post-contact times when sugar and molasses became available.

WILD GREENS

Gatherer-hunter Indian women and children foraged regularly for hundreds of edible wild plants. Even those tribes that relied primarily on agriculture often gathered plants seasonally for use as supplementary foods. Sprouts, leaves, stalks, blossoms and seeds were all used. Some of the most popular greens are listed here.

Rocky Mountain Beeweed

One of most important plants used by the Pueblo Indians of New Mexico, Rocky Mountain beeweed was celebrated in traditional songs alongside the "three cultivated sisters": maize, squash and beans. Beeweed grows in the arid forests throughout the West at altitudes of 4,500 to 7,000 feet. Its young leaves were gathered until July, before the flowers appeared. The Navajo, Zuni and Hopi of Arizona dried them for winter use, usually washing them several times to remove the bitter taste. They were often added to stews and boiled with maize; the Navajo also made a stew of beeweed, wild onion and celery and bits of meat.

Cabbage Palmetto

Cabbage palmetto is the most common tree-palm that grows in Florida; its range reaches up the Atlantic coast as far as Southeast North Carolina. When young, this plant contains a large bud about the size of a cabbage. The Indians ate the roundish, shiny, tender black fruits in the center of the crown, either raw or boiled.

Clover

This green commonly used as cattle fodder today was eaten raw or often cooked by Northwest Coast and Northeast cultures. The Apache of the Southwest prepared it in a pit, alternating layers of large heated stones and well-moistened clover, sometimes adding young onions and common grass. However, the practicality of this food resource was in doubt, as one early European arrival remarked, "This attempt to adapt the food of ruminating animals to human wants involves the necessity of consuming it in very great quantities."[27]

Common Purslane

The Apache ate this green primarily raw. When cooked, it was heated merely enough to wilt. The Zuni mixed purslane with white cornmeal or boiled the green and added a paste of white cornmeal with water to thicken the mixture before simmering.

Dandelion

Picked young before flowering in both the Northeast and Southwest, the tender leaves were eaten raw or cooked. The crown, root and blossoms could also be consumed.

Lamb's Quarters

Lamb's quarters was one of the mildest-tasting wild greens available to Indians throughout North America. Its tops were the most tender part. It might be eaten raw or its moist leaves packed around other foods when pit roasting. If prepared alone, it was added to soups and stews. The plant's black seeds were often ground for bread and mush.

Nasturtium

A member of the watercress family, nasturtium has edible blossoms, buds, leaves and seeds. It was noted that "when the covered wagons moved west across the Plains, the settlers found a kind of nasturtium growing in the wild. They named it Indian Cress because tribes of the area used both the blossoms and leaves to give their green salads a special pungency."[28] The term "green salads" takes a bit of license because the Indians did not prepare what could be called salads.

Round-Leafed Sorrel

The Alaska Indians chopped up sorrel leaves with scurvy-grass or watercress to make into a kind of mash that was allowed to ferment before eating.

Wild Spinach

Wild spinach, gathered by the Zuni in early summer, was boiled with a dry toasted corn cob with kernels intact to dispel its naturally bitter taste.

FUNGI

Rich in folic acid and a good source of B vitamins, fungi contributed a unique taste to Indian dishes. In the Northeast, natives gathered round to balloon-shaped puffballs (the largest edible fungus), common mushrooms and morels. Short, white to brown meadow mushrooms were relished by the Iroquois from New York State who peeled, diced and boiled them. Puffballs, found in fields and woods, were eaten in the early stages of their growth raw, boiled or roasted. The Zuni dried them for winter, while the Iroquois roasted and added them to soup. The Omaha of Nebraska cut puffballs into chunks and cooked them like meat. The Dakota gathered elm caps—long, thick mushrooms particularly abundant after heavy rains—from areas of decayed elms or box elders. Bracket fungi—sulphur yellow to orange fungi that grew on the bases of decayed or dead tress—were sliced and boiled by the Dakota who ate only the young ones and avoided those growing on ash trees, owing to their bitterness.

TUBERS

Groundnut or Potato Bean

This starchy tuber, also known as "Indian potato," was the most important gathered plant in the Northeast, although it was also consumed by many other tribes. The groundnut might be as large as an egg, and often several were found together growing low along streams or borders of swamps and marshes. They could be dug at any time of year except spring, when they started to grow. Among the most nutritious tubers found in the "New World," more so than the potato, the groundnut contained about 17 percent protein. Explorers Meriwether Lewis and William Clark noted in their journals that the groundnut "is the true *pomme de terre* of the French and the modo or wild potato of the Sioux Indians, and is extensively used as an article of diet. . . . [T]hese they boil with meat or pound and make an agreeable bread. . . . [T]his pittaitoee may be used in it's green or undryed state without danger provided it be well roasted or boiled."[29] Dried groundnuts kept for several years. English colonist Mary Rowlandson, taken captive by the Wampanoag Indians of Massachusetts, mentions eating groundnuts frequently. As she and her captors were on the run from the British Army, they were either carrying dried stores or the tuber was so readily available that it could be dug most anywhere.[30]

Indian Bread or *Tuckahoe*

Derived from an Indian word for loaf or cake, *tuckahoe*, a highly nutritious tuber that grew on roots of large trees, was sometimes as large as a man's thigh and could weigh up to forty pounds. In Virginia during summer, *tuckahoe* was the principal food. It was dug in fields and marshes throughout present-day Delaware, New Jersey, New York, Pennsylvania, Virginia, North and South Carolina, Indiana, Georgia, Mississippi, Kansas, Arkansas, Texas and Florida. Prolonged cooking neutralized its toxic properties and rendered the gelatinous character of the cellulose tender so it could be ground into meal for making bread.

Digging roots. Courtesy of Library of Congress, Prints & Photographs Division, Edward S. Curtis Collection (reproduction number: LC-USZ62-47003).

ROOTS

Among the large variety of roots gathered by the Indians were pepper-root, Solomon's seal, Indian turnip, skunk cabbage, wild licorice, anise, sweet myrrh, wild artichoke and potato vine. Those that were most highly prized included the following.

Breadroot

This large, starchy turnip-shaped root was one of the most important food plants of the gatherer-hunter culture on the Plains, who practiced almost no cultivation and were therefore dependent on wild foods. Harvested in summer, breadroot was sometimes peeled and eaten raw but also boiled and roasted. Raw slices were strung on strings and dried in the sun for use in winter, when they were ground into meal or cooked with meat.

Wild Onion

The Tewa, Navajo and Hopi of the Southwest, as well as many tribes in the West, ate wild onion raw in salted water with boiled corn dumplings or pieces of *piki*, the Hopi blue corn wafer bread. The Navajo also used them in soups and gravies. Sometimes wild onion was roasted in ashes or dried for winter. The Shoshoni in Idaho were more interested in the greens of the plant than the root, while the Oregon Paiute ate the onion itself raw or cooked and wove its leaves to use as covers for pit ovens. The Northwest Coast tribes cooked some of the bulbs in ashes along with camas bulbs, strips of caribou meat, lupine, carrots and fern.

Biscuitroot

These fleshy roots were known among Indians as *cous* or *cowas*. They were an important food of the Western Indians, and served as chief articles of trade; Lewis and Clark mention exchanging with Native peoples for a supply of "cows," and they certainly were not referring to animals.[31] Wholesome and nutritious biscuitroot was peeled, dried and ground into flour, which was sometimes made into traveling flat cakes.

Wild Leek

In the Northeast, according to one explorer, this root was a common gathering "whidh the *Indians* ufe much to eat with their fifh [fish]."[32]

WATER PLANTS

Wild Rice

Wild rice (actually a grass) grew in the lakes and rivers of Minnesota, upper Michigan, northern Wisconsin, New York, the Great Lakes, Florida and the Upper Mississippi, which reached into Louisiana, Southwestern Missouri and Virginia. It was the only grain native to North America and a staple of the Sioux of the Dakotas, Chippewa (Ojibwe) and Menomini of Wisconsin, and Dakota. Among the Ojibwe, the autumnal harvest of wild rice was of such significance that they named a month in their calendar for the event. Despite the richness of this resource, the crop failed every three to four years. One early traveler observed, "Vaft quantities of wild rice are seen throughout the country [from Lake Superior to Lake Winnipeg], which the natives collect in the month of Auguft for their winter flores."[33] It was such a valuable commodity that large amounts were packed in baskets and traded among various tribes on a regular basis. Consequently, it was also the focus of considerable wrangling. For 250 years, there was almost constant battling between the Dakota and Ojibwe over the rice beds.

Gathering wild rice was a huge, communal undertaking. Nineteenth-century Detroit area citizen and observer Edward Tanner wrote in the *Detroit Gazette* in 1820, "The Indians around Sandy Lake [Aitkin County, Minnesota], in the month of September, repair to Rice lake, to gather their rice. In no other place does it grow in as large quantities as there. This lake is about 5 miles long and 3 broad. It might, perhaps be called a Marrais, for the water is not over 5 feet deep, and its surface is almost entirely covered with rice. It is only in morasses, or muddy bottoms that this grain is found."[34]

Sometimes the Indians moved temporarily to a rice-gathering camp while they pulled stalks, tied them in bunches and secured with strips of bark. Then the grain was stripped off and dried. The entire harvesting process lasted an entire month. The preserved product was used to thicken soups of venison, bear, fish and fowl, or parched and carried by hunters. Early French traveler Pierre Radisson wrote in 1661 that "for each man a handful of that they putt in the pott, that swells so much that it can suffice a man."[35] Some of the grass was buried in water pits in the fall and left there to rot over the winter. When the Indians returned in the spring, they found the taste very much to their liking. Sometimes the grain was eaten with maple syrup or used for a dish known as *tassimanonny*, a mixture of rice, corn and fish boiled together.

Yellow Pond Water Lily

Also called the yellow lotus, this pond lily blooms with huge yellow flowers followed by the formation of oval-shaped pods with seeds about the size of acorns. Lewis and Clark noted that "of the root of this plant the Indians prepare an agreable dish," and also "dried by being expose to the sun and air or at other times with a slow fire or smoke of the chimnies, it shrinks much in drying . . . six to ten inches wide," Lewis and Clark found that the long, starch-filled rootstock developed in the fall and late spring and was much prized by Indians who boiled or baked it.[36]

The seeds were a staple for the Klamath Indians of Oregon, who gathered the pods as they matured and named the roasted seeds *wokas*. They kept for several years when dried. Lewis and Clark wrote that "each of these cells [in the seed pod] contains an oval nut of a light brown colour much resembling a small white oak acorn smothe extreemly heard, and containing a white cernal of an agreeable flavor; these native frequently eat either in this state or roasted. . . . [I]t is esteemed as nutricious as the pumpkin or squash and is not very dissimilar in taste."[37] Stored for winter use, *wokas* were sometimes kept in wigwams in caches of twenty to thirty bushels.

Klamath Marsh in Oregon contained about 10,000 acres of solid growth of pods that were harvested from dugout canoes. The profusion was so thick that the Indians could not use poles to convey their canoes. When fully mature and filled with a sap-like substance, the pods opened at the base and the seeds were larger, whiter and more palatable. The most-prized seeds were known as *spokwas*. Using a kind of wicker spoon, the women scooped and put them in a special basket. At the end of the day, the *spokwas* were placed in a pit in the ground and allowed to ferment. Then the women transferred them to a dugout canoe, added water and stirred the whole concoction so that the seeds dropped to the bottom and floating refuse was skimmed. The seeds were then spread out on a mat to dry prior to storing.

White or Tuberous Water Lily

Originally found along pond margins and slow streams of the Platte and Missouri Rivers, the white water lily, according to Lewis and Clark, "are either boiled to a pulp in their soupe" or less boiled eaten with bear oil or venison and bear flesh—"they sometimes pound it and make a bread of it."[38]

Cattail

These tall stalks grow in marshes, swamps and ponds from low to high elevations all over America except the coldest regions. They provided highly nutritious food throughout the year. The rootstocks, tips of new leaves, inner layers of stalk, green bloom spikes, pollen and seeds were all edible. Cattails produce a greater yield than modern potatoes, wheat, rye or other grains. In late winter or early spring, their sausage-shaped brown heads burst into fluffy masses of tiny seeds dispersed by the wind. In spring, the Indians ate the tender young shoots as a vegetable. They also collected the flowers to eat raw or boiled. For the Paiute of California in March, cattails were the first fresh plant food of the season, signaling an end to winter. The women pulled up the young shoots; the soggy outer leaves were ripped off and the crisp white stems eaten raw. Most important as a food source, however, were the creeping rootstocks, which were easy to pull up and full of starch when harvested in late fall and early spring. These formations were often boiled or baked and the cores dried and ground into flour for bread. This flour was equal to that of maize in food value. The Pima cooked cattail pollen in small pits: once the fire burned down, the ashes were pushed aside, then cold water was sprinkled, followed by a layer of pollen. The layering of water and pollen continued until it was finally covered over with leaves and baked.

Arrowhead

This water plant found all over North America and used especially by Northwest tribes produces potato-like tubers in the mud bottom of shallow lakes and pools. The Chinook of Washington named these nutritious, starch-rich bulbs *wapatoo*. The bulbs are not easy to harvest because gatherers must wade into the water to dig them. As a shortcut, the Indians sometimes raided the secreted stores of muskrats. Once obtained, *wapatoo* were prepared like potatoes— boiled or roasted, or strung on strings to sun-dry if not needed immediately.

Eelgrass

This fully submerged flowering saltwater vegetation is the only known grain from the sea to be used as a human food source. It grows along all the coasts of North America, particularly the northern Gulf of California, and was consumed primarily by Northwest Coast Indians, becoming one of the primary foods of the Seri in California. In spring, the eelgrass fruit (known as *xnois*) broke free and floated close to shore where it was collected. After gathering, it was spread out to dry and the women threshed it with wooden clubs and winnowed the fruit to remove debris before storing it in pottery jars to be eaten during the fall rains. If desired for flour, eelgrass was winnowed a second time to separate the chaff from the seed which was then milled on a grinding stone. After cooking the *xnois* with water to make gruel, the pulp was eaten with sea turtle oil. *Xnois* contained protein and starch like other grains and had an unusually low fat content.

Rockweed

Popular particularly in the Northwest, this brown seaweed was gathered in late spring and dried in the sun until crisp and black. It was most prolific on rocky shores, although some floated on the water surface because of air-filled sacs. Rockweed is rich in minerals and vitamins, specifically iodine and B_{12}.

NUTS

All gathered nuts were prepared and used primarily in the same ways—ground into meal and flour; mixed with water so oil on the surface could be skimmed; made into pastes, butters and bread; and used as thickeners of stews and soups.

Acorn

Acorns from the white oak were the most important food for the California tribes, including the Northern Paiute, Southeast Salish, Pomo, Tubataulabal, Yokut, Yosemite, Yurok and Washo. They were also much appreciated by the peoples of the Southwest who often ate them raw; those of the Northeast, where the Iroquois valued them as highly as maize; and natives living in Minnesota, Wisconsin, Nebraska, North and South Dakota, Arizona, Nevada, Louisiana and Utah. Apache women cracked the nuts on a flat stone by rolling over them with a stone cylinder. Batches of acorns were boiled together in a tight-meshed basket to produce the mush that constituted a meal.

Acorns provided a huge fall harvest but required special processing called leaching before they were edible. The high natural concentration of tannic acid in the nuts made them extremely bitter and toxic, causing indigestion. The Indians, however, by discovering leaching were able to transform an inedible food into a primary one. After drying the acorns, cracking them open and grinding the nuts into meal, they washed (leached) it in water multiple times. At first washing, the water was yellow, indicating tannic acid. When it finally ran clear, the women knew that most of the tannins had been leached

California Pomo Indian woman cooking acorns. Courtesy of Library of Congress, Prints & Photographs Division, Edward S. Curtis Collection (reproduction number: LC-USZ62-103072).

out. The resulting sweet meal could then be pounded into flour that made a heavy, unleavened bread.

Acorn oil was valued as much as meal. When the nuts were boiled, their oil floated to the surface, where it was skimmed into pottery jars, gourds or skins for storage. Early records suggest that collection of oil was facilitated with ashes. English traveler John Josselyn writes that the New England Indians used ashes of maple. "The Natives draw an Oyl, taking the rotteneft Maple Wood, which being burnt to athes, they make a ftrong Lye therewith wherein they boyl their white Oak-Acorns until the Oyl fwim on the top in great quantity; this they fleet off, and put into bladders. . . . [T]hey eat it likewife with their Meat, it is an excellent clear and fweet Oyl."[39]

The high fat content of acorns makes them calorically superior to most grains; one pound of meal contains 2,160 calories. Although they have less protein than wheat or barley, they are comparable in carbohydrates. Acorns were easily stored either in dwellings or in raised outdoor granaries and lasted sometimes for as long as two years.

Additional Nuts

Many other nuts figured in the subsistence of various tribes. They provided a reliable food source in the fall. The Kickapoo of Wisconsin were fond of pecans and hazlenuts (also known as filberts); nuts of the ironwood tree were gathered in the Southwest; those of the evergreen shrub jojoba in the South were valued for their 50 percent oil content; chestnuts, hickories (favorites of the Iroquois who made them into a kind of milky substance), walnuts and butternuts in the Northeast. Josselyn commented that chestnuts were "very sweet in tafte, and may be (as they usually are) eaten raw."[40] At the time, the American chestnut grew abundantly in the Northeast, although it was later eradicated by blight. Chestnuts were sometimes boiled and their mealy interior used for puddings or their dried meats pounded into flour and mixed with meal to give bread flavor. The Tennessee Cherokee chestnut specialty was a dough of corn flour with chestnut pieces baked in cornhusks.

Pecans grew in the well-drained alluvial soils of the Mississippi and its tributaries from Illinois and Iowa south to the Gulf Coast of Louisiana and west to part of Texas. The crushed nuts were boiled in water and the oil skimmed off, leaving a mass of mashed remains in the bottom of the vessel. These remains were eaten as porridge or made into cakes and dried for winter. The tribes in this area also ate the milky liquor, called *powcohiccora*, made by mashing the nuts in water.

SEEDS

Seeds were collected primarily to eat raw or to grind and pound into flours to be used in bread or as thickeners in soups and stews. The variety included sunflower, pumpkin, squash, ocotillo (a large thorny shrub that grows in the Southwest) and amaranth, but the seed that developed a reputation of its own was that of the pinyon pine.

The seeds of the cones of the pinyon pine were gathered in California, Utah, Arizona, New Mexico, Idaho, Nevada and Colorado. A staple of Southwest Indians, remains of pinyon seeds have been excavated from most ancient burial sites. The Navajo collected the most pinyon of Southwest tribes, climbing to the mountains to find them. Another species was a staple for Great Basin peoples and an incidental but highly desirable item for California Indians.

In fall and early winter, the tribes migrated to the pine groves to gather the crop. Boys were assigned to climb the trees and shake down the cones. For the higher limbs, the men beat the branches with long poles. The harvest was considered indispensable to tribes such as the Paiute who stayed in the region throughout the winter. It was noted that "in cases where for any reason a failure of this crop occurs, some tribes or bands have been brought nearly or quite to starvation for the want of the nutriment they afford."[41]

Pinyon were enjoyed raw or cooked. The Navajo roasted them in a shallow vessel until they cracked, or ground them carefully to break their shells and then winnowed them in a basket. The "nuts" were also sometimes parched by placing them in a basket with live coals and shaken. Otherwise, pinyon might be boiled into a gruel; dried, it could be formed into cakes. Once ground into meal, pinyon could be used for both bread and porridge. Many, of course, were dried and stored. For snacking, pinyon could not be beat. They provided more than 3,000 calories a pound and consisted of 50 percent carbohydrates, 12 percent fat and under 10 percent protein. One nineteenth-century observer wrote, "A handful of pine-nuts to an Indian child is as much of a treat as are sugar-plums to our boys and girls."[42]

BULBS, BLOSSOMS AND BUDS

Squash Blossoms

Considered part of the squash harvest, the infertile blossoms were gathered because the Indians knew that they would dry up, and as Buffalo Bird Woman put it, "become a dead loss."[43] Once collected, they could be cooked fresh or laid out on grass to dry and stored in animal skin bags for the winter. The Navajo added large quantities of squash blossoms to boiled meat and soups for flavoring. Buffalo Bird Woman gave the following recipe for boiled blossoms: A little water was brought to boil in a clay pot. A handful of blossoms, either fresh or dried, was tossed into the pot and stirred with a stick. Once they shrunk quite small, another handful of blossoms was tossed in. This was continued until a small basketful of the blossoms had been stirred into the pot. Into this a handful of fat was thrown, or a little bone grease was poured in. The mess was then allowed to boil a little longer than meat is boiled, and a little less than fresh squash is boiled. The mess was then ready to eat.[44]

Camas Bulbs

The starchy bulbs of the camas lily plant were collected mostly by Northwest Coast Indians of Cape Flattery, California; the Nez Perce of Idaho as well as those of Pitt River; and the Plateau Indians in parts of Idaho, Oregon, Washington and Montana. The bulbs were second only to salmon in importance in their diet. Each spring the meadows of the Northwest were covered with the blue flowers of the camas. The tribes went looking for them in early spring, an activity that involved the entire village. When the blossoms withered, the women dug out the bulbs and twisted the roots from the ground with willow digging sticks. The bulbs were eaten raw, roasted or pulverized into flour and made into cakes that were then boiled. In pressed form, camas kept for a year or more. Camas bulbs were also often baked in pits lined with flat stones. A fire was made in the bottom, and after the stones got hot, the ashes were removed, and the pit lined with green leaves and then partially filled with bulbs that were covered with more leaves and earth. After about thirty-six hours, the dirt was removed along with the bulbs. Camas were said to have a kind of sweet taste and became the focus of many community feasts and festivals. The gathering and preparation of camas continued to link groups like the Nez Perce to their traditional foodways long after they were relocated to a reservation.

Cholla Buds

The Pima and other Southwest tribes gathered buds of the cholla cactus in March when they were the only available vegetable food. Once the thorns were removed, the buds were placed in a sifter basket along with several small pieces of sandstone. The basket was stirred or shaken to separate the inner part of the buds from their coverings. These tender morsels were pit-baked overnight in layers alternating with hot stones and saltbush. Finally, they were sun-dried. Two tablespoons of buds contain forty-eight calories and more calcium than a glass of milk.

WILD FRUIT

There may have been more than 250 species of berries and fruits eaten by the Indians. These included huckleberries, squawberries, chokecherries, bear berries, wild strawberries, gooseberries, salal berries, currents, service-berries, elderberries, wild grape, whortle-berries, dew-berries, hackberries, sugarberries, mulberries, blackberries, raspberries and juneberries, wild crab apple, plums and cherries. All are rich in vitamins A and C, especially when eaten raw. They were often dried and ground into meal.

Berries

Huckleberries. In the Northeast and West, these abundant berries were a necessary food source. Different species grew in each area, and the Indians made long trips to the growing regions to gather them for drying for winter use.

Chokecherries. Sour fruit that varies in color from dark red to almost black, chokecherries were gathered in the Southwest, Northeast, Southeast and California. The Jicarilla Apache of Arizona ground dried berries into meal and fashioned round cakes about six inches wide. These could then be stored and reconstituted by soaking in water, boiling and straining off the juice.

Strawberries. Among the first wild fruit to ripen in the Northeast and Southeast, strawberries were so welcomed that the gathering time was celebrated in some tribes as Strawberry Moon. The plants thrived in natural meadows and open woodlands and the tiny, intensely sweet berries were gathered in large quantities for festivals and strawberry bread. An early Long Island description noted that during June it looked as if the fields had been died red.

Other Fruit

Persimmons. Taken from the Plains Indian word, persimmon is an acid, plum-like fruit that sweetens as it ripens in the fall. It was often

Mandan women gathering buffalo berries. Courtesy of Library of Congress, Prints & Photographs Division, Edward S. Curtis Collection (reproduction number: LC-USZ62-46987).

dried for winter use and made into pudding or bread by the Eastern Algonquian.

Wild Grapes. Grapes grew profusely in various parts of North America. Most were small, seedy and sour. The fox grape grew along streams and in low woodlands from Maine westward to Michigan and southward to the Gulf of Mexico. These fairly large purplish-black to brownish-purple fruits were pleasantly sweet and musky, the parent of the Concord grape. In the Southeast, the purplish-black to bronze muscadine grape measuring almost an inch in diameter was a great favorite of the Indians. It had a tough skin but was sweet and musky.

Plums. In the Southeast, many thickets of Chickasaw plums ripened in June or early July.

Cactus Fruits

Saguaro. These crimson fruit with tiny black seeds grow in late spring on the crowns of the towering saguaro cacti in the Southwest and are a challenge to harvest. In June, entire villages of Pima and Tohono O'odham moved to the saguaro forests for two to three weeks, a time that signaled the beginning of a new calendar year. Using two ribs from a dead saguaro spliced together and mounted with a transverse stick of the creosote bush, the fruits were knocked off, splitting when they hit the ground. Pulp was scooped out, then tossed into a basket and soaked in water to loosen the seeds so they could be sun-dried separately and ground for bread or mush. The pulpy part was spread out on a mat to dry after most seeds had been

Two Pima women harvesting saguaro cactus fruit. Courtesy of Library of Congress, Prints & Photographs Division, Edward S. Curtis Collection (reproduction number: LC-USZ62-101252).

removed. It was then cooked and strained through loosely woven baskets that allowed the juice to pass through into a pottery vessel. This was slowly boiled until it was reduced to a thick syrup that became the basis for a fermented drink described in the beverage section. Each saguaro fruit contains about 34 calories (2 tablespoons of dried seed have 74 calories) and a high amount of protein, fat and vitamin C.

Yucca Fruit. These long, banana-shaped fruits are considered one of the most important wild plants used by Indians in the Southwest. They were eaten raw, boiled, dried and ground into meal, and also used ceremonially. The Apache gathered them before they were fully ripe and laid them out on twigs to ripen in the sun before roasting them in hot ashes. The Navajo made a cake out of the fruit. The Zuni picked them in September or October when they were reddish yellow, washed, peeled and boiled them until they turned dark brown. When fully cooked, the fruits were kneaded into logs or rolls and dried for winter storage.

Prickly Pear or Indian Fig. Juicy red fruits known as *tuna* grow on the prickly pear cactus, which is found throughout the Southwest and West. According to Navajo legend, a hair must be plucked from the gatherer's head so the plant will give up its fruit willingly without twisting its heart. The Zuni picked Indian fig from August through September, using wooden tongs to remove the fruit. The women brushed off the spines with branches of creosote bush. The fruit, sweet and juicy, were eaten raw as thirst-quenchers. They might also be cooked, and their parched seeds used as soup thickener.

BARK

Although the bark of trees may seem like an incredibly strange foodstuff, the juicy inner layer (most often of the Ponderosa pine) was eaten by some tribes seasonally. The early European explorers found large stands of stripped white pine on the east coast; the name of the upper New York State tribe "Adirondack" means "tree eaters"; they were said to eat bark in great quantities. Northwest Coast Indians often ate the bark of shore pine, whereas the Rocky Mountain Indians ate the Ponderosa.

After cutting a line around the tree as high up as one could reach and another down low, the bark was removed in strips. The inner bark was the sap-carrying layer where a sticky film, a mixture of cells and half-formed wood, developed in the spring and could be scraped off. Sometimes, it was eaten raw, but more often the inner bark was cooked and ground into flour for making bread. Whether eating this substance was an act of desperation, a last defense against starvation or a seasonal food is a matter of debate. William Clark noted in his journal in 1805: "I made camp at 8 on this roade & particularly on this Creek the Indians have pealed a number of Pine for the under bark which they eate at certain Seasons of the year, I am told in the Spring they make use of this bark."[45]

LARGE WILD GAME

Hunting the largest animals possible made the most sense for Indian subsistence because they provided the greatest amount of flesh in return for the least energy expenditure. The ability to preserve huge quantities of meat meant fewer hunting trips each year. Among those animals not detailed here are elk, caribou (in Idaho among other places), moose, bighorn sheep and mountain goat (in the Northwest).

Bison

The wild ox, misnamed "buffalo" by the Europeans, belongs to the *B. bison* genus, and is properly called bison. It was the major food animal for those tribes who lived between the Mississippi River and Rocky Mountains. Not surprisingly, the Blackfoot called bison the "real food." It is hard to imagine more ideal prey. Millions of bison populated the Great Plains during early times, spilling over into the Northeast forests. One Indian captive wrote, "Buffaloes are so numerous about this place, that I often killed them with a bow and arrow, though I hunted on foot, and with no other aid than that of dogs well trained and accustomed to hunt."[46]

A "bison culture" evolved among the Plains Indians, who were so dependent on the animal that they worshipped it, celebrated it in myth and legend and endowed the creature with its own magic signs and symbols. Winter was the best hunting time, partly because the tribes could ambush the animals as they came down steep, snowy trails. The hunt typically began with a ritual prayer after which a scout was dispatched to pinpoint the herd while other hunters waited downwind. Once located, the animals could be killed in a number of ways—for example, chased onto a frozen lake where they would fall through. Each animal could weigh up to a ton. During the winter of 1702–1703, the Sioux ran 1,000 bison onto the ice. This single hunt supplied enough meat to feed all villages throughout the winter. Consequently, the hunters only occasionally needed to work. The Indians were adept at herding bison, moving them where they wanted them. At times of the year when water was not frozen, the hunters might drive the animals into a pond and then set fire to surrounding grass except for a narrow passage where they were easily killed with bow and arrow as they tried to escape. Using this method, the Miami of the upper Mississippi could slaughter as many as 120 bison a day. This translates into 50,000 pounds of meat, enough to supply a hunter with six pounds daily for twenty-five years. Another strategy was to drive a herd off a cliff. Because the Indians ate only the tender bison cows, leaving the tough bulls to rot, this could mean that a large percentage of the kill was wasted. Yet another hunting strategy involved driving the bison into corrals—circles of logs sometimes 100 feet across. Or the Indians might make themselves into decoys, donning bison robes with heads attached while imitating the cry of a calf. The herds were easily deceived. Some hunters were so successful that they killed more than 2,000 bison a year, enough to feed a village of 400 people.

In addition to eating the flesh, the Indians consumed the entrails and organs, drank the blood, sometimes eating the still-warm brains. A typical hunt provided an on-site feast. A Quaker missionary who lived among the Kiowa Indians wrote, "After loading ourselves with meat from the slaughtered animals—many choice bits being eaten raw by my friends—we turned our course toward the north, and arrived at Otter Creek in the middle of the afternoon, where we cooked some meat, and took supper."[47]

The most popular ways to prepare bison meat were jerky and *pemmican*. Jerky was made by smoke-drying the meat slowly during the day. At night the women took it off the racks, laid it on the ground, covered it with a bison robe and trampled the hide to squeeze out the blood. By day, it went back on the racks again.

Pemmican, an Indian word, was a high-protein, high-energy food made often by tribes such as the Blackfoot. The best and leanest dried meat was pounded into bits over which melted bison tallow (the animal fat) and marrow were poured. After the meat had been fire-dried until brittle, it was pounded on the bison-skin threshing floor with a heavy stick. Some women melted tallow from the bison cows' udders while others prepared *pemmican* bags, sometimes made of the skin of unborn calves. The meat and tallow were poured into the container in a ratio of about fifty pounds of meat to forty pounds of tallow. If chokecherries or service berries were available, they were often added to the mix. Then the concoction was stirred to spread the meat particles and remove air bubbles. When cooled, the *pemmican* bag was sewn shut. One pound of *pemmican* contained the same food value as five pounds of meat. It could be eaten directly from the sack or boiled in water; in smaller portions, it was easily transportable.

Bear

Bear was a primary food in the Northeast, valued not only as meat but for its high fat content. It was most often hunted in fall after it had fattened up on acorns or in winter while hibernating. Hibernation afforded a relatively safe opportunity to take a bear unaware. However, it was still a tricky procedure, in which the hunter entered the den through the very narrow opening. English traveler John Josselyn wrote, "The *Indian* as foon as he finds them, creeps in upon all four, feizes with his left hand upon the neck of the fleeping *Bear*, drags him to the mouth of the Den, where with a club or fmall hatchet in his right hand he knocks out his brains before he can open his eyes to fee his enemy."[48] Sometimes the method backfired. One brave, Black Robin, surprised a not-quite-comatose bear who attacked; Black Robin had his "buttock torn off."[49]

The Indians also took advantage of fully awake bears they encountered. An Indian captive wrote how he and his captors passed a tree that contained telltale claw marks. The Indians chopped the tree down and found two cubs secreted in a hollow. They were promptly killed. As one Indian captive wrote, "Their entrails were taken out, and after the hair was thoroughly singed from their carcasses, heads and feet, they were roasted whole." He pronounced the meat "excellent eating."[50]

Bears were especially prized for their fat content. One early observer noted that after the skin was removed from one animal, the fat was six inches deep in several places and required two people to carry it. To make oil, fat taken from the bear was cut into chunks, put into a wood or pottery vessel and simmered until it was liquid, then poured into a gourd or skin bladder container. The Indian captive explains, "It is the habit of these Indians to treasure up all the bear's oil which they collect during the hunting season, and carry it to their villages for home use. It is put up in deer skins, which are stripped from the animal with as little splitting as possible, and the openings necessarily made are carefully and securely closed. . . . The oil is eaten with jerked venison, and is as palateable an addition to that article of food, as butter is to bread."[51]

Deer

Various kinds of deer were hunted almost everywhere in the United States—mule deer in the Southwest; white- and black-tail in the Northeast, east of the Mississippi and in California. The sheer abundance of this game was staggering. Some Indians in Texas were said to kill 200 to 300 at a time, according to one Spanish observer.[52] Around 1750 in South Carolina, it was recorded that Indians exported 30,000 pounds of deer skins annually. As late as 1819–1820, the tribes who lived in Northwestern Illinois and Northeastern Mississippi took 28,680 deer skins. Like bison and other meats, deer was sun- and smoke-dried, made into jerky and *pemmican* and combined with corn and other vegetables in soups and stews.

SMALL WILD GAME

A great many small animals were also game for the Indians. Chief among these was the beaver, known for its high fat content, rabbit, porcupine, muskrat, grouse, prairie dog, rat, woodchuck, pack rat, raccoon, skunk and otter. Groundhog was one of the most important meat animals among several Native American tribes because it was more plentiful and easier to capture than deer. Squirrel was also a favorite and made into soup by the Seminole of Florida. A recipe for squirrel soup was included in an early American cookbook, *The Carolina Housewife*: "Take a squirrel cut it up and put it on to boil. When the soup is nearly done add to it one pint of picked hickory-nuts and a spoonful of parched and powdered sassafras leaves—or the tender top of a pine tree, which gives a very aromatic flavor to the soup."[53]

BIRDS AND FOWL

Passenger Pigeon

The passenger pigeon, a seasonal native food of the Northeast Indians of New York and Pennsylvania for thousands of years, was the most prolific bird in North America during pre-Columbian times, with a population estimated at 3 to 5 billion. (Today the species is extinct.) In the spring when the newborn birds were ready to fly, the parents abandoned the nests for a crucial window of a few days during which the Indians could easily capture the young. By either chopping down the densely nested trees or throwing themselves against them, the hunters brought the birds to the ground. Women and children participated by pushing nests out of smaller trees with long poles. Passenger pigeons made up the bulk of the diet for some communities such as the Indians at Lamoka Lake in south-central New York State, where archaeologists found that these birds' bones made up 75 percent of the fragments discovered.

Turkey

Called furkee by some of the colonists, and *gun-na* by the Cherokee, this wild fowl, native to the eastern United States, was a sacred bird to some tribes. English trader James Adair wrote, "The wild turkeys live on the small red acorns, and grow so fat in March, that they cannot fly further than three or four hundred yards, and . . . we speedily run them down."[54]

Waterfowl

Birds such as cormorant, shape or sharke could be hunted on the water from a canoe. At night, according to New England traveler John Josselyn, "the *Indians* will eat them when they are fley'd, they take them prettily," although "I cannot recommend them to our curious palats."[55]

FISH

For many of the coastal tribes, fish was the staple. The Northeast Indians migrated to rivers and the ocean each spring for the fishing season to catch cod, trout and bluefish, among other prey; in the

Northwest, salmon, halibut, perch and flounder were abundant. Seafood in general was an excellent source of vitamins A, D and niacin. Vitamins A, B_1 and B_2 are concentrated in many fresh fish roe. Whole fish is a good source of the mineral fluorine. As with game, every part of the fish, including head, tail, eyes and guts, was consumed.

Salmon

For both Northwest Coast and California Indians, salmon was the primary food. During fishing season, which extended from May to November, the natives temporarily relocated to summer villages on the banks of streams and rivers. The water teemed with salmon swimming upstream to spawn. The fishers poised on either side of the water with spears raised. They also set up weirs, traps consisting of two open willow fences spanning the river. Fish heading upriver were able to navigate through the lower grid but became penned by the upper one. Then, wielding three-pronged harpoons, it was easy to catch dozens of fish at once. After gutting the salmon, the women splayed them open and mounted them on upright poles around an open fire so they could smoke-dry for about ten days. The dried fish could be stored for year-round use.

Oolichan

For prestige and value among the Northwest Coast tribes, no food outranked these tiny fish, sometimes called candlefish, favored for their oil. Many Indians made the annual fishing pilgrimage to the lower Nass River in British Columbia, where oolichan were caught through holes in the ice. The cold, strenuous, round-the-clock preparation of oil and grease was a specialty of the Niska. An entire year's supply was manufactured at once. First, the oolichan were dumped into bins and left to decompose. As they softened, the grease oozed out and was then boiled and skimmed. The flavor varied according to how long it was allowed to spoil. The Niska traded oolichan to other tribes in exchange for dried fish, meat, tanned hides and soapberries. Oolichan grease also had a symbolic role representing blood in warmaking ceremonies among some tribes. The men drank from huge dippers to underscore their intention to take the life blood of the enemy.

Tui Chub

This abundant, important fish often fed the people of the western

Great Basin. The fish were an easy and reliable catch by net in spring, summer and fall. Tui chub were dried and stored for winter.

Herring

In the Northeast, the Wampanoag looked forward to the herring run in spring, when the fish swam to spawn in area ponds. The Indians set up temporary homes along the rivers, bogs and estuaries that line the southwest side of Cape Cod.

Eel

These highly prized, nutritious fish were indigenous to fresh and salt waters of the Atlantic and Gulf coasts. In early spring, these semi-amphibians migrated up the coast, even crossing land to reach freshwater habitats. Wampanoag Chief Earl Mills recalled, "We'd get the eel spears out, making sure each spear was firmly attached to its handle. . . . With the eel spear, we could only catch a certain size because we'd have to fight in the mud for them and thrust the spear back and forth. Sometimes we'd have three or four eels on that spear in between those hooks, and we'd bring that up and have our hands full."[56]

MOLLUSKS AND CRUSTACEANS

The tribes that lived near coastal areas harvested a wide variety of shellfish. In New England, these included the hard-shelled round clam or *quahog* (a name derived from a Narragansett word), soft-shelled clam, razor clam, mussel, periwinkle, oyster, scallop, cockle, conch, whelk, lobster, crab and oyster. One mid-eighteenth-century traveler noted that "The *Indians* who inhabited the coast before the arrival of the *Europenas* have made oysters and other shellfish their chief food."[57] These peoples had access to rich clam banks on the Connecticut shoreline with the largest at what is today Milford, Connecticut; around Narragansett Bay, Rhode Island; dozens of spots on Cape Cod; and Maine. Many of these beds were three feet deep and ranged over ten to twenty acres.[58] When excavated, it was found that 95 percent of these heaps were made up of soft shell clams with *quahogs*, razor clams and mussels making up most of the remainder. The largest deposits of oyster shell heaps have been found along the Damariscotta River in Maine, an area that contained an almost unlimited supply. One seventeenth-century traveler noted, "*Oysters* which are delicate breakfaft meat fo ordered, the *Oysters* are long fhell'd, I have had of them nine inches long from the point to the roe, containing an *Oyster* like thofe the Latines called *Tridacuan* that were to be cut into three pieces before they could get them into their mouths, very fat and fweet."[59] They were even found along the East River in New York City. Old and infirm inland villagers would journey to the shores to gather shellfish as the mainstay of their winter diet. Although the task was performed at low tide, it was often cold and troublesome because clams bury in mud. Once the shellfish were collected, the women shucked them with a deer or moose antler or bone sharpened to a point. In colonial times, Roger Williams, founder of Providence, Rhode Island noted that "at low water the women dig for them: this fish and the naturall liquors of it, they boile and it makes their broth and their Nasaump (which is a kind of broth), and their bread seasonable and savoury instead of Salt."[60] For future use, the meat was pierced on a green branch and set on a drying rack, or for lobster, crab, oyster and clam, often over a smoke fire. The Penobscot in Maine then packed them in birchbark boxes for winter use. For immediate eating, lobster and crab were roasted in their shells.

INSECTS

Insects were considered a major dietary item among Native American tribes in the Great Basin, but they also were valued by many others. Some of the most popular were locusts or grasshoppers. The Navajo removed their legs, wings and heads and browned the rest in ashes. The Zuni dug them out of the ground, soaked them overnight and roasted them by the "bucket" (about four cups), then mixed them with cornmeal mush. The Cherokee gathered locusts at night immediately after they had left their shells, washed and fried them in a small amount of grease. For the peoples of the Basin-Plateau, in some years, grasshoppers and a kind of cricket were extremely abundant and could be collected in quantities large enough to last for months. When Major John Wesley Powell, director of the Bureau of American Ethnology, visited the Ute and Southern Paiute between 1868 and 1880, he wrote,

> Grasshoppers and crickets form a very important part of the food of the people. Soon after they are fledged and before their wings are sufficiently developed for them to fly or later in the season when they are chilled with cold, great quantities are collected by sweeping them up with brush brooms, or they are driven into pits by beating the ground with sticks. When thus collected they

are roasted in trays like seeds and ground into meal and eaten as mush or cakes. Another method of preparing them is to roast great quantities of them in pits filled with embers and hot ashes. . . . When these insects are abundant, the season is one of many festivities. When they are prepared in this way, these insects are considered very great delicacies.[61]

Blister beetle was eaten by the Navajo, yellow caterpillars were braided into long ropes by the Shoshone in California and roasted between heating stones, tobacco worms were made into soup among the Pomo, or fried until they were crisp and brown. Vegetables, meal and seed were usually added. An early Iroquois ethnologist wrote, "The writer has seen this tribe gather bushels of the worms for immediate consumption, or to be dried and pounded up for winter stores."[62]

FATS AND OILS

Fats and oils were highly prized by the Indians and celebrated in myth and legend. Many animals and fish could supply these substances both for cooking and for use as condiments or ingredients. These included bear, groundhog, beaver, mountain goat, seal, oolichan, whale and salmon. Oolichan or smelt could also be processed into a rich oil that was poured over almost everything and ladled onto fires by Northwest Coast cultures. A gift of grease given from one tribe to another incurred the greatest debt in return. Oil rendered from boiling fat and grease made dried foods softer and more palatable, added zest to uninteresting foods, became an ingredient in boiling pots of meat and fish, and was sometimes served for dipping hot or cold dried food. There was hardly any food that was not perceived to be enhanced by adding oil. Pieces of fat cooked until they were hot and crisp were a great treat. When cooled and included in a hunter's on-road pack, fat could keep him alive when all else failed.

Salmon grease was obtained from either the heads or whole fish. A thin oil made a good preservative and could have a mild enough flavor to be used even with fruit. Humpback salmon was used almost exclusively for grease in the Northwest. One member of the K'san tribe explained, "To make this grease, we soak salmon heads (usually spring salmon heads) for several days in cold water until they are soft. Then we boil them and boil them until all the grease comes out and rises to the top of the boiling water. We skim this grease off. We may have to repeat this several times to get a clear, colourless, mild grease."[63]

An Eskimo cookbook prepared by schoolchildren in Shishmaret, Alaska, includes a recipe for cooked blubber, a favorite of the old people who remembered earlier foods. Pieces of seal blubber were put in a cooking vessel, doused with hot water, and cooked until the oil was extracted.

Nuts were also used for their oil, especially hickories in the Northeast. English trader James Adair wrote, "At the fall of the leaf, they gather a number of hiccory-nuts, which they pound with a round stone, upon a stone, thick and hollowed for the purpose. When they are beat fine enough, they mix them with cold water, in a clay basin, where the shells subside. The other part is an oily, tough, thick, white substance, called by the traders hiccory milk and by the Indians the flesh, or fat of hiccory-nuts with which they eat their bread."[64]

SWEETENERS: MAPLE SYRUP

It is most likely that maple syrup's properties were discovered fortuitously when some Indians sampled the liquid trickling from holes drilled in the sugar maple by sapsuckers in the Northeast. The syrup had multiple uses as a seasoning, summer drink and preservative for fruit. Above all, it was a sweetener. The Upper Lakes tribes made syrup during March, April and May, and during that time lived almost exclusively on that food, sometimes consuming as much as a pound a day. The Iroquois tapped the birch and several other trees as well as the sugar maple. The maple, however, was the only tree venerated by Iroquois—considered a special gift of the Creator, the only one to which a ceremony was dedicated and offerings were made. Each spring at the foot of the largest sugar maple in the village, a ceremonial fire was set and a prayer chanted by the Keeper of the Maple Thanksgiving ceremony. The running of the sap initiated a new year and signified the Creator's renewed covenant.

During the sugaring season, camps were set up as far as six miles from home, and all family members were involved in the four-to-six-week labor-intensive enterprise. Tapping took place while the tree was dormant by making a slanted gash in the tree trunk. Then a flat stick was driven into the gash. The flow of sap into a bark tub was triggered by a thaw following on a hard frost in the sunny late-winter.

Maple sap camp in the Northeast. Courtesy of Library of Congress, Prints & Photographs Division, Detroit Publishing Company Collection (reproduction number: LC-D419-151).

The collected sap was boiled in a clay vessel or wooden trough by stone-boiling (heating stones and adding them, then replacing cooled stones with hot ones). The reduction technique (by evaporation) boosted the sucrose content from 3 to 62 percent. It took thirty to forty liters of sap to make one liter of syrup. The sweetener was a good source of carbohydrates, calcium—containing between 40 and 80 milligrams, as much as whole milk—three to six milligrams phosphorus, ten to thirty of potassium and four to twenty-five of magnesium.

There has been a longstanding debate among anthropologists about whether Native Americans made maple sugar in addition to syrup. Sugar requires much higher temperatures to evaporate 94 to 98 percent of the water compared with only 34 to 35 percent for syrup. Some scientists have argued that bark and wood vessels could not withstand the high heat necessary for this rate of evaporation. It is now generally agreed that without the technology of metal kettles supplied by the Europeans, the Indians could not have manufactured maple sugar. According to French traveler Father Pierre-François-Xavier de Charlevoix who observed the syrup-making process in 1721, "It is very probable that the Indians . . . have at all times, as well as today, made considerable use of this liquor. But it is certain, they were ignorant of the art of making a sugar from it. . . . They were satisfied with two or three boilings, in order to thicken it a little, and to make a kind of syrup from it, which is pleasant enough."[65]

SEASONINGS

Salt

Salt, where it could be found or made by evaporation, was an important substance. It was considered essential as a meat preservative for winter by some tribes. The salt lake in New Mexico was the most sacred of all lakes to the Navajo. It was the presumed home of Salt Woman, one of the Holy People who, according to myth, traveled around the country, leaving deposits of salt wherever she rested until she reached the lake and settled there. The Navajo, Hopi, Zuni and other tribes made annual pilgrimages to the site to gather salt, which was valued highly for ceremonial purposes. The Zuni allowed only men to gather salt as part of initiation rituals. The Navajo ground native salt with a stone on a *metate*. In California, wars were fought over access to the salt beds on the Pacific shores. The Pomo of California owned a salt deposit where salt crystallized each summer from brackish groundwater seeping from a particular acre. The Pomo did not mind sharing but wanted gifts in return and would attack anyone who tried to steal. The Paiute scraped up salt from alkali flats and mixed it with water to make a paste, molded flat cakes about eight inches in diameter and then dried and stored them or used the patties for trade. They even carried some across the Sierra to trade with other tribes to the west for such items as acorns. In the Southeast, there was a great abundance of salt. It was made by evaporation in special pottery salt pans and was a common article of trade. The Chitimacha in Louisiana were one of the few tribes that used salt from local deposits rather than drying or smoking to preserve game. The Great Salt Spring was located in what is now Southern Illinois. There is also some evidence of early salt trade from the Gulf Coast tribes reaching as far as the Cherokee trail system.

Interestingly, use of salt was to some degree a matter of preference. Although it existed in New York State, salt was seldom or never used by Northeast Indians. The Iroquois adopted it only in the late historical period. The Mandan, although their territory abounded in salt, were also nonusers. For a dish of white corn and beans, Buffalo Bird Woman reported that "spring salt" was added. "A small palmful of the salt was mixed with a little water in a horn spoon; this dissolved the salt and let the sand and dirt drop to the bottom. The dissolved salt was poured off through the fingers, held to the mouth of the horn spoon; this strained out the sand and dirt. The salt turned the mush slightly yellow."[66]

Other Seasonings

Among other items used for seasoning were maple syrup, bear's oil (the fat rendered down into liquid) and grease (particularly from the intestines area), wild garlic, mint, juniper berries, marjoram, wild onion, sage, wintergreen leaves and berries, ginger, spicebush (wild allspice) and dried cornsilk. Bear oil was used as butter or ketchup is used today—to enhance or add flavor to practically anything. New Englanders did not use salt, but as a substitute, they used a thickened broth of boiled clams called *nasaump* to flavor bread.

BEVERAGES

Water

Spring or lake water was the preferred beverage of most Indians. According to a nineteenth-century anthropologist, "Of their drink not much can be said, for the reason that, generally speaking, they had nothing but water, and curiously enough, they preferred it warm and stagnant."[67] Some, such as the tribes in Virginia, flavored their water with ginger, sassafras or dried fruits.

Broth

Diluted bouillion in which meat or crushed animal bones had been cooked was also a popular drink. One early historian commented, "The common drink of the Indians at their meals is nothing but the broth of the meat they have boiled, or spring water."[68]

Fat

It was not unusual to skim fat from boiled bear or beaver meat and drink it. Bear's oil was also popular.

Manzanita Cider

A drink made of the berries of the manzanita bushes found throughout the chapparral belt of the coast range, northern mountains, and Sierra foothills was the principle beverage of the California Indians. The berries were placed in a dish, crushed and leached with water. The juice was drunk without sweetening.

Cactus Juice

In the Southwest in the dry season, pulpy, juicy cacti often provided liquid refreshment. The fruit, fleshy leaves and joints of the prickly pear cactus contain a high proportion of water. Also used was the pulp of the barrel cactus stem, the young stems of the agave and yucca as well as other desert plants.

Tea

Many kinds of tea were made from various barks, roots and berries such as red sassafras, wild allspice, red sumac berries, wintergreen, sweet fern, rose hip, wintergreen, and catnip. In the Northeast and Southeast, cranberries and blueberries might be mixed with soup broth or cornstalk juice. Labrador tea was made from a small, dwarflike plant with slender green needles that grows on the tundra in the Northwest. Chaparral tea came from an infusion of the flowering tops of this plant. The long, green stalks and leaves of the ephedra plants were used by almost all Southwest Indians. Navajo tea was made from the cota plant, found in the Southwest from May to October on grassy plains, mesas and open woodlands from 4,000 to 5,000 elevation. Wild stalks were collected and bundled together to dry and then boiled up with water whenever tea was desired.

Atole

Popular in the Southwest, *atole*—the Spanish name for corn soup liquor or corn soup—usually refers to a hot drink made of maize and water. It was made by the Zuni by mixing blue corn meal with water.

Mesquite *atole*, a mixture of mesquite meal and water, was consumed daily by Indians of the Sonora desert in southern Arizona to sustain them through the winter. Some tribes drained off the liquid in which maize bread had been boiled and stored it in pottery jars to drink. The Iroquois preferred beverages made from herbs or maize to water, and often mixed gruel with cold water until sufficiently liquid to be drunk.

Fermented Drinks

Many Native Americans gathered wild fruits that had a high enough sugar content to allow fermentation to take place. This process takes place so quickly that it is thought the discovery could not have been avoided even if there were no containers to store the products.[69] A traveler writing between 1808 and 1814 claimed that the Virginia Indians made wine from grapes and added liberal amounts of ginger, black cinnamon and sometimes sassafras. The Iroquois apparently fermented maple sap. Early-twentieth-century archaeologist Arthur Parker wrote, "Maple sap was drunk as it came from the tree and fermented, was sometimes used as an intoxicant, the only record of such a thing which the writer has been able to find as used anciently by the Iroquois. When fermentation went too far a vinegar was produced which was highly esteemed."[70]

Saguaro Wine. In the Southwest, the Pima and Tohono O'odham fermented fruit of the saguaro cactus annually during a two-day summer celebration. The juice was mixed with four times as much water and fermented while heated for seventy-two hours. Each family contributed a jar of boiled juice to the huge jars kept in the council house. For ritual reasons, to "bring down the clouds" or make rain, the men drank large quantitites of this wine, called *navai't* (it had a very low alcoholic content) specifically to induce vomiting. The logic was that because the saguaro is the tallest plant in the desert and therefore nearest the clouds, consumption of its fermented fruit and vomiting it back onto the earth was a good way to cause rain. As one Tohono O'odham elder speaking in 1979 explained to an anthropologist, "When *I'itoi* [the Creator] gave the Indian people the saguaro cactus wine, he gave it to them for two days, to have a dizzy effect for only two days, to use as medication. *I'itoi* knew that to stay dizzy for days was not good for man."[71]

Indians of the Southwest also sometimes made a fermented drink out of dried, pounded and ground mesquite mixed with water. Some tribes fermented the pulp from the agave. After pit-roasting, the pulp was pounded, placed in a hide pouch and buried for two days. When removed, the juice was squeezed out and allowed to ferment for another two or three days.

Tiswin. This maize beer, made by soaking kernels for twenty-four hours, figured prominently in the ceremonial dances of the Apache. The production involved digging a hole in the ground of a wigwam, laying dry grass on the bottom, placing the maize on top and covering everything with grass, then sprinkling it with warm water four or five times a day. At night, the family slept over the pit to increase the warmth and cause sprouting. After four or five days, the mixture was considered done. The fermented grain was then dried, pulverized, placed in a cooking vessel and boiled for about five hours. When cooled, flour and sweetener were added and it was left to ferment for another twelve hours, after which it was finally considered ready to drink. After the lengthy preparation, the beer had to be drunk within a few hours or the alcohol would turn into acetic acid, giving the drink a sour taste.

NOTES

1. James Adair, *History of the American Indians*, ed. Samuel Cole Williams, LLD (Johnson City, TN: Watauga Press, 1930), 439.

2. Sidney Mintz, *Sweetness and Power: The Place of Sugar in Modern History* (New York: Penguin Books, 1986), 9.

3. Ibid., 11.

4. L. J. Rementer, *Lenape Indian Cooking with Touching Leaves Woman* (1907; reprint Dewey, OK: Touching Leaves Indian Crafts, 1991), 3.

5. Gilbert L. Wilson, *Buffalo Bird Woman's Garden: Agriculture of the Hidatsa Indians* (Minneapolis: Bulletin of the University of Minnesota, 1917), 42.

6. Ibid., 58.

7. Arthur C. Parker, *Parker on the Iroquois*, ed. William N. Fenton (1910; reprint Syracuse, NY: Syracuse University Press, 1968), 19.

8. Ibid.

9. Ibid.

10. John Josselyn, *New-England's Rarities Discovered* (London: Printed for Giles Widdows at the Green Dragon in St. Paul's Church-yard, 1672), 53.

11. Betty Fussell, *The Story of Corn* (New York: Knopf, 1992), 11.

12. Wilson, 48.

13. Ibid.

14. Parker, 5–6.

15. Wilson, 27.

16. Rementer, 12.

17. Wilson, 86.

18. John Heckewelder, *History, Manners, and Customs of the Indian Nations Who Once Inhabited Pennsylvania and the Neighboring States* (1876; reprint New York: Arno Press, 1971), 194.

19. Peter Kalm, *Travels in North America, the English Version of 1770* (Reprint New York: Dover Publications, 1987), 517.

20. F. W. Waugh, *Iroquis [sic] Foods and Food Preparation* (Ottawa, ON: Government Printing Bureau, 1916), 112.

21. Wilson, 21.

22. Ibid., 20.

23. Ignazz Pfefferkorn, *Sonora: A Description of the Province* (Germany, 1794–1795; reprint Tucson: University of Arizona Press, 1989), 60.

24. Ibid., 61.

25. Earl Mills Sr. and Betty Breen, *Cape Cod Wampanoag Cookbook: Wampanoag Indian Recipes, Images & Lore* (Santa Fe, NM: Clear Light, 2001), 152.

26. Heckewelder, 194.

27. Edward Palmer, "Food Products of the North American Indians," *An Ethnobiology Source Book: The Uses of Plants and Animals by American Indians*, ed. Richard I. Ford (1887; reprint New York: Garland, 1986), 423.

28. Yeffe Kimball and Jean Anderson, *The Art of American Indian Cooking* (Garden City, NY: Doubleday, 1965), 117.

29. Meriwether Lewis and William Clark. *The Journals of the Lewis and Clark Expedition*, ed. Gary E. Moulton, 13 vols. (Lincoln: University of Nebraska Press, 1983–2001), 2:223–224.

30. Mary Rowlandson, "A Narrative of the Captivity and Restoration of Mrs. Mary Rowlandson," *Norton Anthology of American Literature*, ed. Nina Baym, 5th ed., 2 vols. (New York: Norton, 1998), 1:297–330.

31. Lewis and Clark, 7:227.

32. Josselyn, 54.

33. Albert Jenks, *The Wild Rice Gatherers of the Upper Lakes: A Study in American Primitive Economics* (Lincoln, NE: J&L Reprint Co., 1977), 61–62.

34. Ibid., 69.

35. Carolyn Raine, *A Woodland Feast: Native American Foodways of the 17th & 18th Centuries* (Huber Heights, OH: Penobscot Press, 1997), 19.

36. Lewis and Clark, 2:221.

37. Ibid., 2:223.

38. Ibid., 2:224.

39. Josselyn, 49.

40. Ibid., 51.

41. J.S. Newberry, "Food and Fiber Plants of the North American Indians," *An Ethnobiology Source Book: The Uses of Plants and Animals by American Indians*, ed. Richard I. Ford (1887; reprint New York: Garland, 1986), 35.

42. Newberry, 36.

43. Wilson, 75.

44. Ibid., 77.

45. Lewis and Clark, 7:227.

46. John Tanner, *A Narrative of the Captivity and Adventures of John Tanner During Thirty Years Residence Among the Indians in the Interior of North America, Pt. 1* (1830; reprint Ann Arbor, MI: Xerox University Microfilms, 1975), 63.

47. Thomas C. Battey, *The Life and Adventures of a Quaker Among the Indians* (1875; reprint Norman: University of Oklahoma Press, 1968), 280.

48. John Josselyn, *An Account of Two Voyages to New England* (London: Printed for Giles Widdows at the Green Dragon in St. Paul's Church-yard, 1674), 91–92.

49. Ibid.

50. Charles Johnston, *Incidents Attending the Capture, Detention, and Ransom of Charles Johnston of Virginia* (Cleveland, OH: Burrows Brothers Company, 1905), 56.

51. Ibid., 66–67.

52. Lucien Carr, *The Food of Certain American Indians and Their Methods of Preparing It* (Worcester, MA: C. Hamilton, printer, 1895), 184–185.

53. Sarah Rutledge, *The Carolina Housewife* (Charleston, SC: Babcock, 1847), 46.

54. Adair, 387.

55. Josselyn, *An Account*, 102.

56. Mills, 140.

57. Charles Willoughby, *Antiquities of the New England Indians, with Notes on the Ancient Cultures of the Adjacent Territory* (Cambridge, MA: The Peabody Museum of American Archaeology and Ethnology, Harvard University, 1935), 211.

58. Howard Russell, *Indian New England Before the Mayflower* (Hanover, NH: University Press of New England, 1980), 123.

59. Josselyn, *An Account*, 110.

60. Roger Williams, *A Key to the Language of America* (Ann Arbor: Gryphon Books, 1971), 104.

61. David Madsen, "Hunting Hoppers," *American Antiquity* 3 (1988): 595.

62. Palmer, 427.

63. People of 'Ksan, *Gathering What the Great Nature Provided: Food Traditions of the Gitksan* (Seattle: University of Washington Press, 1980), 50.

64. Adair, 439.

65. Pierre-François-Xavier de Charlevoix, *Journal of a Voyage to North America* (London: Printed for A. and J. Dodsley, 1761), 48.

66. Wilson, 61–62.

67. Carr, 182.

68. Waugh, 144.

69. Ibid., 147.

70. Parker, 103.

71. Bernard I. Fontana, "Ethnobotany of the Saguaro: An Annotated Bibliography," *Desert Plants* 2, no. 1 (1980), 1.

CHAPTER 3

FOOD PREPARATION, PRESERVATION AND STORAGE

Native Americans often went beyond simply making raw ingredients palatable. The agrarian cultures were settled enough to evolve some cuisine, based on loosely codified "recipes" passed down orally from one generation of women to the next. Some types of dishes were common to almost all cultures: porridge, stew, soup, bread, roasted and boiled meat and fish and fruit pudding. Relying primarily on a maize-based diet and using limited cooking methods and equipment, meals might have become monotonous. Indian women, however, introduced some innovation in devising dishes appealing to the palate, creativity for which they have received scant credit. The variety and abundance of food must have been inspiring. Maize was prepared in so many different ways and combined with so many other foods (chopped meat, shredded fish, ground nuts, other vegetables and maple syrup, for example) that the fare would not have been boring. The Navajo were reported to have several dozen ways of preparing meat, all the more surprising as their culture was largely vegetarian. Although most early European arrivals disparaged Native American fare, there were significant exceptions. One glowing reviewer wrote, "The Delaware woman spent a good deal of time and ingenuity in the preparation of food, [and] she was unsurpassed as a cook. Her two meals a day were prepared with a nicety that astonished Europeans."[1] They were considered especially skilled in regulating the fire and selecting the right wood for different dishes and tastes.

This chapter covers cooking equipment and utensils; processing techniques used as a prelude to actual cooking; prepping methods, both mechanical and chemical (including leaching, alkali processing to remove hulls from maize, food coloring and fermentation); cooking methods; and techniques for preserving and storing food for winter and lean times.

COOKING EQUIPMENT

Cooking Vessels

Pot or Kettle. Made from a variety of materials, the kettle was the single most important piece of cooking equipment. Holding between two and ten gallons of food, this vessel was in almost constant use from dawn to dark, as boiling was the primary cooking method in those cultures where water was plentiful.

Among the gathering-hunting cultures, kettles were sometimes made of materials that actually became part of the meal. The Plains Indians used the hump of the bison, dried into the shape of a large bowl, for their cooking. Some tribes adapted the carcass of a freshly slain animal suspended upright over the fire as a container for water and vegetables. After cooking, both contents and container were consumed. The nomadic tribes also often made cooking vessels of wood because they were light, not easily broken and could be transported. These advantages were offset, however, by the possibility that they would burn in the fire.

Soapstone and baked clay, either alone or in combination with powdered shells to withstand the heat of the fire, were also favored materials. The Southwestern tribes and the Mandan in Missouri, among others, fashioned pottery vessels. Whether the practice of making ceramic pots spread northward from what is today Mexico, or was invented independently by American Indians, is unknown. Early accounts of the Zuni report that basket trays used for parching corn were lined with clay to keep the basket from burning. This lead to finding that the clay form, hardened by fire exposure, could be lifted out of the basket and became a vessel in its own right. In the South, Indian women made huge pots, glazing them by placing the kettles over a large fire of smoky pitch-pine that produced a smooth black surface.

Some cultures like the Southwestern Apache made their kettles from baskets woven so tightly that water could not seep through. In the Northwest, the women wove these baskets underwater. Keeping the fibers submerged while working caused them to swell and ensured that the grasses in the dried vessel would shrink and tighten, becoming leakproof. The Northwest Indians also used cedar to make boxes that were used both for cooking (boiling) and serving.

Kettles were either hung over the fire or set on the ground, sometimes supported by stones, and then surrounded by fire. The pot was filled with water and then maize and other vegetables, flesh, fish and/or fruit might be added and boiled together to make the ubiquitous stews.

Bark Bread Bowl. This vessel was made from bark peeled in the spring when it was soft and could be bent into the required shape of one to two feet in diameter and four to nine inches deep. The bowl was bound around the edge with a hoop of ash bark sewn on with a cord from the inner elm tree. The vessel was sometimes used for cooking, but more often for mixing cornmeal for bread loaves before shaping and boiling and also for holding finished baked loaves.

Wooden Bread Bowl. This vessel carved from pine or maple, sometimes from maple knots, was the same size as the bark bread version and used for the same purposes.

Piki Stone. This griddle stone, about four inches thick by twenty-nine inches long and eighteen inches wide, was a special piece of equipment used by the Hopi of Arizona to make their sacred blue maize *piki*. The griddle was made with much care of sandstone quarried ten miles away from the village and smoothed by grinding with coarse gravel. Then the *piki* stone was polished with cottonseed oil, heated and seasoned with pinyon sap and treated again with oil. Preparing the stone was a ritual that had to be performed properly by a woman on her own. Finally, the stone was placed on four legs above a cedar and juniper fire. Each precious *piki* stone was handed down from one generation to the next. Although other Southwest tribes also made wafer bread and used a special griddle stone, nowhere did this food take on such symbolic and religious significance as among the Hopi.

Among the Zuni of Arizona a few old women were keepers of the secrets related to making the griddle stones. They alone were charged with quarrying the stone and manufacturing it. When finished, the stone was carried into the "kitchen" by two of the women who had made and tempered it, leaned facing east against the wall and introduced to ears of maize placed on either side, exorcised with rituals, invested with prayer-meal and sprinkled with water. Finally, it was installed on four columns of masonry in the corner of the hearth.

Making Piki or Wafer Bread: An Art Unto Itself. This quintessential blue maize staple of the Hopi was baked in a special *piki* house or room on the special *piki* stone placed above the fire, a method in use for at least eleven centuries. Although other colors of *piki* (white, yellow and red) were made and brought to children as gifts by dancers representing the spirits of the Kachina cults, they are nowhere near as prevalent as blue and certainly do not have the symbolic value. The dough was made by combining finely ground (powder-like) blue maize meal, adding hot water and culinary ash (*chamisa*, a source of alkali) until blue hue is achieved, then kneaded to the thin consistency of pancake batter. To intensify the color, the Hopi placed white limestone rocks in the fire until it died down. Then they were moved to a vessel, sprinkled with water and covered with cloth overnight. The next day the rocks would have turned to powder, which was sifted to make it even finer. This powder had the chemical ability to heighten the blue color. If the powder were intended for immediate use, it was mixed with water and then only a few drops were needed to turn the *piki* dough blue.

When the dough was ready, a fire was built under the *piki* stone. Then the baker, kneeling or sitting, dipped her hand in the batter, rubbed off the excess, and quickly smeared it with her flat palm across the top of the stone from far to near in successive arcs. The process built up heat-resistant calluses so that after a while, fingers did not get burned. It took little time for the crepe-like bread to bake, and then it was quickly peeled off and either folded or rolled and placed in a pile. A brush of alkali sacaton grass was used for cleaning the stone.

There was a ritual to the first use of a new stone. As the heat intensified, an old woman used her saliva to test the stone to see whether it was hot enough. A pot of thin paste, made of hot water and fine flour from all six varieties of maize, was set to cook while the bread-bowl was filled with a similar but thicker paste made in cold water. If the stone was ready, it was scoured with salt, greased and rubbed with an old rag. The woman took drops from each of the pots of paste and scattered them in the fire as a sacrifice. One of the old women dipped her fingers first in the hot paste and then the cold one. Then with a skimming motion of her hand along the surface of stone, she applied a paper-thin batter that cooked very quickly. She removed each sheet as it was done, rolled it up and placed it on a straw mat. For the Hopi women, *piki*-making was a daily, laborious activity that might be performed communally. It took great skill and art and also conferred status. It was the definition of what it meant to be a woman in this matrilineal society. A woman who excelled at *piki*-making held a special status. She could marry anyone outside of her clan no matter how high in status. One contemporary anthropologist observes, "The importance of *piki* to the gender identity of Hopi women cannot be lost in an understanding of the selective forces at stake in nurturing a food processing technology that ushered in an even greater sanctity for the role of maize products in the secular and sacred life of the Hopi."[2]

Preparation and Cooking Utensils

Tongs. Made from wood, bone or antler, tongs were essential to pick up and place heated rocks into kettles to make water boil, and to remove the rocks as they cooled.

Narrow Stirring Paddle. This utensil carved from hard wood and sometimes decorated (the designs were sacred to the Iroquois of New York State) was used for stirring soups and dried, hulled white or yellow maize mixed with water.

Stirring Sticks. Made from a bundle of thin sticks of sage, saltbush or greasewood in the Southwest, these *adistsiin* (Navajo for "stirring sticks") were used exclusively for maize dishes. Uneven numbers (from one to eleven) were preferred. For other dishes, several arrowweed stalks were tied together as stirring implements.

Wide Bread Paddle. The Cherokee of North Carolina were one of many tribes who baked their unleavened maize bread in the ashes (ash cakes) on a long-handled greenwood paddle. The moist newness of the wood reduced the possibility of burning the implement. When baked on one side, the bread was turned over to bake the other side.

Ladle/Dipping Spoon. Made of wood, horn or gourd, this utensil was used for dishing up soup and stew. Artist George Catlin, who traveled for eight years in the mid-nineteenth century among the Plains Indians, noted in his writings a ladle of particular beauty in a Mandan village. "In this dish laid a spoon made of the buffalo's horn, which was black as jet, and beautifully polished; in one of the others there was another of still more ingenious and beautiful workmanship, made of the horn of the mountain-sheep. . . . [I]t was large enough to hold two or three pints, and was almost entirely transparent."[3]

Wide Lifting Paddle. This sometimes beautifully carved and ornamented utensil, might be either round or rectangular with a hole in the middle. It was used for lifting maize bread out of the kettle where it had been boiled, allowing the water to drain off through the hole.

Scraper. In the Northwest, shells and stone knives were used to scrape the singed hair and flesh from a sea lion before removing organs for eating. A mussel or oyster shell, stone knife or lower half of a deer jaw was often used by other tribes to remove green maize (young, unripe) kernels from cobs.

Hulling Basket. Measuring about eighteen inches deep and broad, and tapering to twelve inches at the bottom, this basket was used for washing hulled corn.

Hominy Sifter. Made of cane splinters, this sifter measured about a foot square at the top and tapered to ten inches at the sievelike bottom, which had openings of about ³⁄₁₆ of an inch.

Meal Sifter. This tool with openings of ¹⁄₁₆ inch wide was used for sifting maize meal.

Winnowing Basket. A winnowing basket was a large, shallow basket used most often for hulled or pounded corn. When the basket was tossed upward in the air, it acted as a separator so that the lighter kernels came to the top and the heavier hulls concentrated at the bottom. After winnowing, the hulled kernels could easily be picked off the upper layer.

Grinding Stone and Roller. In the Southwest, the large, flat stone on which grain was ground and the smaller stone grasped in both hands like a rolling pin for grinding came to be known by the Spanish names *metate* and *mano*. Most often, three *metates* were lined up side by side, one for a coarse grind, the second for finer meal and the third for flour so the grinder could quickly progress from one to the other. A smaller stone (about four inches by three inches) was designated for grinding grass and flower seeds in a circular motion.

Mortar and Pestle. These tools used for pounding foods—most often maize—were made from both stone and wood. Stationary stone mortars, worn into the face of a rock outcropping, were common

Pounding fish with a mortar and pestle. Courtesy of Library of Congress, Prints & Photographs Division, Edward S. Curtis Collection (reproduction number: LC-USZ62-113089).

near village sites south of Ohio. Among the Kickapoo of Wisconsin, the Kansa of Kansas and Osage of Missouri tribes, each village had a large communal stone mortar at the center of settlements. This instrument was operated while standing, using a long stone or wood pestle that was sometimes ornamented with carvings.

The process for making wooden mortars that were smaller than stone and portable was recorded by English trader James Adair in 1775. The Indians "cautiously burned a large log to a proper level and length, placed fire a-top, and with mortar around it, in order to give the utensil a proper form, and when the fire was extinguished, or occasion required, they chopped the inside with their stone instruments, patiently continuing the slow process, till they finished the machine to the intended purpose."[4] A wooden mortar was sometimes referred to as a beater by the Cherokee when it was used to pound damp maize into meal. A muller—a short wood pestle or pounder with a flat rounded base—was usually used for pounding in the smaller wooden mortars.

Both grinding stones and mortars were used to make berry and fruit puddings by either macerating the fruit or pounding it and then cooking the thin pudding over low heat until it thickened. Fruits were often ground whole with their pits but then leached (washed through with many baths of water) to remove the poison (hydrocyanic acid) in the pits before being made into pudding.

Husk Salt Bottle. This vessel, made of tightly woven maize husks with a piece of cob for a stopper, was used by the Iroquois to hold seasoning substances for soup and bread, and was valued for its ability to keep salt dry.

FOOD PROCESSING

Food processing includes everything that is done to foods between harvesting (gathering, capturing or killing) and cooking—winnowing, grinding, sifting, washing, peeling, grating, straining. Prepping refers to things done to food to prepare for cooking.

Husking

Maize required a great deal of preparation before cooking. Husking was a communal activity among women, often accompanied by song and dance as the workers moved from house to house, where they were served maize soup for their labors. Husks were never discarded, but dried and stored for many uses.

Scraping

When it was not dried on the cob, maize was most often shelled when it was green or immature. Using the scraper, the milky kernels were removed before being pounded into a semi-liquid state. This became the basis for many dishes such as creamed maize and green maize pudding and one of the two main types of bread, the well-known corn-in-the-milk bread. Once sufficient green maize had been scraped, it was shaped into loaves and baked near the hearth.

Grinding

Corn, nuts, seeds and beans (including mesquite pods) were often ground or cracked into meal or flour before combining with other ingredients and cooked. Grinding was accomplished on the *metate*, using the *mano* in a pulling motion toward oneself repeatedly every day, often for hours. Because the diet for the agricultural tribes was maize-based, meal was a staple that needed to be on hand at all times. If flour was desired, the women used three *metates* successively to go from a coarse to a medium to a fine grind, using a grass brush for sweeping up the meal toward the top of the *metate* each time it was to be re-ground. Grinding maize was a female ritual, often accompanied by the men singing grinding songs. Anges Dill of Isleta Pueblo remembered, "And in the grinding songs they tell you almost what to do. And you have to grind to the beat, to the rhythm of the songs."[5]

Three *metates* (for coarse, medium, and fine grinding) were kept in each home and handed down for generations. Maternal grandmothers were charged with teaching their granddaughters how to grind at early ages so they would be able to perform without assistance at their puberty ceremonies.

The following Hopi method for making blue maize flour gives an idea of the process:

1. Shell dried blue maize.
2. Wash maize until water runs clear.
3. Coarsely grind maize on grinding stone.
4. Put ground maize in shallow basket or pottery pan and bake until it puffs and smells like popcorn.
5. Pour maize out of container and cool.
6. Grind puffed maize on grinding stones until fine as flour.
7. Store flour in covered container in cool place.[6]

Hulling Maize

Each kernel of maize is encased in a tough outer shell known as the hull. Native Americans removed these hulls before using maize as an ingredient. Hulling was accomplished either by chemical or mechanical means.

Chemical Method. The most important of these was the chemical alkali-processing technique, practiced to some extent by all maize-growing American Indians. The technique had profound nutritional consequences that will be discussed in detail in Chapter 6. In this method, wood ashes were combined with water, which produces lye, a strong alkaline solution with a distinctive odor. When mixed with unhulled fresh or dried maize, the lye chemically loosens the hulls, producing hominy or hulled corn. This technique was practiced throughout Mexico. However, it is not known whether it was also discovered independently by American Indian cultures at different points in time or diffused northward from Mexico.

Buffalo Bird Woman of the Hidatsa tribe in Missouri explained the process: "I collected about a quart of ashes; only two kinds were used, cottonwood or elm wood ashes." She then boiled water, added the ashes and stirred the mixture with a stick. After the pot had settled, the lye was poured off into a clean vessel that was returned to the fire. Shelled ripe, dried maize was added and the whole boiled until the hulls slid off and kernels appeared white. Twice, the lye was drained and the maize placed in a hulling basket and washed in water. Then she rubbed the kernels between her palms and sloshed the basket vigorously up and down in a tub of water until the hulls were free. Now the maize was ready to be boiled, made into baked hominy bread, become part of a stew or dried for further use.[7]

Culinary ashes called *chamisa* (made from burning branches of the four-wing saltbush) were used by the Hopi because of their ability to fix the blue color of blue maize. These sacred ashes were stored in a special building.

Mechanical Method. The mechanical method of hulling involved pounding unhulled maize together with ashes and water in either a stone or wood mortar and then clearing the hulls by winnowing. To make hominy for a family of five, a quart of flint corn was thrown into a mortar and moistened with a ladle of water. White ashes were added and the whole pounded until the hulls loosened. When they began to come off easily, the pounding was accelerated until the kernels were in coarse pieces. Then the maize was ready for the hominy sifter. Once sifted, the coarse grains could be thrown back into the mortar to be repounded and sifted again. After the second sifting, the uncracked kernels were thrown to the birds and the pounded maize placed in a winnowing basket and tossed so the lighter pieces came to the top and the heavier hulls settled at the bottom.

Mashing

Some foods were prepared by pounding in a mortar. Meat and berries, for example, might be mashed. When they were pounded together and tallow was added, this became *pemmican*. The Sioux of the Dakotas made their feast dish *wash-en-ena* from pulverized dried meat mixed with marrow and combined with sun-dried, pounded cherries. The Kiowa of Texas used the thrashing technique for mesquite pods. An early account reported, "They prepare it by pounding it into a coarse meal, put sugar with it [obviously written after European arrival], and mix it with water, then let it slightly ferment, and dry it. They undoubtedly have other methods of preparation, but this gives it a pleasant vinous taste, not disagreeable to the palate. They sometimes break these small cakes, reducing them to meal, and boil in the water in which meat is cooked, making a kind of mush."[8]

Nuts were also pounded in mortars and used as an ingredient in bread or broth, or mixed with hominy. To make hickory milk, hickory nuts were pounded to pieces in a stone mortar, tossed into boiling water, passed through fine strainers to extract most of the oil and used as a beverage or an ingredient in maize cakes or mixed with hominy.

Leaching

Leaching—drawing out bitter tannins, most often from acorns and camas bulbs—was an invaluable technique for turning naturally toxic foods into edible staples, particularly among the California Indians, who depended on acorns for sustenance. Sometimes the process was accomplished in a sand-banked leaching pit where unrefined acorn meal was placed. Then water made hot with heated stones was poured into the hole. This water washed the tannins through the meal so that they were absorbed into the sand base. The women watched the water as it was poured in and continued pouring until its color turned from yellow to clear, indicating that the tannins had been removed. Then the meal was placed in a woven cone with its narrow end set down on a flat stone; a second stone was used as a pestle so that a number of acorns could be ground into fine meal at once. Another approach to leaching involved placing coarse meal in a tightly woven basket, submerging it in a digging hole along the sandy bank of a river and allowing water to flow through for several days.

This traditional recipe for acorn mush is adapted from one from the Miwok tribe of California.

Acorn Mush

Ingredients:
Black oak acorns
Water

Preparation:
1. Harvest acorns in the fall, dry well.
2. Shell and pick off red skin on acorns.
3. Find an acorn pounding rock.
4. With a good sized basalt pestle, pound away until the acorns are crushed into a fairly fine grain/powder.
5. After pounding acorns, they must be leached. Make a sand volcano, flatten the top and make a rim around edge. Cover with a mat. Spead a thin layer of acorn mush over the mat and using a pine needle branch as a water breaker, carefully pour cold water over. The water will seep through fairly quickly. After a few leaches, taste to see that the bitterness has gone away.
6. Make a fire pit and heat up rocks.
7. Put the pounded and leached acorns into the cooking basket.
8. Add water in the ratio of 2 cups to each 1 cup of meal.
9. Using two poles or an antler as tongs, pick up a rock and quickly dip it in fresh water to remove the ash; then place in the cooking basket.
10. Repeat until acorn mush is cooked (about 5 minutes), adding hot rocks and removing cold ones to maintain the temperature. Serve.[9]

Masticating

Many world cultures, including some American Indian ones, practiced mastication—chewing food and spitting it into a vessel before cooking. This process produces a dramatic chemical change in food by mixing it with saliva, which contains the enzyme salivary amylase, a compound that converts carbohydrates into simple sugar. Not only did mastication sweeten food, but it also allowed subsequent fermentation (which requires sugar) to take place. The Navajo made their white maize tamales by first masticating cornmeal for sweetening.

Mastication is used in this recipe for *adeya: mu'le* (squash blossom flower cake), supplied by a Zuni woman: "Roast the blue corn. Grind the corn into a fine flour. Have the flowers cleaned and ready. She said they would have the flour in their mouth and wet it with their own saliva. She said it will produce a sweet taste. So what they chewed on will have to go into the flower pockets. Line them (the flowers) up depending on how much you want to make. Put them on top of a . . . hot griddle and brown. Turn over and brown on both sides."[10]

Leavening

As some American Indian tribes figured out how to ferment sugar-containing foods, it seems probable that they discovered yeast, the byproduct of fermentation. This living, microscopic, single-cell organism that converts its food into alcohol and carbon dioxide is contained in the froth or sediment of fermenting liquid. Whether American Indians made much use of yeast in their cooking or baking is hard to determine.

Early Zuni anthropologist Frank Cushing, who lived as a member of the tribe for many years, wrote, "The most prized leaven of his [the Zuni] time, however, was chewed *Sa'-k'o-we* [very coarse meal] mixed with moderately fine meal and warm water and placed in little narrow-necked pots over or near the hearth until fermentation took place, when lime flour (made with lye) and a little salt were added. Thus a yeast in nowise inferior to some of our own was compounded. In addition to its leavening qualities, this yeast had the remarkable property, when added to the meal of the blue corn or black, to change the color during cookery to a beautiful green hue, or, mingled with yellow-corn flour, to render it light blue."[11]

The Zuni ground hulled maize with water, making a fine, sticky batter to which lime (lye) yeast was added. Then clumps of the mixture were wrapped in corn shucks, folded over, tied at the ends and boiled. This solidified batter dish known as *tchu'-tsi-kwah-na-mu'we* is said to have had the quality of gelatin.

Wrapping

Meal was frequently packaged in maize husks or grape leaves before boiling, baking or steaming. This wrapping held the food together in a shape, sealed in moisture and lent the food a pleasing flavor. Among the Navajo, green corn was made into mush and wrapped in two folded green corn husks; the packets were then laid face-down in a hollow in the coals or boiled. One early European observer noted that "better flavored bread I never ate in any country."[12] This was also the way the Cherokee prepared green corn dumplings, called broadswords. Leaf bread tamales were made by beating green maize to a milky paste, patting it into shapes, wrapping it in husks, and dropping it in boiling water. They were then often dried for winter use.

COOKING METHODS

Many foods were eaten raw where they were gathered or hunted. These included not only plant foods, but also flesh and organs of game animals, oysters, salmon and herring. Most food, however, was cooked. In fact, a Moravian missionary to the Lenape (Delaware) in the 1700s observed: "Food which they prepare must be well cooked and well done; they do not like anything rare or raw. Meat and even fish must be so thoroughly cooked that they fall apart."[13] For some foods, the high heat of cooking was essential to transform it from poisonous to edible.

Much culinary attention was, of course, lavished on maize. A missionary in the late nineteenth century recorded twelve ways in which he observed Native Americans preparing corn:

1. Boiling in the husk.
2. Boiling quickly (really parboiling) in the husk, removing the husk and boiling again.
3. Roasting the ear in the husk in ashes as soon as it came off the stalk.
4. Pounding kernels small and then boiling them until soft.
5. Grinding unhulled corn into flour using a wooden mortar and pestle which removes the hulls.
6. Kneading corn flour with cold water, shaping the dough into a cake about a hand's breath round and an inch thick, wrapping it in leaves, and baking in hot ashes. This was one kind of bread made by the Indians.
7. Mixing dried bilberries with the corn flour to enhance the taste.
8. Chopping roasted or dried deer's flesh or sometimes smoked eel, and boiling it with the corn.
9. Boiling coarsely ground corn with fresh meat.
10. Boiling unripe corn until it swelled, drying it, and putting it aside for future use in soup.
11. Roasting whole corn when mature but still full of juice.
12. Roasting corn in ashes until it became brown, then pounding it into fine flour, and pressing it forcibly into a bag.[14]

Fire Making

This essential first step was usually a male responsibility. Fire making was accomplished by friction, using an instrument today called a pump drill—a weighted spindle of resinous wood inserted into a greased socket and foot in the notch of a piece of dry tinder. A slack bow string was fastened to the top of the contraption, the bow hanging at right angles to the weight. By twisting the bow string and then quickly pressing down on the bow itself, the spindle was set spinning. As the string unwound, it was automatically re-wound in the opposite direction. The bow was quickly pressed down again and the motion repeated until the rapid twirling created enough friction to ignite the dry wood. The fired wood was quickly touched to a pile of kindling.

There were various methods of sheltering the fire so it would stay lit; most often, it was built in a pit. Sometimes wood was kindled in a rock-sheltered circle or between two logs. The job of keeping the fire going fell to the women, who might spark it with a liberal dose of grease or fat.

A Northeast winter method of fire building using snow as a shelter was described by seventeenth-century English traveler John Josselyn:

> The men pitch upon a place near fome fpring, and with their fnow fhoos fhovel the fow away to the bare Earth in a circle, making round about a wall of fnow; in the midft they make their *Vulcan* or fire near to a great Tree, upon the fnags whereof they hang, their kettles fil'd with the Venifon; whilst that boils, the men go to sleep; The women tend the Cookerie, fome of them fcrape the flime and fat from the skin, cleanfe the finews, and ftretch them and the like, when the venifon is boiled the men awake, and opening of their bags take out as much *Indian* meal as will ferve their turns for the prefent; they eat their broth with fpoons, and their flefh they divide into gobbets, eating now and then with it as much meal as they can hold betwixt three fingers.[15]

Boiling

Boiling is one of the earliest cooking methods, accomplished either by direct fire or stone-boiling. It could be practiced only in geographic locations where water was plentiful. Direct-fire boiling was more prevalent in the Southwest and Northeast, where pottery was made. Stone-boiling was dominant in the Northwest and California cultures. On the Prairies and in the Northeast, the Indians boiled most meat along with plant foods. The women often rose before dawn to fill their water jars at springs, returning with the pots balanced on cloth rings on their heads. Northwest Indians stone-boiled pieces of blubber from sea lion in tightly woven baskets that could hold water. The precious oil was skimmed from the top and poured into a bottle made from the animal's stomach and hung from the rafters. The oil might be used to season leaves of the yellow dock plant that had been boiled and beaten to a pulp. Maize and pumpkin pudding, a favorite of the Iroquois, was made by boiling parched or yellow cornmeal mixed with maple syrup and pumpkin or squash. *Someviki*, a traditional dish of the Hopi, was made from blue maize meal that was placed in dried husks and boiled. The Iroquois and many other tribes made boiled corn dumplings. Their preparation is described by an early ethnologist: "Moisten a mass of corn meal with boiling water and quickly mold it into cakes in the closed hand moistened in cold water. Drop the dumplings one by one into boiling water and boil for a half hour. Dumplings were the favorite thing to cook with boiling meats, especially game birds."[16]

One well-known boiled dish of maize and beans, adopted by the early colonists and still made today, was known to the Narragansett as *sukquttahash*, later anglicized to *succotash*. A winter version was made from dried hulled maize, beans and winter vegetables (such as squash), whereas the summer variant contained fresh shelled beans and green maize. Bits of fresh meat were sometimes added, and the whole thickened with ground sunflower seeds. Grease or oil was included for seasoning and flavor.

This simple adapted recipe for *i-ya-tsu-ya-di-su-yi se-lu*, Cherokee succotash, comes from Tu'ti, a member of the Southeast Kituwan Nation, who learned it from his grandmother:

Cherokee Succotash

Ingredients:
Beans
Corn
Pumpkin (optional)

Preparation:
1. Shell some corn.
2. Boil corn and beans separately, then combine.
3. Add pieces of pumpkin (if desired) and boil until desired degree of tenderness.[17]

In the Southeast, a boiled maize dish called *sagamite* by the French and *samp* by the English was made from coarsely ground dried hominy. The kernels were pounded in a mortar and then boiled with any kind of dried or fresh meat or fish, sometimes oil, fresh or dried pumpkin and finely chopped beans, peas and other vegetables. In the spring and early summer, green maize was the primary ingredient. When made with bear oil, it was reputed to be "delicious."

Roasting

The lack of water in the Southwest made "roasting" (either on a spit or in a pit) the favored technique there, but it was also practiced elsewhere. Among the Mohican and Delaware, an early writer observed, "Their roasting is done by running a wooden spit through the meat, sharpened at each end, which they place near the fire, and

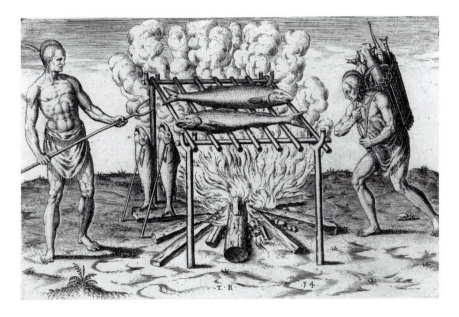

Roasting fish on a wooden frame over a fire. Courtesy of Library of Congress, Prints & Photographs Division (reproduction number: LC-USZ62-053339).

occasionally turn."[18] The Iroquois also roasted maize in-the-husk in quantity by digging a trench where the fire was built, then placing a stick lengthwise over the embers and laying on the cobs.

Foods such as tubers and roots were "roasted" by burying them directly in the coals or ashes. Pumpkin or squash might be placed whole in the hot coals until tender and then sliced. All tribes that grew maize roasted some of it green in the husk.

Pit Roasting. A roasting pit was constructed by digging a hole in the ground and building the fire there; this provided much more concentrated heat. Pit roasting was popular in areas where water was in short supply, like the Southwest, but it required a great deal of human energy.

This method for pit-roasted venison has been adapted from one described by a descendant of the Passamaquoddy tribe of Maine who notes that the technique has Miwok (a California tribe) origins:

1. Early in the morning, dig a deep pit, put rocks in the bottom and build a roaring fire on top.
2. When the fire burns down, put down willow and fresh bay leave branches.
3. Wrap the venison in a hide or rush mats to keep it clean and place it in the pit.

4. Cover the meat with more bay branches and earth. Let the venison roast all day.

5. Dig up the roasted venison for dinner.[19]

Baking

Baking was accomplished either on a griddle stone or in the embers of the fire. The word pone, as in cornpone, is derived from the Algonquian word *apan*, which means baked. Native Americans did not have ovens, nor did they need them to make their unleavened corn breads, which can be baked on a flat surface. To make one type of cornbread, the maize was first pounded into meal, then sifted and combined with water to make a dough; bear oil and fresh or dried fruit might be added. Then it was wrapped in leaves and baked in the ashes or on broad earthen baking stones placed near or over the fire. Maize was not always the primary ingredient for bread; it might also be chestnuts, beans, acorns and sweet potatoes. Acorn meal could be molded into patties and fried, or the flour could be dried and made into a stiff dough that was baked into a dense bread in the smoldering fire. Some tribes mixed acorn flour with water to make a thick paste and then poured it into a circular depression made in sand with raised edges to shape a round loaf of bread. A fire was built over the cake so that it would half-bake and half-steam. The Delaware and midwestern tribes also bake-steamed meat, fowl and fish in clay jackets, then cracked them open, stripping away the scales, fur or feathers.

This recipe for ash cake, common to many if not most agricultural Indian cultures, is adapted from a Cherokee cookbook: Make a stiff dough of cornmeal and warm water. Rake ashes back, spread hot stone at base of fire with oak leaves, put pone of bread (flattened cakes of cornmeal and water, the everyday breads of southern tribes) on the leaves, cover with more and pile on red-hot ashes. Remove pone when done.[20]

Popping

Popping popcorn was a cooking method in the Southwest, where the Indians raised the special maize.

Steaming

Steaming is a sealed, moist method of cooking. The Kwakiutl on the Northwest coast steamed both goat meat and salmon heads in covered pits. When the outside of the pit was covered with earth, it was known as an earth oven, and food was often steamed in it overnight. One popularly known example of steaming in a pit often attributed to American Indians is the clambake, a New England tradition. Shellfish and corn are steamed, alternating layers of seaweed and food. However, serious doubts have been raised that this method of pit steaming can really be traced to Native Americans. Excavations of Indian sites on Martha's Vineyard, Massachusetts, have uncovered pits of clam shells but this is not proof that the people did, in fact, steam clams in holes. Perhaps they were refuse pits. Far more likely was that the Indians made their clambakes aboveground on a circle of rocks. Excavations in Illinois have turned up unused piles of freshwater mussels, "heap ovens," covered with clay that seemed all set for steaming. Similar evidence has been found in the Tennessee River Valley.

It is agreed that the Indians probably did their steaming aboveground, not in pits. Among the Wampanoag (Massachusetts) Indians, the clambake process began with the collection of rockweed, a greenish-brown seaweed, desirable because its pockets held salt water that provided moisture during steaming. Rocks were arranged in a circle with a fire kindled on top until it burned down. Layers of rockweed were alternated with layers of shellfish and everything covered over with more rockweed, which had to be continually kept wet during the cooking to insure steaming. Once the mound heated up, the steamers (a type of clam) would break open and their juice helped steam the food.

Putrefying

Intentionally allowing food to spoil is not usually thought of as a preparation method, but some tribes preferred to eat certain foods this way. No doubt the technique was discovered accidentally when some food went bad but was all there was to eat. The Mandan were said to like ripe-to-rotten bison meat. One chronicler of the Iroquois wrote, "They do not hesitate to eat stinking and almost rotten meat when they have no other. They never skim the pot, in order to lose nothing."[21]

Fermenting

Fermentation was sometimes used as a food preparation method. *Sofki*, a symbolically important food to the Creek, began as a watery maize gruel made of water, crushed flint corn and ashes, simmered for several hours until thick, then allowed to sour for three days. This dish allegedly had a sharp, bitter taste and a strong vinegary, beerlike odor. It was eaten from bowls at every meal and given to anyone who was hungry. The Creek believed that no meal was complete without *sofki*. The Seminole of Florida fermented the tuber koonti after pounding it to pulp. The Sioux fermented wild rice after winnowing it, leaving it to rot in water. When they returned in spring, they thought it was very good even though it had a terrible odor.

FOOD PRESERVATION AND STORAGE

None of the tribes would have survived if they had not been able to develop effective ways to preserve and store food, some for lean times, some for trail food. Before the methods could be invented, however, there had to be a surplus above and beyond what was needed for daily subsistence. The Iroquois traditionally grew and harvested much more maize than they needed so they could build up stores both for emergencies and trade. The Iroquois Confederacy—the Mohawk, Oneida, Onondaga, Cayuga and Seneca—had an agreement whereby any one tribe would come to the food aid of the others if they fell short.

Food storage locations were a matter of the utmost secrecy. The social purpose was to protect the food from greedy or lazy neighbors and warring enemies, as well as hungry animals attracted by scent. The Plains and Northeast Indians were said to have tens of thousands of underground caches. The discovery of some of these was recorded by French explorers on the St. Lawrence and Illinois-Mississippi Rivers, the Pilgrims at Plymouth colony and American explorers Lewis and Clark on their mission west. When French explorer Samuel de Champlain uncovered Iroquois pits in 1682, he estimated they contained enough maize to supply the villages for three or four years. Preservation and storage had profound social consequences for the tribes because they helped set the stage for a more settled existence, not so dependent on the vagaries of seasons, droughts, crop failures and dwindling supplies of fish and game.

Preservation Techniques

Drying. Drying food, either in the sun, close to the fire or by wind, was the most commonly used preservation method. In the villages of the Hidatsa and many other tribes, maize was dried on a raised stage in front of each lodge. The Hopi dried it on their rooftops, turning the cobs often to make them dry quickly and completely. The women then removed the husks and tied them into bundles secured with yucca

Drying meat on a stick frame. Courtesy of Library of Congress, Prints & Photographs Division, Edward S. Curtis Collection (reproduction number: LC-USZ62-113093).

or husk strips, to be stored for use as wrappers. Usually, enough maize was dried to last through two cropless winters. Other tribes in the Southwest dried maize by stringing cobs on long yucca threads and hanging them outside for several weeks or baking cobs in the ashes before drying. Dehydrated, powdered maize was saved both for food and, when mixed with water, for drink. Maize dumplings could be fire-dried and stored to be reconstituted at a later time into instant porridge.

On the Plains during bison hunting, wooden frameworks were erected where strips of meat were dried either in the sun or over the fire. Fire and smoke hastened drying and kept away flies and other pests. One hundred pounds of fresh meat reduced to only twenty pounds dried. The meat could be eaten dry or made into *pemmican*. Melted fat was poured over the *pemmican*, which was then packed into rawhide containers. Most was consumed within a year.

On hunting and fishing expeditions, whatever food was not consumed on site was dried and stored for future use. Salmon, halibut, codfish, perch and even eel and oysters were dried. Otherwise, fish would spoil rapidly. The Indians of the Northwest invented elaborate huge wooden racks that towered over villages for drying large amounts of salmon. Or the fish might be cut open, splayed on sticks and set close to the fire to dry. Clams were strung on skewers and taken back to coastal camps where they were fire-dried and then often transported inland to be traded to the Yakima. When soaked in water, the clams became soft again and were then boiled to make a favorite food of the Eastern Washington Indians.

Also in the Northwest, the tribes invented a method for drying their favorite fruit, huckleberries, so they could be used all year as a sweetener for baked *wappato* or camas bulbs. A large slab of bark was peeled off an old log that had fallen to the ground. The log was set on fire, and when smoldering, the bark was positioned on its edge a few feet away facing the log. The huckleberries were placed in large reed baskets between the bark and what was called the "drying log."

Huckleberries might also be dried quickly by setting fire to a large fire-killed, fallen fir tree. As it had already been burned, the log would give off a steady heat to the crushed huckleberries spread on stones nearby. Berries were also frequently dried by crushing them into a paste, spreading the mixture on bark or stones in the sun, and then storing them in sacks. During the winter, this sweet paste provided variety in a diet that might otherwise have consisted solely of dried fish.

Another preservation technique was a combination of cooking and drying as in this formula for dried yucca fruit from the Navajo. First, the fruit was gathered, peeled and seeds discarded. Then, according to a Navajo woman: "Bake skin and pulp over fire until very brown, stirring constantly. When it takes on the consistency of applesauce [clearly this is a modern rendition] remove to another pan and cool. Grind thoroughly on a *metate* until very fine and sticky, then mold by teaspoonfuls on a flat board and dry for five days in the sun thus forming small, red, slightly sticky cakes. Knead these cakes into a hard dough and mold into loaves like bread, making a lengthwise hole through each loaf, dry again for five days in the sun, and store in boxes for the winter."[22] When reconstituted with water, these dried cakes were something like fruit preserves.

Parching. Parching was a way of thoroughly drying maize by placing already air- or sun-dried kernels in containers above the fire. It was favored by the Indians for lending sweetness and preventing mildew; it also concentrated nutrition. Parching maize in a vessel used specifically for that purpose was the earliest form of pot cooking in the Americas, originating in Peru. In the Northeast, next to meat, parched maize was the most important food item. Before parching, ears of ripe field or flint maize were taken, their husks pulled back, the silk removed, husks tied together and the ears hung in a warm, dry place until completely dry, a process that took a few weeks. Then the kernels were removed and placed a handful at a time in a shallow vessel over an open fire where they were parched, stirring often so they would not burn. When parched, the kernels turned a golden brown and puffed up slightly, making them crunchy but easy to chew. Using this method, maize could be preserved almost indefinitely. All varieties of maize, including blue and immature green, were parched.

The Zuni parched maize by heating sand in a pot, adding dried maize and stirring the mixture over the fire with a bundle of stirring sticks until the corn popped and smelled toasted. A slotted dipper was then used to sift out the sand and the parched maize placed in a basket. Either a corn cob or brush dipped in salted water was used for applying seasoning. This method was said to lend a deliciously sweet and nutty flavor.

Wokas, the seeds of the yellow pond water lily, were also parched by the Klamath in Oregon by taking a handful or two of fermented *wokas* known as *lolensh*, putting them in a shaker and roasting them over the fire until browned. Then the kernels swelled and cracked their coats. In this parched form they were known as *shnaps*, and often eaten dry, but usually moistened with water.

Smoking. Actually a kind of slow, low-temperature cooking, smoking was also used for preservation of meat and fish, particularly in the Northwest where salmon were commonly smoked slowly in a small, closed hut. The chemistry of smoke preservation involves complex toxic substances that inhibit the growth of microbes while simultaneously drying the meat. Of course, the process also added the distinctive smoke flavor.

Smoke-dried meat was called *jerk* by the Indians. To prepare it, thin slices of meat were laid on a grate of sticks placed over a fire kept low and constant. The pieces were turned occasionally to ensure even drying. The process took eight to twelve hours. One early European visitor, who had the chance as a captive to observe this method first-hand, wrote, "The Indians killed a bear and two does that day . . . they brought the meat of all to the camp that evening, and some of them was busily engaged in cutting the meat off the bones and drying it on a little rod or stick over the fire to make what the Indians call Jerk—dried meat to carry with them."[23] On another deer hunt,

Jerking meat. Courtesy of Library of Congress, Prints & Photographs Division, Edward S. Curtis Collection (reproduction number: LC-USZ62-113094).

the same captive noted that after smoking all the meat, they soon had 4,000 pounds of dried venison.[24]

Salting. Salt has long been used for preservation because it inhibits microbial growth in foods by drying up the microbes. The use of salt for preserving fish is mentioned only for Northeast and California tribes. An early observer witnessed the combined use of salting and drying preservation:

The Indians "skinned the bull [bison] and cut off all the meat in broad thin pieces, which we laid on the hide, and sprinkled salt thereon, letting it lay till we made a long [burning] fire. We then put a row of forks on each side of the fire, and placed poles on the forks. Small sticks were then laid on them, and the meat laid on the sticks over the fire, where it remained until half cooked; it was then turned over and left to lay till morning, for by this time it was in the night. . . . In the morning we put the meat in bags and carried it home."[25]

Roasting. For centuries, the Hopi preserved sweet (mature) maize by roasting it in pits before storing. Among the Northwest Coast Kwakiutl, salmon, codfish, kelpfish, perch and flounder were often roasted and then dried. The tribe seemed to prefer to eat these fish dried rather than reconstituting them with water.

Fat. Northwest Coast Indians used oolichan grease made from candlefish as a preservative, packing dried fish in oil and coating crabapples and firm berries, then setting them in a cool place in wooden boxes to congeal. The grease kept air away from the fruit and slowed decay.

Fat itself was stored for future use as this formula for bear lard details: First, it was necessary to cut bear fat into chunks. Then it was cooked until all the grease was cooked out. Next, slippery elm tree strips were taken from between the outside bark and the tree and tied into three-inch rolls. The bear lard was stored in a container lined with slippery elm bundles to keep the lard fresh.

Fermentation. One of the oldest food preservation techniques, fermentation extends the shelf life of foods with high sugar contents. Fermentation also enhanced nutritional quality, substantially increasing protein and many B vitamins; it eased digestion by breaking down factors like tannic acid. No doubt fermentation was discovered serendipitously. Production of vinegar (acetic acid) from aerobic fermentation of alcohol is one of best known methods of food preservation (pickling); vinegar produced from fermented maple sugar sap was used as a preservative for meats in the Eastern Woodland areas. Writing about the Ojibwe, English Colonel James Smith, a captive of Northeast Indians said, "It is allowed to become sour to make a vinegar used in their cookery of venison, which, when afterwards sweetened with maple sugar [clearly this is after European arrival], corresponds to the German fashion of sweet-sour meat."[26] Once maple sap had tuned into vinegar, the Iroquois gained a product highly esteemed.[27] Roots of camas were fermented by Indians of the Northern Plains in underground pits into which hot stones had been placed.

On the Northwest Coast, preparation of *wokas* for storage involved two processes—fermentation and parching. First, *woka* pods were emptied into a hole in the ground about two feet square by two feet deep. When filled, the pit was covered with grass and the pods were allowed to ferment until all of the seeds spilled out. Then the slippery *wokas* were scooped out and put in a canoe with water that was rocked from side to side until the seeds settled in the bottom. When the liquid was poured off, only the wet seeds were left to be removed and placed on a mat to drain.

Now they were ready to be made into the dish known as *lolensh* and stored. The seeds were placed in wicker trays and parched over live coals. Then they were ground lightly between two millstones that cracked off the outer hulls, exposing the kernels. Kernels and hulls were deposited in the *woka* shaker, a round tray woven of grass, and then were winnowed. The wind blew away the hulls but left the kernels, which were then parched a second time and finally packed away for later consumption.

Storage

Many foods were stored in dwellings, hung from ceilings. These included maize, seaweed and corn cakes wrapped in hemlock bark. Maize might also be stored on rooftops or, as the Iroquois did, braided in bunches and hung from ridgepoles or crossbeans in the longhouses, the large Iroquois dwellings constructed of elm-wood poles and elm bark (18 to 25 feet in width and 50 to 150 in length). The Huron put their tree bark chests of maize, some holding between 100 and 200 bushels, directly in their dwellings.

Stores could not give off an alluring scent if they were to remain safe from animals, which increased the popularity of underground pits. In the Northwest, storage cellars were dug in hillsides for this purpose. Human predators were also a danger. The Navajo traditionally removed food from their caches only before dawn so the location would remain secret, known only to family members. The Navajo stored dried shelled maize in a round hole in the ground lined with shredded juniper bark, covered over with more, then a thin layer of rock and another of dirt. They stored squash and sunflower seeds in the same manner in a hole three-and-a-half feet deep and twenty inches in diameter; roots and other seeds were stored either loose or in sacks in an unlined hole (previously dried out with fire). The Hopi removed all old maize from their storage bins every year, cleaned them and prepared for the new maize. In a traditional system of rotation, the Hopi placed newly harvested maize in the bottom of the bin so the year-old cobs would be consumed first. Underground pits might be dug hastily when the Indians found themselves on the run from warring enemy tribes or colonists. Jesuit Pierre-François Charlevoix wrote of the Miami, "When they are obliged to be from home for any time, or when they apprehend some irruption of the enemy . . . make great concealments under the ground."[28]

The permanent underground storage pit was constructed in a number of ways. In the Northeast, early colonists discovered these caches about four to five feet deep, lined and covered with tree bark or earth, from Cape Cod, Massachusetts, in the north to the Virginias in the south. This style protected the contents from frost; they were used by the Northeast tribes to store vegetables, pumpkins and other fruits. Lewis and Clark found elaborate bell-shaped food caches where maize, beans, sunflower seeds and dried squash were preserved over the winter among the Mandan. The narrow opening was large enough only for someone to lower himself down.

Gradually, as the population increased, social organization changed and food was collected centrally for redistribution. The character and design of storage areas were revamped. In the Mississippi Valley, for example, the style evolved from household storage pits in the sixth century BC to central-communal pits in the late ninth century AD to above-ground granaries in the tenth century.

Storage Vessels

Vessels for storing food needed to be made as airtight as possible. Some Native Americans used gourds with stoppers or clay pots. Among the Tohono O'odham in southern Arizona, sealed jars were used for parched and sun-dried seeds and beans that would later be ground into flour. Storage baskets, each capable of holding between a pint and four bushels, were woven by many tribes from rushes, maize husks, bark and wild hemp, sometimes decorated with birds, beasts, fish and flowers. Among the Northwest Coast tribes, birch bark cut into squares was used like aluminum foil to separate layers of dry-smoked fish so that if one layer happened to spoil, the adjacent one would not be affected. The idea for this novel wrapping came from the observation that bark left on a fallen birch protected the underlying wood from rotting. The reason, it was believed, was that the bark was water- and airtight. It also proved an effective sealer for dried berries, which it preserved for decades.

The Eskimo made good use of seal poke (the skin) for storage. According to one Eskimo cookbook, "The inside of the seal together with the head and all, is cut and taken out through the head part of the seal skin. The skin is then turned, cleaned and blown up for drying. This is then used to put the meats, berries, leaves or other foods for storing in winter."[29]

Corncribs, storage bins elevated off the ground, were invented by the Indians. A hole was first dug in the ground about one-and-a-half feet deep, surrounded by small five-inch-diameter posts set closely together so no animals could intrude. The hole was packed with dirt to the level of the surface of the ground. This receptacle was then filled with corn-on-the-cob and poles were laid straight across the top. Flat pieces of elm bark removed in spring and seasoned over the winter were placed over the poles. Shelled, dried maize was also sometimes preserved in bark barrels. The Seneca created another kind of above-ground granary made of bark, elevated and pierced on all sides so air could circulate and prevent moisture from rotting the maize.

Transportable Food

Not all preserved food was destined for the storage bin. Some was specifically intended as trail food to be carried on journeys, whether hunting, fishing or war parties. Preserved foods to fill this role needed to be dried, light, compact and loaded with concentrated energy. *Pemmican* and parched maize were ideal. On the trail, the maize could be pounded into meal, and water added to make a satisfying dish. The Narragansett called parched cornmeal *nokechick*, meaning "it is soft." Roger Williams, founder of Providence, wrote, "Parch'd meal, which is a readie very sholesome food, which they eate with a little water, hot or cold; I have travelled with neere 200 of them at once, neere 100 miles through the woods, every man carrying a *little Basket* of this at his *back*, and sometimes in a hollow *Leather Girdle* about his middle, sufficient for a man for three or four daies."[30] It would keep indefinitely and was said to be so nutritious that two or three spoonfuls mixed with water furnished a man with food for a day. When the Indians could get maple syrup, they mixed that with the parched meal and considered it a great improvement. The colonists respelled *nokechick* as "no cake." Pone, a flat baked corn cake, was also convenient to carry.

The Cherokee and, no doubt, other tribes made corn bread baked on bark when they were traveling. According to a Cherokee cookbook, "When it was time to cook bread one of the men would carefully cut pieces of bark from a chestnut tree. The dough was put on the inside of the bark and this was stood up before the fire to cook. The combination of bark, wood smoke and hunger made the bread about the best any Indian ever ate."[31]

Biscuitroot, said to taste something like parsnip, was dried so that it became brittle and white and then easily reduced to flour that would keep for several months. When the roots were pounded fine, the flour was pressed into flat cakes with a hole in the middle so they could be tied to other trail gear. It was such a trail staple that it was sometimes called bread root.

NOTES

1. L. J. Rementer, *Lenape Indian Cooking with Touching Leaves Woman* (1907; reprint Dewey, OK: Touching Leaves Indian Crafts, 1991), 5–6.

2. Barrett P. Brenton, "Fermented Foods in New World Prehistory: North America," in *Diet and Subsistence: Current Archaeological Perspectives; Proceedings of the Nineteeth Annual Conference of the Archaeological Association of the University of Calgary*, eds. Brenda V. Kennedy and Genevieve M. LeMoine (Calgary, AB: University of Calgary Archaeological Association, 1988), 10.

3. George Catlin, *Letters and Notes on the Manners, Customs, and Condition of the North American Indians*, 2 vols. (New York: Wiley and Putnam, 1841), 1:116.

4. James Adair, *History of the American Indians*, ed. Samuel Cole Williams, LLD (Johnson City, TN: Watauga Press, 1930), 416.

5. Betty Fussell, *The Story of Corn* (New York: Knopf, 1992), 212.

6. Juanita Tiger Kavena, *Hopi Cookery* (Tucson: University of Arizona Press, 1980), 16.

7. Gilbert L. Wilson, *Buffalo Bird Woman's Garden: Agriculture of the Hidatsa Indians, an Indian Interpretation* (Minneapolis: Bulletin of the University of Minnesota, 1917), 64–65.

8. Thomas C. Battey, *The Life and Adventures of a Quaker Among the Indians* (1875; reprint Norman: University of Oklahoma Press, 1968), 283.

9. Native American Technology and Art, http://www.nativetech.org/food.

10. Rita Edaakie, comp., *Idonapshe = Let's Eat: Traditional Zuni Foods: Stories and Recipes* (Albuquerque: University of New Mexico Press, 1999), 45.

11. Frank Hamilton Cushing, *Zuni Breadstuff* (New York: Museum of the American Indian, Heye Foundation, 1920), 283.

12. Lucien Carr, *The Food of Certain American Indians and Their Methods of Preparing It* (Worcester, MA: C. Hamilton, printer, 1895), 180.

13. Rementer, 6.

14. Ibid., 9–10.

15. John Josselyn, *An Account of Two Voyages to New England* (London: Printed for Giles Widdows at the Green Dragon in St. Paul's Church-yard, 1674), 138.

16. Arthur C. Parker, *Parker on the Iroquois*, ed. William N. Fenton (1910; reprint Syracuse: Syracuse University Press, 1968), 73.

17. Native American Technology and Art website.

18. John Heckewelder, *History, Manners, and Customs of the Indian Nations Who Once Inhabited Pennsylvania and the Neighboring States* (1876; reprint New York: Arno Press, 1971), 196.

19. Native American Technology and Art website.

20. Mary Ulmer and Samuel E. Beck, eds., *Cherokee Cooklore: Preparing Cherokee Foods* (Cherokee, NC: Museum of the Cherokee Indian, 1951), 19.

21. F.W. Waugh, *Iroquis [sic] foods and food preparation* (Ottawa, ON: Government Printing Bureau, 1916), 49.

22. Flora Bailey, "Navajo Foods and Cooking Methods," *American Anthropologist* 42 (1940): 288.

23. Peter Henry, *Accounts of His Captivity and Other Events in Further Materials on Lewis Wetzel* (Bowie, MD: Heritage Books, 1994), 3.

24. Ibid., 95.

25. O.M. Spencer, *Indian Captivity: A True Narrative of the Capture of O.M. Spencer* (New York: Waugh & Mason, 1835), 21.

26. Col. James Smith, "An Account of the Remarkable Occurrences in the Life and Travels of . . . during His Captivity with the Indians, in the Years 1755–59," in *Indian Captivities*, ed. Samuel G. Drake (New York: Derby & Miller, 1851), 295.

27. Parker, 103.

28. Pierre-François-Xavier de Charlevoix, qtd. in Warren R. DeBoer, "Subterranean Storage and the Organization of Surplus: The View from Eastern North America," *Southeastern Archaeology* 7 (1988): 1.

29. Students of Shishmaref Day School, Shishmaref, Alaska, *Eskimo Cook Book* (Anchorage: Alaska Crippled Children's Association, 1952), 26.

30. Fussell, 193.

31. Ulmer and Beck, 50.

CHAPTER 4
FOOD CUSTOMS

Societies could not survive without rules to govern eating behavior. Otherwise, there would be violence and possibly murder committed over rights to food. American Indians established complicated codes that ensured meals would be peaceful and everyone would get their fair share. The rules also covered such things as who eats with whom and when, who is served first, special treatment for the elite, young and old, taboos, hospitality and reciprocity.

It was not unusual for a tribe to have one set of rules for everyday meals and another more elaborate code for feasts when guests were present. Food customs varied from culture to culture, and helped build tribal identity and bind the community together. The codes were passed down from one generation to the next so each member grew up knowing what was expected. The rules were deeply ingrained and violations were taken seriously. Among the Crow who lived in Montana, a transgressor was shunned and despised. From an anthropological point of view, food customs are considered part of the civilizing process.

In this chapter, the custom of food sharing will be discussed first; followed by rules for eating behavior at mealtimes; then habits relating to elite tribal members, lifecycle customs, taboos, hospitality, feasting, and the unusual practices of eating dog and ritual cannibalism, sanctioned by some tribes under particular circumstances.

FOOD SHARING

The custom of sharing food, what one early European observer called "the communism of food," was all but universal among Native Americans.[1] Among the Mandan in North Dakota, any tribal member could enter any lodge, including the chief's, and help himself to food, even if he had been lazy about hunting. The tradition evolved out of religious beliefs. One early missionary among the tribes in Delaware and Pennsylvania noted, "They [American Indians] think that he (the Great Spirit), made the earth and all that it contains, that when he stocked the country that he gave them with plenty of game, it was not for the benefit of the few, but for all."[2]

Status might be expressed in special foods made and served only to chiefs, hunters, warriors, elders or men. Where food was redistributed by a chief, he might allocate the choicest maize for himself and the ruling elite. Among the Kwakiutl of the Northwest Coast, nobles had the right to eat and drink before others. All tribes of this area reserved organ meats, including the heart and liver of sea lion, for the elders. Among the Ten'a of Alaska, only older men and women were allowed to eat mink and otter. The elderly were not always treated with such respect. Among the Kwakiutl, pectoral and anal fins of fish as well as tails and salmon-heads were given to older tribal members.

Among the tribes of the Northwest, it was incumbent on the hunter or fisherman to share equally with all family heads; this garnered tremendous prestige for the procurer. Among the Blackfoot of Montana, when a hunter killed a bison, any tribal member who approached could help himself to meat; if the hunter was alone, he could take half the flesh home, leaving the rest for others. If there were two hunters, each was permitted to take a third. The robe and tongue always belonged to the hunter who made the kill. If he brought meat back to the lodge, it was up to the hunter whether to be generous to those who asked for some.

Gluttony was taboo, a restriction that supported sharing, and was taught from the earliest age. Among the tribes in the Iroquois Confederacy—Mohawk, Oneida, Onondaga, Cayuga and Seneca—children were warned that eating too many maize cakes soaked in maple syrup would provoke an ominous visit from the bogeyman Longnose.

The sharing prescription was sometimes sabotaged. For example, among the Mandan, a hunter who slew a deer or other game might leave it some distance from home and send his wife to bring it back.

As she was not obliged to share the meat, she could retrieve it for her family alone.

As populations increased, food sharing based on informal face-to-face negotiations became less workable. Food collection and redistribution was entrusted to a chief. After maize was harvested, for example, the chief might decree that all should be delivered to him. Then he would set aside a certain amount for the poor and needy, another portion for hospitality (entertaining), and a third lot for defraying common expenses. The remainder was either dried and stored or distributed among tribal members.

MEALTIMES

Some tribes, particularly in the earliest times, had no such thing as regular mealtimes. Pots were kept simmering all day, and people could eat whenever they were hungry. One English captive of Northeast Indians reported that they had no such thing as breakfast, dinner or supper.[3]

The disadvantages of day-long eating-on-demand soon became apparent. Among other drawbacks, there was no time when the tribe came together as a community. The Iroquois of Upper New York State converted from no set mealtimes to once a day, around 10:00 or 11:00. The Mandan ate twice daily. In some tribes, the number and timing of meals varied with seasonal hours of daylight. The Upper Lakes Indians ate at sunrise, noon and sunset during the long days of summer but only twice daily during the shorter days of winter. When provisions were scarce, these meals might condense to one or none. Among the Crow, breakfast was the principal and only regular meal for a time. Usually, infrequent meals were supplemented by handfuls of dried food like parched maize that were available all day as high-energy snacks.

Although some leeway was allowed for children to eat whenever they were hungry, this was not always the case. Among the Zuni of New Mexico, breakfast was not a custom. If a hungry child began to snivel, the elder would say, "There now, never lie around longing for food; never whine for it—*dogs* do that! Wait till the heat of day; it will enliven your sense of the taste of good things. Food whistles on the spit and sings in the cooking-pot when it is ready, and only women know its music or understand its language; *little children* should wait for *them* to interpret!"[4]

129

Two Apache women at a campfire. Courtesy of Library of Congress, Prints & Photographs Division, Edward S. Curtis Collection (reproduction number: LC-USZ62-101172).

Such strictness was remarkable to ethnologist Frank Hamilton Cushing who studied the Zuni in the early twentieth century. He commented, "I do not exaggerate when I say that I have repeatedly seen one of these old men get his *two-year-old* grandson on his knee and talk to the little fellow about the amenities of eating time, as though he were a well-grown youth about to enter the solemn precincts of a sacred feast." The result, according to Cushing was "admirable self-control."[5]

Mealtimes offered opportunities for tribe members to express and practice food customs, and also to teach them to the young. In general, it was expected that people would not be stingy with food, eat modestly, not talk during meals, accept some of any food offered, go lightly on scarce items, not clean their plates and show appreciation by smacking their lips or giving a loud burp.

The Indians were not above criticizing each other's manners, which provided reinforcement. Cushing wrote, "A little idiosyncrasy like an undue fondness for some particular kind of eatable—a peculiarity of serving or taking food, even the ill-timed utterance of a word connected with it will be seized upon and converted into a sobriquet so pithy as to last a lifetime."[6] Native Americans were even more critical of the habits of Europeans, who returned the favor. "The American eat food with fingers and knives of metal, and talk much while eating," a Zuni priest told Cushing. He added, "Insolent and godless must be a people whose children affront the 'Givers of Food' by making light of it with much chattering while partaking of it."[7]

It was most common for men to eat first. Among the Mandan, it was customary for male diners to eat either sitting cross-legged, with their feet under their bodies, or reclining, resting on one elbow with dishes spread on the floor of the lodge. When the men were finished, the women, children and dogs ate together. Among the Northwest Coast cultures, when eating from a spoon, a man was required to squat with his right elbow resting on his right knee and sip carefully from the tip.

In addition to eating in separate shifts, men and women sometimes ate different foods. Among the Ingalik of Alaska, roasted food was reserved for men and boiled for women; the women of the Ten'a of western Alaska were not allowed to eat the head or neck of a bear. Different tribes had different customs about what was served when. Among the Shoshone in Nevada, usually only one food was served at a meal, generally a mush made of the dominant staple to which greens, seeds and berries might be added. Among the Kwakiutl, milky-salmon spawn was eaten at noon and evening but not in the morning because its fat was supposed to make diners sleepy.

Often, meals were consumed out of a communal bowl. People talked little, but focused on the fairness of the process. Among the Iroquois, pointed sticks (primitive forks) were employed to pick up dumplings. In the Northeast, clam shells were often used as spoons, whereas the Hidatsa in Missouri employed horn spoons or mussel shells. Otherwise, fingers, hands, leaves and bones were used. Just how challenging eating with fingers could be was discovered by Frank Cushing when he was invited to share his first Zuni family meal. "Everyone dipped his fingers into the hot, greasy, meaty, pepper-dyed [this is after Spanish introduction of chile peppers] soup with such perfect unconcerned dexterity, that I essayed: Great goodness! It seemed as though my nails were scalded off. I jerked my hand out with such instant and unconscious vigor that my elbow struck the broomy head of a boy by my side so hard that he howled." This is how Cushing received the epithet "He-Who-Eats-From-One-Dish-With-Us-With-One-Spoon."[8]

Gradually, most Native American tribes began to fashion individual dishes and spoons of wood, bark, earthenware, gourds or woven reeds. Among the Kwakiutl on the Northwest Coast, implements were used to enforce ideas about rank and family identity. Small, ordinary dishes were made in the shape of canoes, and used by one person or shared by husband and wife. Elaborate "house dishes" were treasured heirlooms reserved for great feasts, handed down as an inheritance in aristocratic families. Chiefs seated themselves around large dishes and ate with elaborately carved and decorated spoons of wood, mountain goat horn or shell while the common people ate from small vessels. Large spoons were used by men, smaller pointed ones by high-born girls who were not supposed to open their mouths too wide.

LIFECYCLE CUSTOMS

As part of the rites associated with particular life events from birth to death, most tribes endorsed appropriate special food customs.

Birth

Cornmeal, the most precious substance to the Pueblo Indians of New Mexico, was rubbed on newborns. Among the Hopi in Arizona, maize rituals preceded the naming of a new baby.

Coming of Age/Initiation

At puberty, among the Hopi, the girls had to grind maize ceremonially for four days. Similarly, the boys had to run all night to place cornmeal offerings on distant shrines and return to the village before dawn. In the Navajo tribe of Arizona, cornmeal was sprinkled over the kinalda cake (made for a girl's puberty rite) in the belief that it would prevent burning; burned foods were taboo.

Courtship

Among the Creek in Florida, girls began making the symbolically important food *sofki* (a gruel of corn and water) at the age of courtship. When a girl agreed to make *sofki* for a boy, the courtship period had begun and might result in marriage. After marrying, the making of *sofki* marked a woman as head of her household. If she ever stopped the practice, it signaled the end of the marriage.

Betrothal and Marriage

Among the Hopi, when a girl proposed to a boy (an interesting role reversal), she made a plate of *piki* bread. Escorted by her mother and maternal uncle, she delivered it to the boy's doorstep. If his family took it in, the proposal had been accepted. The next step was for the girl to take a pan of white cornmeal and basket of blue *piki* to the boy's house. From that day on until the wedding, the women of the village ground maize for the wedding feast. When parents arranged a marriage for their daughter, a bowl of *sofki* was placed under the projecting shed of the corn crib in sight of the boy's home. If the girl allowed the boy to eat a spoonful, she had accepted the marriage. The couple spent the first night in the corn crib.

Among the Zuni and the Hopi, girls about to be married were put to a test to see how well they ground maize. The results were evaluated by the fiance's family who then asked the girl to prepare a meal of their choice from her ground meal. The Hopi bride-to-be ground parched blue maize for her wedding cake called *someviki*.

Pregnancy

The Zuni prepared two different "magical" teas to influence the sex of an unborn baby. If the pregnant woman wanted a boy, she would drink one tea, and for a girl the other one.

Death

Among the Sioux in Minnesota, when someone died, mourning persisted until the closest relative gave a medicine feast and dance. Only then could the family member collect bones from the bier and bury them. Among the Crow, women were always buried alongside either a bowl or dish. In the Navajo tribe, members of the burial party were required to eat from separate dishes from the rest of the family for four days of mourning. Among the Intuit of the Northwest Coast, people made offerings of food either at the grave or at festivals for the dead because they believed that the soul persists and retains human needs like eating. Some continued to leave offerings for four to five days because they thought the soul hung around in the area for that amount of time. In a Mandan village, Indians "fed the dead." Each woman knew the skull of her husband or child and usually came every day with a dish of the best cooked food her wigwam could afford to leave before the skull at night. In the morning, she would return for the dish.

TABOOS

Some eating rules were expressed as taboos—bans on specific foods either permanently or under specific circumstances. These prohibitions, deeply ingrained in the culture, often had a magical-religious basis. Violations of taboos were taken very seriously and punished. Permanent taboos usually included indigestible or toxic foods—in which cases the rules clearly had survival value but they were not necessarily nutritionally sound. Some edicts outlawed consumption of unfamiliar foods from another geographic locale. Such unknown foods had not been submitted to the tribe's trial-and-error method of testing over time and were therefore far more likely to produce illness or death. Taboos, like other eating rules, served an important social purpose to express solidarity and strengthen cultural identity. For a religious taboo, the banned items had to be things fairly desirable and obtainable or there would have been no point in forbidding them. These rules, according to one scholar, "helps keep the sacred sacred."[9] Some researchers believe many taboos got their origin because they had adaptive value at some point in time. In other words, taboos were there for a reason and that reason was usually based in biology, whether practitioners consciously realized this or not.

Permanent Taboos

Toxic Foods. The proscription against eating foods discovered to be toxic over hundreds of years of trial and error was foremost in all American Indian cultures. These essential rules were passed down from one generation to the next. Among the Hopi, all food was neatly classified into one of two categories: *nuh:sioka* ("that which may be eaten") and *ka-nuh:sioka* ("that which is not to be eaten").[10]

Mother-in-Law Taboo. The prohibition that prevented a man from accepting food from his mother-in-law was all but universal among Native Americans. It may have been an incest taboo. Among the Crow, although it was permissible for a mother-in-law to prepare food for her son-in-law, she was not allowed to hand it to him; instead, she passed it to her daughter to give to her husband.

Particular Foods and Tribes. Many taboos applied to specific cultures and foods. Among the Hopi, boys were not allowed to eat blue corn mush from the corn stirring sticks, whereas girls could; if a boy violated this taboo, it was believed that his hand would tremble when taking aim in hunting. A food preparation taboo existed among the Zuni and Hopi, who were prohibited from making blue corn marbles in the summer if it were raining because this was believed to provoke hail that would destroy the crops (the Hopi got around this by flattening the marbles). For the Navajo, all burned foods were taboo, but burned bread in particular was believed to produce "baked blood," which could kill the eater. Some Navajo avoided bear meat, saying it would make the diner too "mean." Among the Cayuga in New York State, the flesh of a pregnant animal would not be eaten because it was said to cause diarrhea. Eating animals who lived near burial grounds was thought to be bad luck because spirits of the dead inhabited them. Some Plains Indians refused to eat the thymus gland of the bison because it was thought to be a piece of human flesh stuck in the throat of the last mythological bison to eat human flesh. The Kiowa and Comanche of Texas did not eat birds, fish or bear. One early observer noted, "They are forbidden, in the code of *laws*, as unclean—tabooed—or, in plain Indian 'bad medicine.' Hence with them the wild turkey is valuable only for its feathers, which they use to wing their arrows."[11] The Iroquois had a taboo against picking up dropped food during a meal, believing it should be left for the dead. They were thought to suffer from hunger and, if neglected, would continue to haunt the living, making people sick. There were many taboos related to hunting and fishing to guarantee success. Among the Kwakiutl, for example, a husband could not tell his wife where he was going when he hunted because the animals would hear and, therefore, get away.[12] More important was the prohibition against eating for days before an important hunting expedition. When the Apache gathered and baked agave, sex and drinking were forbidden in the belief that these activities would prevent rain.

Temporary or Situational Taboos

Temporary or situational taboos often involved a lifecycle event, rite of passage or a particular group of people and only applied during that period. Salt taboos are a classic example. The Western tribes observed this prohibition during pregnancy, birth, boys' and girls' puberty rites, menstruation, boys' initiations, vision quests and mourning. These taboos were seldom found all together in one tribe but it was rare not to have at least one in each culture. The same applied to eleven Southwestern cultures.

Puberty. Boys in the Oneida tribe of New York State were not allowed to eat salt or anything hot when their voices changed. Young girls at puberty in the Northwest Coast cultures were forbidden meat. Among the Ten'a of Alaska, women of childbearing age were not allowed to eat mink or otter. Otter was considered very powerful; a violation of the taboo would keep the animal away and inflict misfortune on the man who caught it. Young, unmarried girls were not allowed to eat lynx.

Menstruation. As with many cultures, the mysterious event of menstruation among women became the focus of many taboos. Among the Cayuga in Upstate New York, the Delaware and cultures of the Northwest Coast, menstruating women were not allowed to touch or eat meat. Members of the 'Ksan tribe warned, "If they eat fresh meat their family would have bad luck in everything they did."[13] Delaware girls were not allowed to do any cooking during their periods; if they did, no one would dare eat this "unwholesome" food for fear of abdominal pain. The Creek had an elaborate code of behavior surrounding menstruation. Women had to live apart at this time and eat from separate dishes and utensils rather than the communal bowl. They were not allowed to cook for men. If anyone violated this taboo, she could be accused of any misfortune that befell the tribe. One chief told an anthropologist, "A man should never use a plate that a menstruating woman has used. This will make people sick." A woman said, "If these rules are forgotten, men will get sick and maybe die."[14] The Mohawk in New York State prohibited women from pounding maize and touching food during menstruation. Otherwise, various illnesses would result. As with Western North American Indians, there were restrictions among Southeastern Indians for a low-sodium diet during menstruation.

Pregnancy. Pregnant Ten'a women were not allowed bear meat. Among the Delaware, pregnant women were not to look at certain animals like oppossum and rabbit or the baby would be born with a harelip.

HOSPITALITY

Entertaining members of other villages or tribes required the full set of eating rules, a more elaborate code than was used for ordinary meals. Food was the common currency of hospitality. One European captive wrote, "If any one, even the town [village] folks, would go to the same house several times in one day, he would be invited to eat of the best—and with them it is bad manners to refuse to eat when it is offered."[15] There was inherent and serious danger in having an unfamiliar guest at the table. Sitting close to each other made tribe members vulnerable to someone who might brandish a concealed weapon. To neutralize this, hospitality protocol required that all feelings of enmity be put aside when guests were present.

The Indians frequently socialized. One early European observed that Native Americans "undertake long journeys, visit distant tribes, to renew their friendship. Such visits are received with ceremonious feasting, and valuable presents are exchanged."[16] Among the Indians on the Southwest Pueblos, hospitality dictated that under no circumstances could a visitor refuse food or, having asked for it, be refused. A guest was always fed before he was expected to announce the reason for his visit. Among the Indians along the Missouri River, if a relative returned after a hunt, war or prolonged absence, his wife immediately set food before him. Only after having eaten was it considered polite to ask where the man had been and what he had done.

These rules of hospitality extended even to enemies. According to an early account, "Though he [the chief] may be barbarous in the extreme, no stranger seeking repose or refreshment in his lodge will be turned away unsheltered or unfed. In his lodge, an enemy is a brother, warmed by his fire and sharing his food."[17] The Zuni and Navajo shared a mutual hatred, but if a member of either tribe showed up at the dwelling of the other, he would be greeted with the words, "Enter, sit and eat." Zuni anthropologist Frank Cushing recalled a visitor from a Navajo to a Zuni household who was fed four times in one day even though he had killed the host's uncle; the Zuni in turn had killed the Navajo's father.

Guests were expected to show their appreciation with the usual smacking their lips, lingering over the marrow bones, taking loud and long sips of soup and eating a large and equal amount of each item. Most important, guests were expected to reciprocate with meals of their own to keep things in balance.

FEASTING

Feasts were held for any and all occasions—the celebration of the huckleberry season, the bison slaughter, harvesting of acorns, or honoring an outstanding warrior or hunter. Foods served differed in both quantity and quality from ordinary meals. The sheer amount was staggering. At one village feast, an early observer recorded consumption of twenty deer and four bears. At another, 170 fish, most large as salmon, were eaten.[18] Dishes were prepared in elaborate, time-consuming ways. Often the entire village was involved in the preparations. Feasts were a special kind of ritual, times when people came together to celebrate, express and reinforce what they held in common. Feasting on a grand scale when guests were invited is considered an important turning point in food history because it was only possible when societies were able to produce and store huge surpluses. This bounty could then be used to form relationships or impress guests. Most feasts had a religious component such as thanking the spirits for the harvest (see Chapter 5).

The Ten'a of Alaska celebrated an eagerly awaited annual end-of-summer feast. Once a date was set, everyone talked of the good time they would have. Anticipation of the feast would spur on the men to work hard at the tiring activity of duck hunting. If they were not able to catch a sufficient supply of ducks, the feast was automatically canceled. This feast served many social purposes—recreation, entertainment, exchange of news and gossip and to remind people of their unity in collecting food.

Among the rules that applied to a formal feast, it was incumbent on visiting chiefs at a Northwest Coast celebration to give eloquent addresses at the end of which they praised their hosts and expressed appreciation. As usual, the men were served before the women and children. If there were guests, the hosts stood during the meal while the women waited on people. It was obligatory to provide more food

CHAPTER 5
FOOD AND RELIGION

American Indian spiritual beliefs evolved from the need to ensure the food supply. It is not surprising, therefore, that religion focused on the natural world. Land, religion and life were one; agriculture was sacred and hunting holy. Wisdom was gained by divining spiritual messages from the living world, plants, animals, germination, the skies, sun, rain and wind. Their significance was explored in endless discussions with other members of the community.

The religious leaders were the medicine men or shamans who acted as intermediaries between the realms of the physical and spiritual. They were regarded as possessing gifts for healing and prophecy. In spite of the diversity among the tribes—hundreds of religions were created over thousands of years—certain common themes and rituals emerged. Creation stories and myths, the concept of the spirit world and supreme beings and the sacredness of the land were among those shared beliefs. Most tribes held rituals to invoke rain, ensure plentiful hunting and bountiful harvests, and express gratitude for food.

This chapter first looks at the origins of religion among Native Americans, then moves on to shared themes, ritual practices, feasts, ceremonial foods and fasting.

EARLY ORIGINS OF RELIGION

Native American religious concepts were shaped thousands of years ago. Taking into account the vagaries of nature that could impact the procuring of meat, fish and edible plants as well as growing crops, American Indians did not take food for granted. Sustenance crops, particularly maize, beans and squash, were considered gifts from sacred beings.

About 3,000 years ago, most tribes increased their reliance on domesticated crops and storage technologies, which lead to a more settled existence. Then it was possible for more leisurely contemplation of human existence. Permanent ceremonial dwellings were erected, such as the underground *kivas* in the Southwest, and rites and rituals became more standardized. Ceremonial calendars were developed. Funeral and burial processes became more elaborate.

About 1,000 years ago, the shamans of the Mississippian culture, located in the Mississippi River's rich bottomland, focused on symbols of the sun as the source of all power because it made plants—most often maize—grow. Maize was sacred. The priests found the sun a convenient symbol to relate the elite powerful warrior class to the producers of food, the farmers. Agriculture became a holy labor, capable of bringing the people into profound contact with the powers of life. Shamans sought the blessings of the spirits for this endeavor, oversaw planting at the right time, recited prayers when planting seeds, conducted ceremonies that linked the life cycle of maize and sacrificed sacred foods at the beginning of each year's harvest.

While this maize-based, sun-centered religion was evolving in the St. Louis, Missouri, area, a similar phenomenon was taking place in the Southwest among the Anasazi Indians (Ancestral Puebloans) in Arizona. The priests carefully observed the movements of the stars, moon and sun. Subterranean ceremonial rooms called *kivas* housed ceremonies to honor the Indian Triad—maize, squash and beans. Practices and legends were passed down from one generation to the next. One Puebloan Indian anthropologist observed, "For a people so intensely agrarian for so many centuries of their existence, all life does result from happenings within the earth, from the union of earth, water, and sun."[1]

SHARED THEMES AND BELIEFS

Creation Stories

Native Americans formulated a spiritual explanation for the origins of the world, humans and all forms of life in their many different creation stories. One of the oldest and most widespread is the Earth-Diver story, which tells of a deep-diving animal hero who at the beginning of time swooped down into the water to retrieve the land. From this first earth, the first people and food emerged. In other stories, the world is shaped by the All-Father sun. In Zuni theology the Fourth Sphere is associated with the Earth Mother, giver of all vegetation. Their creation story relates a momentous decision by the chief about whether the world should be entirely water; he opted for some land to provide food. This choice proved to be life-saving during a great flood, when the only safe, dry place was Corn Mountain. The rising waters, according to this story, were held off by the sacrifice of a boy and girl who scattered cornmeal as they walked.

The Huron of upper New York State told a creation story in which a female deity fell into the world when it was only water. She was rescued by the animals who put her on Turtle's back so she would not drown. Frog brought her a piece of earth, which she touched, magically transforming it into land. When this divine woman died in childbirth, food sprung forth from the place where she was buried, pumpkin vines from her head, maize from her breasts and beans from her arms and legs. This ascribing of plant food origins to an all-giving mother figure, sometimes known as Corn Mother, the spirit of fertility, was a popular concept among the agricultural tribes of the Northeast.

A Navajo creation story pinpoints the origins of First Man and Woman to the underworld called First World. This domain was filled with strife, which drove out the first humans. They left accompanied by two supernatural companions on a journey through additional underworlds until they reached the Third World, where they witnessed the creation of six sacred mountains, still revered by the Navajo today.

In the Southwest Pueblos of New Mexico, life was thought to have begun in the fire located in a sunken pit under the roof opening of the *kiva*. A small hole nearby was thought to be the point where the umbilical cord attached man in life and death to the Place of Beginning in the Underworld. The center of the *kiva* was a sacred place from which the people of maize emerged and returned after death.

Mythic Time

The entire creation period was known as mythic or Distant Time. People were able to access that time of spiritual power through certain ceremonies and rituals. Repeating the myths over and over was one such sacred process; these legends were not regarded as having been created by human beings, but by superhuman powers.

Rituals involving prayer and drumming could also recapture mythic time by creating a suspension of secular time. The creation period was thought to have occurred a very long time ago, when animals and humans spoke the same language and animals shared meat from their kills with humans. When members of the Koykon tribe in Alaska found some caribou killed by wolves but hardly eaten, they believed that this harkened back to the myth that wolves sometimes left food for humans. Many legends had to do with famine, as the Indians were so often hungry, if not starved, in the winter, during times of drought and flood. There are many versions of the story of the flight of the Corn Maidens from the Zuni, an event that produced famine. The people sent out emissaries to recover the maidens, who agreed to give maize to the people. In the Rain Ceremony held every four years and in harvest rituals held each fall, as well as in the Shalako Ceremony held at winter solstice, the personification of the Corn Maidens is a key element.

A familiar character in gatherer-hunter mythology was the Trickster, a shape-shifter, part god, part culture hero. In the cycle of trickster Raven myths of the Northwest Coast, the story of the mythical food quest was retold with a moral. The Raven was a glutton, constantly preoccupied with hunger. In one myth, the Raven was anxious because he believed that all the fish in the world were about to become extinct. To make sure his grandmother did not starve, he took her a fish. To his surprise, she was outraged, and told him that if he were so greedy, there would not be any fish left for tribal descendants.

Among the Creek of Florida and other Southeast tribes, a myth about the Corn Mother was prevalent. This divinity was believed to feed her children from maize that grew on her legs, as it does on cobs, that she scraped off daily. When the boys in the tribe secretly spied on her and saw her scraping off the maize, they were horrified and killed her. Then they ran away to live as warriors hunting in the forest. The murder of the Corn Mother symbolically separated mothers from adolescent boys.

Sacred Land

Land was not only sacred, but also alive and sustaining. Prayers of thanks were offered for this wondrous earth, so necessary for growing food. The link to the land, however, was not portable and could not simply be transferred to another location. In keeping with a settled agrarian culture, land was attached to specific sacred sites. A place-name often evoked a particular story, memories of beloved foods, family reminiscences, vital gods and particular ancestors. One Navajo elder said in 2001, "When we talk about place—we talk about Earth and we have to consider what's under the Earth, what's on the Earth, what's above the Earth."[2] Reconnecting with the land at regular intervals was considered a holy act. In northern Wisconsin, at the season when wild rice was harvested from the swamps, the Anishinaabeg (also known as Ojibwa and Chippewa) felt they were reenacting their connection with the land in the same way as their ancestors had for many centuries. It recalled vividly and spiritually all the ricing seasons past, and became an important way to "recharge their own Indianness."[3]

Time as a Cycle

The ceremonial calendar was based on the natural, seasonal cycle of time and the lunar cycle. Most tribes named the months after the lunar cycle. For the Zuni, this included the April Moon of Plants, August Sturgeon Moon, September Corn Moon and December Hunting Moon. Rituals revolved around the cyclical processes that sustained life—hunting, gathering, fishing, planting, growing and harvesting. The Southwest Pueblos followed a strict ceremonial calendar with seasonal reenactments of rituals during which tribal members impersonated, thereby becoming, sacred beings. If the Indians did not scrupulously follow this calendar, they believed that the world would die. The Sun Dance performed on the Great Plains honored the source of life so that the cycles might continue.

Supreme Being

Most Native American tribes had a concept of a supreme being called the Great Spirit. This may have evolved from hero-worship of actual men, perhaps chiefs or warriors. The earth belonged to the Great Spirit, who established the various tribes in their locations and gave food as his gift. He was often called on for advice and help especially in the winter, which was often a time of starvation. One European captive wrote in the early nineteenth century, "It was not until our sufferings from hunger began to be extreme, that the old woman had recourse to the expedient of spending a night in prayer and singing. In the morning she said to her son and *Waw-be-be-nais-sa* [an indolent hunter], 'Go and hunt, for the Great Spirit has given me some meat.' . . . Go, my sons, you cannot fail to kill something, for in my dream I saw *Wa-me-gon-a-biew* [her son] coming into the lodge with a beaver and a large load of meat on his back." The men were not enthusiastic about setting out again because they were discouraged, hungry and cold, but the woman gave each a medicine sack that she said could not fail to work. With this magic, they did, in fact, meet with success and brought back a moose.[4]

The Cardinal Points and Symbolic Colors

Many Native American religions recognized six deities in addition to the supreme being, of which four had no visible shape because they were the winds. They ruled the corners of the earth, the sanctified cardinal points, bringing rain and sun, overseeing the seasons and wealth. Most festivals made reference to the four points or directions. Among most tribes, two other directions were also venerated: Above (the Sky or Zenith) and Below (the Earth or Nadir). Altogether, the six directions permeated American Indian religious thinking. They were associated with particular colors, animals, birds, mountains and/or plants, depending on the tribe. The Apache in New Mexico and Texas designated black for East, white for South, yellow for West and blue for North; the Cherokee, who spanned parts of Tennessee, North Carolina, Kentucky and Virginia took red, white, black and blue respectively for the same points; the Navajo selected white, blue, yellow and black, with white and black for Below and blue for Above. Many beliefs and legends were attached to each color. Among the Tewa along the Little Colorado River and the Rio Grande, parents dedicated their children to one of the maize groups: white (East), black (North), yellow (West), blue (South). The adult members of the groups blessed the children during the first solstice ceremony following their births.

In the Southwest, a legend told of the miracle of the Seed People. After dancing and singing, seven prayer plumes were supposed to have turned into maize plants, all sisters—yellow was the eldest, followed by blue, red, white, speckled and black, until the youngest, who was sweet corn. In Zuni maize planting, the Sun Priest took six kernels, each a different color, wrapped them in a husk with a plumed wand and went to his field. There he made four deep holes, the first to the North, second to the West, third to the South and fourth to the East. Two more were for the Sky and the Lower Regions. Standing in the central space, he faced East and used the prayer wand to mark a cross on the ground to symbolize the four cardinal points. Then he took three grains of each of the six colors of maize and placed them with the kernels already in the husk, reciting the planting chants along with each color. When his work was finished, the priest fasted and prayed for four days.

This was not the only Zuni ceremony that made use of the sacred directions and colors. Each of the six *kivas* was represented by beans of colors that symbolized the four compass directions. At puberty, boys were required to bring back a bowl of the right color of beans for the *kiva* they planned to enter once initiated. The *kachinas*, dancers representing supernatural beings with vast powers to confer abundant harvests, used the colors in their religious ceremonies.

The Spirit World

The worship of the pantheon of supreme beings was complemented by the spirit world, in which every animal, fish, tree and plant was endowed with a soul. This animism is often credited as one reason the Indians generally treated the environment with respect. Among the Mandan of North Dakota, it was common to feed bison heads or skulls a ceremonial meal that was intended to appease the spirits of the dead animals while reassuring those of the living about to be hunted. Hunters always made a small food offering to a skull before the hunt.

There were a great many fears about the consequences of crossing the spirits of certain animals. Some tribes, for example, believed that the carcasses of mink or muskrat needed to be thrown on the ground or the animals would be offended and not allow themselves to be taken any more. A porcupine who came prowling around the hunters' camp should not be molested because he was thought to be the bearer of news. Bears were regarded with great respect. Hunters sought to avoid alienating their spirits because then it might not be possible to catch them. In the east it was thought that humans who abused game animals would suffer terrible consequences. There was also the belief among many tribes that eating bear or deer would confer on the diner the qualities of that animal. This was based on the magical belief that we are what we eat.

Many animal and bird dances encouraged the Indians to think more deeply about their relationship to nonhumans. The capture of newborn passenger pigeons by the Northeast Indians of New York and Pennsylvania was regarded as a feast provided by the parent birds. Consequently, the hunters left gifts at the nesting sites to ensure the birds' return the next season. The Seneca, who lived in New York State, attributed human qualities to the birds and honored them in ceremonies, myths, legends and dance.

Among the Northwest Coast tribes, the salmon was believed to be an immortal being who voluntarily sacrificed itself for the people's benefit. If the fish was treated with respect and not killed unnecessarily, it would return to its village under the sea and encourage others to give themselves up. When a Kwakiutl of British Columbia took his first salmon of the season, he recited the Prayer of the Salmon Fisher: "Welcome, Swimmer. I thank you, because I am still alive at this season when you come back to our good place; for the reason why you come is that we may play together with my fishing tackle, Swimmer. Now, go home and tell your friends that you had good luck on account of your coming here and that they shall come with their wealth bring, that I may get some of your wealth, Swimmer; and also take away my sickness, friend, supernatural one, Swimmer."[5]

Similarly, the Indians tried to ingratiate themselves with the plant spirits. The Zuni believed that they could enter into a dialogue with these spirits. At the apex of the plant spirit world were, of course, the cultivated crops—maize, squash and beans, the Three Sisters. Among the Seneca, some of the women joined a society called the Tonwisas and propitiated the three plants' spirits in a ceremonial march. The leader held an armful of maize and a cake of corn bread as she led the parade around a kettle of maize soup. The Iroquois, who lived in an area that stretched from New York State to Ohio and from the Great Lakes to Canada's Georgian Bay, addressed many religious ceremonies to the Three Sisters or Our Life Supporters, thanking them with singing. Some trees like the *pinyon* pine in the Southwest were thought to possess magic powers. At Santa Clara Pueblo in New Mexico, the *pinyon* was thought to be the oldest food, the original food. According to legend, it was not until some tribe members ascended the western mesa and ate the fallen seeds that the people discovered the cardinal directions of north, west, south and east.

FOOD RITUALS

Gathering

The act of gathering plants and roots was considered a sacred ritual and celebrated with ceremonies, both when the women first set out with their sharp pointed digging sticks and burden baskets, and when they returned to prepare their gleanings.

Planting and Agriculture

Many festivals, ceremonies and rituals honored the sacred planting and growing traditions although they might differ in important ways among various tribes. Maize ceremonies, for example, were quite different for the Pueblo peoples versus the Northeast Woodlands Indians because each group had its own concept of maize. For the Pueblo Indians, maize went so far back that it existed before time; for the woodlanders who began cultivating maize later, there was a time before maize. The Pueblo rituals focused on rain; the woodland rituals focused on fire, the moon, stars and planetary events that were crucial for light and warmth, as these Indians were originally dependent on hunting for food.

Among the Crow of Montana, the Planting Festival held on the eve of sowing seed was the most important feast of the year. The hunting season began ten days before planting so that the hunters could bring back marrow bones and tongues to be consumed during the festival. Only those who performed the actual work of planting were allowed to eat. The day immediately prior to planting there was a prescribed series of four dances. Then the seeds were laid down by hand and covered with earth. Three more dances were performed in worship to the Great Spirit.

The Cloud or Corn Maiden Dance among the Tewa Pueblos, usually held in late winter or early spring before planting, honored the maize in a similar ritual way. Eight women carrying ears of sacred corn were dressed in special costumes with headdresses of cloud symbols to invoke rain. The women, corn and clouds were all fertility symbols.

The Iroquois held a meeting each spring about a week before planting in which the Women's Society shook their shell rattles to express gratitude to the Three Sisters. An appointed speaker announced that it was propitious that such a large number of people were still in this life and able to participate in this season of growing. He gave thanks for the maize and all green plants. One early-nineteenth-century observer recorded an Iroquois speech: "We still have the duty and privilege of planting corn, beans, squashes and other vegetables. We ask you, our Father, to supply us this season with food, to send the game birds and animals, as usual. We thank you today as we have the privilege of performing our ceremony."[6] It was the duty of the owner of the field to provide a feast when the women had finished hoeing; each helper was entitled to take some maize soup or hominy home.

The *Powamu* or Bean Dance Ceremony, performed by the Hopi for sixteen days in February, prepared the world for the planting and growth of another season. On the sixteenth day, a public ceremony was held in which the *kachinas* gave out mature bean sprouts. Planting thanksgivings were also common in which the Creator was thanked for past blessings and asked to continue his bounty.

The Corn Sprouting Ceremony held by the Iroquois in May was a food spirit–supplication ceremony that took place three to four weeks after the seed planting, when the new shoots first showed above ground. The purpose was to entertain the spirits so that they would continue to help the crops mature.

Efforts were often made to foretell the outcome of planting. Among the Iroquois, if a lightning bug or cicada flew inside a dwelling, it was taken as a sign of a bountiful harvest. Among the Huron, the shaman, referred to as the Magician in the Country, was consulted to learn what success might be expected from the maize crop.

Agricultural rituals were also common. The Zuni constructed what are called "waffle gardens," beds of four by twelve to twenty feet enclosed by four-inch-high mud walls with cornstalk hedges that enabled the Indians to keep the maize colors pure. The system of earthworks and dams were partly agricultural invention and partly ritual.

Hunting and Fishing Rituals

Many rituals preceded a hunting or fishing expedition to ensure its success. Among the Sioux of South Dakota, a Buffalo Dance was performed to induce the appearance of the animals. One early diarist recorded, "As the buffalo appears at first in small numbers & then gradually encreasing, so they imitate its habits & send two or three at first to dance & then a greater number. Buffalo are found within sixty or a hundred miles of this point."[7]

Among the Apache of New Mexico, deer and antelope ceremonies were held the night before hunts to secure these animals. The Deer Ceremony involved saying prayers and singing songs to the deer in which they were implored to give up their meat.

In the Northwest before setting off on a whale hunt, each participant from the Makah tribe of Neah Bay, Alaska, conducted a religious ceremony to implore his personal spirit as well as the whale itself for help. In this ritual, the man and his wife rubbed their bodies with hemlock needles until they bled in a kind of ritual sacrifice. The hunters rarely ate before the hunt, believing it would make them sluggish.

The Eastern Dakota Indians frequently held the *Wakan*, or Holy Feast, to produce great success in hunting. Guests were summoned by messenger when the food was ready. After the preliminaries, including consecration of the participants' hands and knives in cedar smoke, the food was divided into equal portions and consumed. People who were unable to finish had to pay the host a fine.

Food Offerings

A token gift of food to the spirits was a ritual in most tribes. Among the Zuni, before eating a meal, diners took a piece of food from the pot with their fingers and breathed on it. Then they recited in unison, "Receive! [Oh, souls of] my ancestry, and eat; resuscitate by means of your wondrous knowledge, your hearts; return unto us of yours the water we need, of yours the seeds of earth, of yours the means of attaining great age." Then they threw the food into the fire in a kind of offering. Early-twentieth-century ethnologist Frank Cushing related that he never saw a Zuni take a bite of food without going through this ritual first, and these words were among the first taught to a child. Until his mother had succeeded, no child was ever weaned.[8]

CEREMONIAL FEASTS

Feasts were held both as religious observances in themselves and in conjunction with religious or social gatherings. They might mark any number of occasions: giving thanks, celebrating the first event in a child's life, observing the appearance of the first foods of the season, honoring the memory of a dead person or as the concluding event of a ceremony. Those feasts that had a strong religious link required the use of specific sacred foods such as wild game, fish, berries and maize that was obtained, prepared and served according to ritual prescriptions. Many of the feasts discussed in Chapter 4 contained religious or ceremonial components.

The members of the Iroquois Confederacy—Mohawk, Oneida, Onondaga, Cayuga and Seneca—held five feasts a year: at the time of making maple syrup, after planting when they gave thanks for the season and learned from the chiefs how to ensure a good harvest, the Green Corn Feast, the harvest thanksgiving, and at year's end at the time of the Old Moon around the end of January. This was also the beginning of the new year; the feast lasted for nine days, during which the chiefs reviewed the affairs of the past year and planned for the upcoming one. On the last feast day, the people shared a meal of meat, maize and beans boiled together and eaten directly from the kettles. All feasts served the social purpose of assembling the tribe together and giving thanks to the Great Spirit for blessings.

First Food Observances

These widespread feasts were held at the first appearance or taking of the season of various foods including wild game, salmon and other fish, maize, fruits, berries, roots and wild rice. First Food celebrations were occasions both to give thanks and avoid the danger of eating unconsecrated food. Ceremonies included prayers and offerings and functioned as ritual preparation for harvesting or taking the rest of the catch. The food's spiritual and physical necessity was acknowledged, and forgiveness asked from the spirits assuring them that the food had not been taken wantonly. These observations were considered essential to ensuring the continuation of finding and growing food for the next season and many to come.

Green Corn Ceremonies. Green Corn rituals, almost universal among maize-growing Native Americans, honored the mid-to-late-summer appearance of the immature "green" corn (the milky stage). This recognized a crucial stage in the normal life cyle of maize. At these rites, which ranged from family gatherings to community-wide celebrations and in preparation techniques from the pit-baked sweet maize of the Hopi to the roasted unripened "field" corn of the Mandan, there was a traditional reconciling of any ill feelings among the people. The ceremonies were generally related to giving thanks for the harvest, extending assurance that the crop would mature, preparing the food and extensive eating of green maize. The most extensive and best recorded of these ceremonies took place in the Southeast. For these tribes, including the Creek and Seminole, the annual *Busk* (taken from the Creek verb "to fast") or Green Corn Ceremony was a major traditional religious observance that ushered in the new year. It was a period of renewal, thanksgiving and amnesty for past crimes and misdemeanors with the exception of murder. Everything in the villages was purified and renewed and, most importantly, the old fire was extinguished and a new one kindled.

It may be that the importance of the Corn Mother, or *Selu*, among the Cherokee is related to the dispersion of the Green Corn Goddess from Mexico sometime between AD 900 and 1200. When the maize was green, the Cherokee sent a messenger to pick seven ears for the seven prime counselors to sample. They then announced the date of the feast based on the crop's readiness. Six days of hunting followed while the counselors fasted. On the sixth day, the people harvested fresh green maize and the hunters returned with fresh meat. On the seventh day, seven new ears were delivered to the priest and a symbolic new fire was kindled from the bark of seven trees. Maize offerings were made to the fire before the feast began. When the celebration was over, the priest and counselors fasted for an additional seven days. All the people then participated in a communal one-day fast that concluded the Green Corn Ceremony.

For many groups in the Northeast and elsewhere, Green Corn rites were more important than either planting or harvest rituals. Among the Oklahoma Seminole and the Creek, the Green Corn Ceremony, held for four days in late June or early July, was the principal event of the ceremonial year. The celebration included fasts, feasts, games, building the sacred fire, sacrifices, naming ceremonies and prayers, and ended with the breaking of the fast.

For the Kickapoo of Wisconsin, the feast was an unusual display of atypical gender roles. The older women were in charge, exercising almost unlimited authority. The oldest and most respectable woman prepared the maize and conducted the ceremony. She decided when the tribe could start eating. First, she went to the fields and examined the corn silk to see if the maize was ready. After she prepared some in different ways, she served it to her cronies to test. If the maize was acceptable, she decorated her door with husks to signal the upcoming feast. Then the whole tribe turned out to dance in the fields. They returned laden with cobs that were buried in their husks in the embers until roasted. When done, the maize was removed and seasoned with bear oil, bison suet or marrow. One nineteenth-century European captive wrote, that "no occasion with which I am acquainted, displays in a more manifest degree its social effects than the corn feast. The heart dilates with pleasure even to overflowing, and the guests give utterance to their joys in songs and dances, and continue the hilarity for the remaining part of the day and night and frequently, for the whole of the succeeding day."[9]

In the Southwest, among the Zuni, elaborate rituals accompanied gathering of the first maize. A bowl of prayer cornmeal (cornmeal mixed with ground white shells and turquoise) occupied a coveted place in each dwelling. Each woman dipped in and took a pinch while one, the corn-matron, went to the storage bin and brought back corn-soot (a later stage of corn smut when the fungus breaks down into spores and dust) and sacred new maize, representing male and female. This introduction of the new to the old maize was a common Native American practice during Green Corn ceremonies. Then, the corn-matron greeted the new maize. This "meeting of the children" ritual was performed in memory of the return of the lost mythic Corn Maidens and their welcome back by the Seed-Priests.

First Salmon Rites (North Pacific Coast, including Northern California, Oregon and Washington). Usually the first catch in the spring was taken by a priest who brought the fish to the altar. The salmon was greeted as a guest of high rank, special rituals were performed, a new fire kindled and the fish tasted by everyone present. The first salmon's head and bones were returned to the stream so it could be reborn. As preparation for the Feast of the First Salmon, all sick people were temporarily removed from dwellings, any dead plant or animal was carried away and dwellings were thoroughly cleaned. The salmon was laid out on a new reed mat with a red berry in its mouth and the shaman offered prayers addressing the salmon directly. After the ceremony, all tribe members were free to fish for the season.

Bean Ceremony (Iroquois). The Bean Ceremony, a day-long feast held during the first week of August when the green beans matured, honored the food spirit of one of the three sacred foods. The Indians thanked the spirit for past bounties and entertained with Our Life Supporter Dances so they would continue to provide.

Acorn Feast (Hupa of California). The annual fall Acorn Feast sanctified the first eating of acorns after some had been collected and ritually prepared. The Hupa then repeated certain texts, said prayers and performed sacred acts.

Raspberry Ceremony (Iroquois). This food spirit ceremony was held when the raspberries first ripened to give thanks for the recurrence of the season and supplicate the spirits to continue to show favor.

Root Feast (Confederated Tribes of Warm Spring Reservation of Oregon). Held in April when the women unearthed three different kinds of roots, the Root Feast was a ritual gathering, serving and eating of these foods in which the people gave thanks to the Creator and blessed the roots. Accompanied by ritual and prayer songs, the women boiled the roots in pots on the morning of the feast. The women gatherer/diggers, along with the fishermen and hunters who also provided food for the occasion, carried the dishes all around the longhouse, calling out the names of each and giving people tiny ritual tastings. After the feast, everyone rose, faced east and prayed. Then families were free to gather roots for their own use. The same procedure was followed for huckleberries in August and wild celery in both late winter and spring.

Maple Festival (Iroquois). The maple feast was held when the sap began to flow around the second week in February. The Indians expressed their gratitude to the maple trees, passed the first sap around for tasting, and asked for a continuation of the trees' providing the raw material for the syrup.

Strawberry Festival (Iroquois). Held in mid-June, the Strawberry Festival honored all first fruits, giving thanks for the berries and new life. The juice was drunk by young and old alike. The Creator and spirit forces were thanked and asked to provide future fruition.

Cranberry Day (Wampanoag of Massachusetts). The medicine man decided when the berries were ripe enough to hold this festival on Martha's Vineyard, Massachusetts, with all members of the tribe participating in scooping up the berries.

Whale Feast (Alaska Inuit). The Whale Feast ritual, with four days of taboos and restrictions, was the principal ceremonial for the Alaskan Inuit. It began with the ceremonial greeting of a beached whale, followed by distribution of the meat. The feast was provided by the captain of the group who took the whale and was based on the belief that the whale allowed itself to be taken but that its spirit had to be placated in return.

Saguaro Festival (Pima and Tohono O'odham of Arizona). Held in July, the Saguaro Festival marked the beginning of the rainy season with the ritual making and drinking of saguaro wine. The women collected the fruit, boiled the pulp and strained the juice through a basket. The syrup was then placed in pottery jars and taken to the ceremonial rain house. There the village headman and his assistant presided over the fermentation while the people danced and sang in a large circle outside. The "sit and drink" part of the ceremony took place on the third day, when the sacred wine was poured on the earth. The men passed around the wine and the village headman recited long poems that explained how the wine produced clouds, rain and maize.

Harvest Thanksgiving Festivals

All first foods observances were thanksgivings, of course, but the harvests themselves were also greeted with independent celebrations of thanks. (See Chapter 1 for a discussion of the "first Thanksgiving.")

Yakima of Washington State (Northwest Thanksgiving). The Yakima gave thanks to the Creator for sending food to the children in this feast in which camas roots were baked in underground pits. Hot rocks were placed in the bottom, then covered with prairie grass and a woven mat. The camas roots were piled on top and water added. The pile was then covered with a blanket and earth. The roasting took several hours while the men broiled meat.

Zuni. When the crops were ready to be harvested, prayers were recited in greeting and acceptance, and the new maize was introduced to the old. The entire family then participated in the harvest. At the final ceremonial, four items were placed in each granary: an ear of yellow maize and an ear of white, the two having grown together in a single husk; a large single ear of maize, dunked in sacred Salt Lake water by the Seed-priest and; corn-soot, which symbolized the generation of life.

Iroquois. For this end-of-the-harvest-season ceremony, the people were called to "gather corn bread." Each family baked a batch and

Women resting in a harvest field in the Southwest. Courtesy of Library of Congress, Prints & Photographs Division, Edward S. Curtis Collection (reproduction number: LC-USZ62-115801).

brought it to the main longhouse. A speaker was appointed to congratulate the people on the success of their crops and gave thanks to the Great Spirit. Two men then performed the Feather Dance, followed by a women-only dance to thank the Great Mother and the Three Sisters.

Seneca. The Seneca recited a prayer in which they gave thanks to the Great Spirit, saying, "Those who take care of [the maize, beans and squash] every day asked, too, that they be sisters. And at that time there arose a relationship between them: We shall say, 'the Sisters, our sustenance,' when we want to refer to them. And it is true: We are content up to the present time, for we see them growing. And give it your thought, that we may do it properly: We now give thanks for the Sisters, our sustenance. And our minds will continue to be so."[10]

Hopi (Packavu). Held at least every four years, the *Packavu* festival featured the Bean Maidens carrying large baskets of bean sprouts

159

and oversized symbolic beans molded of cornmeal while marching to the singing of the chief *kachinas.*

Feasts of the Dead

These death rituals were either funeral feasts at the time of death and burial, or memorial feasts held sometime after the funerals to commemorate deceased members of the tribe.

Huron of southern Ontario, Canada. Held at ten or twelve year intervals, the Feast of the Dead was a ten-day ritual involving exhumation of bodies of all people who had not died violently. Each family held a feast in honor of its own dead. Presents for the deceased were displayed. At sunrise on the last day of the ceremony, the bones and grave goods were emptied into a common pit and reburied, accompanied by group lamenting and a final feast.

Iroquois. Conducted twice a year, once in the spring (April) before planting and again in the fall (October) after harvest, the Iro-

Two Native Americans offering food to the dead (burial scaffold with body). Courtesy of Library of Congress, Prints & Photographs Division (reproduction number: LC-USZC4-6139).

quois Feast to the Dead was hosted by a special society of women. A midnight meal of specific foods was offered during the night-long feast. Families held individual ceremonies to feed their hungry dead, as well as small feasts that required a speaker and a woman to prepare the foods. They believed that the dead were present during these rituals, having returned home to eat offerings.

Shawnee from Tennessee. The annual Death Feast was held at home after the Green Corn Dance to honor the spirits of the deceased. The food was prepared and served, and selected persons spoke to the spirits of the dead, telling them that the food had been prepared in their honor and asking them in return not to disturb the living. The food was left out for a number of hours. It was believed that the dead ate only the spiritual portion of the meal, so when the family returned, it was permissible for them to eat the physical feast.

Alaska Inuit and Aleut. At these Feasts to the Dead, also called Memorial Feasts, the spirits of the dead were invited to accept food and other gifts vicariously through their living namesakes, who ate for the deceased.

Potlatch

This complex Northwest Coast ceremony, which included a monumental feast where huge amounts of food were distributed, was in a class of its own. Scholars still debate on whether this was primarily a secular or sacred feast. The word "potlatch" is the anglicized version of *patshatl* from the Nootka of Washington State, which means "giving." Held during the winter ceremonials and lasting sometimes for weeks, a potlatch marked a change in social rank—most often the inheritance of a title and privilege of a higher status. The Northwest Coast tribes were obsessed with rank. Acquiring position and demonstrating one was worthy of a title was the focus of ceremonial life. In each tribe there were several ranked kinship groups called *numayms*, roughly equivalent to clans. A person's *numaym* was officially conferred during a potlatch. The secret societies were the most important religious groups. During the sacred winter season when the winter dances were performed, secret society membership that took precedence while youths were initiated. The potlatch practice sustained reciprocal relationships among noble houses and stemmed from the requirement that leaders must be generous. The religious element consisted partly of the chiefs impersonating munificent spirits. Memorial potlatches were held by a man to comfort the ghosts of his parents and validate his right to bear their names and pass them on to his children. Failure to honor the memory of one's ancestors would invite their hungry and alienated ghosts to hang around and cause trouble. Ghosts were tormented by two things—hunger and loneliness. Any human gathering attracted these spirits, but especially those where food was served. Periodic burnings of food gave nourishment to the ghosts. A person who fulfilled these obligations would be rewarded social approval. Although many material goods, including such things as blankets, were distributed at potlatches, the ubiquitous element was huge quantities of food. The feasts were expected to be so abundant that there was no possibility that guests could finish; they were expected to take the generous leftovers home. Dried salmon was the principal food, supplemented by berries, seaweed, mountain goat, elk, moose, bear, seal, small mammals and halibut, all smoked or dried. At one recorded potlatch, guests consumed fifty seals. There was lavish use of oolichan, the precious rich fish oil that was poured over everything, including the fire (to make it spark and burn brighter). The use of this most valued and scarce item incurred the greatest debt on the part of guests to reciprocate. The accumulation of food and goods to be given away could take years.

Anthropologists have been trying for decades to decipher the precise meaning and social role of the potlatch. It has been thought by some to have been a mechanism for food redistribution, equalizing variations in food supply and productivity, a necessary antidote to scarcity and even starvation. Considerable redistribution of goods took place within the context of festivals and ceremonial displays. The unreliability of the coastal environment to produce food in winter made the potlatch necessary, according to this theory. Under the pressure of scheduled upcoming potlatches, people kept procuring food at high rates. One researcher commented, "Competitive feasting increases production and thus makes available to the redistributor both the food to be distributed and the social occasion for doing so."[11]

Other experts have maintained that the potlatch played a vital role in the socioeconomic life. By giving away food, goods and money, the giver gained high social status, rank, and prestige. In Northwest Coast societies, wealth was not measured by accumulation of goods, but rather by lavish display of generosity. This process created "contracts" in which receivers of goods and food were obligated to repay this generosity during their lifetimes. In this case, the potlatch was viewed as a kind of business meeting.

Still others saw the focus of the receiving and repaying as creating and maintaining bonds among the people. Hundreds, even thousands might attend. Sometimes, the potlatch was a memorial to a dead chief. Among the Gitksan of the Northwest Coast, funeral feasts were used to repay services that a dead person's father's people had performed for the hosts. The names and status of the hosts were then notched upward to fill the new vacancy created by the deceased. Totem pole feasts, the second type of potlatch held by the Gitksan, were supposed to take place four years after the death of a chief, both as a second burial of his bones and a way of honoring all the high-ranking males who had died since the last totem.

A more negative view of the potlatch maintains that it was based on rivalry and competition, a kind of conspicuous consumption gone haywire. Far from demonstrating largesse, the givers of potlatches were perceived under this theory to be ambitious aggrandizers who wanted to maintain and increase their economic supremacy and political control.

By the time anthropologists began to study the potlatch in the late nineteenth century, the custom had evolved into an event at which gargantuan amounts of food were wasted to a degree unknown in any other society past or present. Guests were obliged to eat until so bloated that they had to stagger off and vomit before returning to eat more. Many arriving Europeans found the practice repugnant and totally lacking in any religious or moral precepts. In fact, Canada outlawed the potlatch between 1885 and 1952.[12]

CEREMONIAL FOOD AND DRINK

The foods used in religious ceremonies and feasts were different from those for everyday meals. They might be more elaborately prepared, less easy to obtain, richer in terms of fat content, grown in special fields or simply consumed only for religious rituals.

Maize and Maize Products

In the Southwest, feasts were often offerings to placate spirits. Foods like prayer cornmeal and maize pollen were included. Pollen was thrown into the wind while praying for renewed life. Cornmeal was offered with prayers to the maize spirits. During the baby naming ceremony, a wash of maize pollen was spread over the ground, and some thrown into the air and rubbed into the hair.

The Iroquois used cobs of maize for divination. When a warrior was about to go to war, he would place an ear at the edge of the fire and then walk away. When he returned an hour later, if the cob had been completely burned, it was a sign that he would be killed in battle. On the Pueblos, maize ears were sacred and had spiritual power. They might be adorned as fetish objects that were kept by people throughout their lives. Perfect ears were used in name-giving rituals, initiation rites and cures. Sacred cornmeal was ground from the best ears of white maize. Meal was held on the hand and prayed over before sprinkling on sacred objects and people. It had multiple uses including spreading on killed deer as a sanctifying element.

Salt

For many tribes, salt was sacred. The Navajo made annual journeys to Zuni Lake to gather salt for ceremonial purposes. Members of the Pima tribe in southern Arizona gained personal power and purification by participating in summer salt pilgrimages to the Gulf of California. The journey symbolized the quest for new life by bringing salt from the ocean to the desert. The pilgrims were allowed minimal amounts of food, water, sleep and talk on the trip. Before joining this pilgrimage, participants were forbidden from having sex for a period and were expected to abstain again after they returned. They were required to repeat the pilgrimage for four successive years.

A Zuni myth describes the offending of the Salt Lady by the tribe who polluted her lake with trash. She moved away and set up home in a new location. Because the people had lost their salt, they tried to find her. After much searching, they found her, planted their prayer sticks near her, prayed for forgiveness and promised to keep the lake clean. They were able to take some salt back to their village, where their aunts anointed them. According to one account, "Following that, a special prayer would be made to the Salt Mother that she keep bearing fruit for the well-being of the people around her."[13]

Among the Zuni boys, being taken by their godfathers on a journey to collect salt was part of their adolescent initiation into the *kivas*. The women, who stayed home, prayed for the success of the trip. Once they were at the Salt Lake, the godfathers instructed the boys again about religion. They were required to plant prayer sticks and fast for four days. Once home, the godfather's family performed purification rites and divided the salt among the families. When the new salt was brought into the home, it was placed near an ear of maize and prayers were recited for a long life. It was believed that a chunk of salt placed near a newborn would protect the baby when it was alone. If some was placed near any food, it was thought to ensure a plentiful supply.

Sunflower Oil (Iroquois)

This precious substance was used by the Iroquois principally for ceremonial purposes such as anointing the masks of members of the False-Face Society, a religious/medicine society.

Bear's Pudding (Iroquois)

Prepared from unseasoned yellow cornmeal and mixed with bits of fried meat, bear's pudding was then boiled and used only by members of the Bear Society at their meetings or while performing rites.

Buffalo Dance Pudding (Iroquois)

This dish of pounded cornmeal was boiled and sweetened with maple or corn syrup. It was supposed to reach the consistency of mud trampled by bison where they have stamped the ground to keep away flies. The pudding was eaten only by members of the Buffalo Company, a medicine society.

Black Drink

Black Drink, a hot tea brewed from yaupon holly leaves, was the ritual beverage of the Creek and Apalachee Indians in the Southeast. These tribes appear to have discovered the only source of naturally occurring caffeine in their environment. They perfected the most effective means for extracting maximum amounts by roasting the leaves. To maximize their absorption of the caffeine, they boiled the tea, which raised the level of the stimulant about thirty times over what it would be at room temperature, and then they drank it quite hot. From the sixteenth century to the eighteenth century, well after the Spanish had established settlements in the Southeast, Black Drink was commonly consumed from ritual cups made of large shells acquired by trade with tribes on the Atlantic and Gulf Coasts. The tea was drunk daily by adult males of high social standing for the purpose of ritual purification. The men drank the brew in preparation for the deliberations of the council, which required that men separate themselves from the women. This ritual cleansing prompted vomiting and expulsion of impurities. The Indians may have added a second ingredient to the brew to turn it into an emetic because it did not have this effect on early Europeans who drank it. Black Drink was valued as a potion that would cement friendship among boys entering puberty, who were required to make forays into the forest before receiving their adult war names. Men almost invariably demonstrated their peaceful intentions toward guests by inviting them to participate in the daily Black Drink ritual, and the tea was routinely drunk in large quantities after fasting for religious purposes.

The stimulant was also believed to possess magic properties. One Spanish observer noted an instance when its powers were invoked to win a ballgame against the Yustaga tribe, also of the Southeast. "When the cacina [the Spanish word for Black Drink] arrived it was thrown into the pot with the little sticks, in the name of the players of the opposing team, in order to make them weak and without strength. If the pot should by chance be uncovered while they are playing, they would lose the game for sure."[14]

Saguaro Wine

Among the Tohono O'odham and Pima Indians in southern Arizona, saguaro wine was used religiously in the annual rainmaking ceremony after the harvest of the fruit in midsummer. Lack of rain was the chief anxiety of these tribes. The ceremony marked the end of the dry season and beginning of the monsoons. Making wine from the tallest tree in the desert, drinking it to become intoxicated and vomiting copiously on the earth were thought to bring down the rain. One myth credited the original creation of saguaro wine to the supreme being, Elder Brother. After the women gathered the fruit and made syrup, the men oversaw the fermenting process, which was considered sacred. Carried out in the council house, fermentation took about seventy-two hours, during which the old men sang throughout two nights to protect the wine and encourage its transformation. The drinking of the wine occurred only as an element of a formal group ceremony conducted by medicine men and singers. A filled gourd cup was offered to the first man, who drained it in one swallow and then sang a song before returning the cup. A typical song went as follows:

> Ready, friend!
> Are we not here drinking
> The shaman's drink,
> The magician's drink!
> We mix it with our drunken tears and drink. . . .
> From within the great rainy mountains
> Rushed out a huge black cloud
> And joined with it.
> Pulling out their white breast feathers they went;
> Spreading their white breast feathers far and wide they went;
> Then they stood still and saw.[15]

The intended result of the drinking was intoxication, sometimes extreme. Drunkenness was required for the ritual success of the ceremony, and all of the wine had to be consumed. A drunken man was believed to be in a sacred state, a religious condition he attained for the benefit of the whole group to bring on the critical rain.

DANCE

Dance was fundamental to ritual and worship. Repetitious movements carried out over many hours, sometimes all night, could induce a kind of trance state that was by some tribes regarded as confirmation of supernatural contact. Most performances were held in conjunction with feasts or festivals, and often focused on various foodstuffs.

Corn Dances (Keresan, Tewa and Towa Pueblos in New Mexico)

Held at midsummer, these dances related to germination, maturation and the harvesting of crops as well as praying for the new year. Symbols of maize were placed everywhere. Some of the thanksgiving and prayers were addressed to the rain.

Our Life Supporter/Our Sustenance Dances (Iroquois)

The Food Spirit Ceremony following the Green Corn Ceremony included a series of women's dances honoring maize, beans and squash. The purpose was to entertain the food spirits and thank them.

Soup Dance (Oklahoma Seminole and Creek)

This activity was the final all-night dance of the ceremonial year. Two women were appointed to ritually prepare soup from wild game, which was served with cornbread to participants as morning approached.

Bread Dance (Shawnee)

The principal event of the ceremonial year, this dance was held in spring and fall. In spring the ritual included a prayer for bountiful crops and fertility, whereas in fall hunting was emphasized. Twelve male hunters provided squirrel or other game for the feast while twelve women prepared corn bread. The foods were displayed until the end of the dance, when they were exchanged by the men and women. The ritual concluded with the Bread Prayer dance.

FASTING

Fasting was a widespread religious practice among American Indians, both as a solitary undertaking and as part of a religious ceremony. In fact, refraining from eating was as integrally connected to the Native American culinary cycle as feasting, although fasting was linked to "downward giving"—the sharing of food or redistribution. Fasting was sometimes selective, applying only to particular foods. The Hopi, for example, fasted for four days before every ceremony by not eating any food containing fat, such as meat and nuts, although they were allowed to eat beans, blue marbles (balls of ground blue maize), fruits, greens, *piki* (the paper-thin bread of blue maize that had great symbolic and ceremonial signficance), baked pumpkin, squash and sweet maize mush. The Hopi believed that self denial would bring about a closer relationship with the Creator, both by purifying the body and strengthening the will. Fasting was also practiced to gain access to the spirit world, for fulfilling a vow, offering a sacrifice, preparing for a religious role, asking for spiritual assistance before a difficult decision, seeking solutions to serious problems, praying for peace, invoking the Great Spirit's blessing on a bison hunt, before a girl's puberty, searching for wisdom from higher powers and countless other reasons. Fasts varied in duration and frequency depending on the individual, tribe and purpose. The physical sacrifice and humility of a three- or four-day fast was believed to open people up in a direct manner to contact spiritual essences. A late-nineteenth-century European traveling among the Delaware and Mohican of Delaware and New York State noted the use of fasting for purification: "I do not recollect that it has already been mentioned, that previous to entering upon the solemnity of their sacrifices, the Indians prepare themselves by vomiting, fasting, and drinking decoctions from certain prescribed plants. This they do to expel the evil which is within them, and that they may with a pure conscience attend to the *sacred performance*, for such they consider it."[16]

One specific use of fasting for spiritual guidance was the vision quest, a specific kind of fast practiced as part of male pubescent initiation rites. Women also went on vision quests, but they were not as rigorous. For the Sioux, the ritual for a young boy meant first undergoing a purification rite in the sweat lodge, then walking to a distant hilltop and spending four days and nights there alone without food while crouched in what was called a vision pit. There, the boy begged the spirits for a dream. The power might appear to him as a bison, bird or other creature. When the boy returned to his village, the medicine man interpreted his vision, seeking clues to the adult name the boy would take. The vision quest was repeated throughout life as a person felt the need for help from spiritual powers, before a raid, during a child's illness or in a time of doubt.

NOTES

1. Betty Fussell, *The Story of Corn* (New York: Knopf, 1992), 56.

2. Quoted in Lois Ellen Frank, *Foods of the Southwest Indian Nations: Traditional & Contemporary Native American Recipes* (Berkeley, CA: Ten Speed Press, 2002), 17.

3. Albert Jenks, *The Wild Rice Gatherers of the Upper Lakes: A Study in American Primitive Economics* (Lincoln, NE: J & L Reprint Co., 1977), 12.

4. John Tanner, *A Narrative of the Captivity and Adventures of John Tanner During Thirty Years Residence Among the Indians in the Interior of North America, Pt. 1* (1830; reprint Ann Arbor, MI: Xerox University Microfilms, 1975), 72.

5. Franz Boas, *Ethnology of the Kwakiutl, Based on Data Collected by George Hunt* (Washington DC: Government Printing Office, 1921), 1319.

6. F.W. Waugh, *Iroquis [sic] Foods and Food Preparation* (Ottawa, ON: Government Printing Bureau, 1916), 13.

7. Frank Blackwell Mayer, *With Pen and Pencil on the Frontier in 1851: The Diary and Sketches of Frank Blackwell Mayer* (St. Paul: Minnesota Historical Society, 1932), 199.

8. Frank Hamilton Cushing, *Cushing at Zuni: The Correspondence and Journals of Frank Hamilton Cushing*, ed. Jesse Green (Albuquerque: University of New Mexico Press, 1990), 305.

9. John Dunn Hunter, *Manners and Customs of Several Indian Tribes: Memoirs of a Captivity among the Indians of North America, from Childhood to the Age of Nineteen: With Anecdotes Descriptive of Their Manners and Customs, to Which Is Added, Some Account of the Soil, Climate, and Vegetable Productions of the Territory Westward of the Mississippi* (1823; reprint New York: Johnson Reprint Corporation, 1970), 274.

10. Joseph Epes Brown with Emily Cousins, *Teaching Spirits: Understanding Native American Religious Traditions* (New York: Oxford University Press, 2001), 98.

11. Peter Farb, *Man's Rise to Civilization as Shown by the Indians of North America from Primeval Times to the Coming of the Industrial State* (New York: E. P. Dutton & Co., 1968), 153.

12. Ibid., 271.

13. Alvina Quam, *The Zunis: Self-Portrayals* (Albuquerque: University of New Mexico Press, 1972), 206.

14. Charles M. Hudson, ed., *Black Drink: A Native American Tea* (Athens: University of Georgia Press, 1979), 49.

15. Chandler Washburne, *Primitive Drinking: A Study of the Uses and Functions of Alcohol in Preliterate Societies* (New York: College and University Press, 1961), 182.

16. John Heckewelder, *History, Manners, and Customs of the Indian Nations Who Once Inhabited Pennsylvania and the Neighboring States* (1876; reprint New York: Arno Press, 1971), 213–214.

CHAPTER 6

CONCEPTS OF DIET AND NUTRITION

Foods consumed by American Indians were determined largely by energy needs, hunger, taste, availability, storability and cultural traditions. Native Americans had no conscious understanding of the biology of a balanced diet or appropriate percentages of various nutrients. Yet, whether they were nomads or agrarian farmers, they managed to consume nutritionally sound regimens. Over thousands of years, largely by trial and error or accidental discovery, these early peoples developed strategies to obtain maximum nutrition from their gathered, hunted, fished and farmed foods. They even learned how to convert toxic and nutritionally limited foods into beneficial ones. These adaptations enabled them to extract optimal nutrients from their environment. Moreover, these behaviors were reinforced by cultural traditions and passed down from one generation to the next. This is the mystery of indigenous nutrition.

This chapter focuses first on a description of nutritional adaptation, followed by some general thoughts about Native American diets, then moves on specifically to the gatherer-hunter diet, its benefits and risks, the agrarian diet, with its limitations and positive adaptations, and finally to the crucial role of culture. The last section discusses how nutritional stress—food scarcity produced by factors such as drought, crop failure and war—impacted diet, and examines the use of emergency or famine foods.

NUTRITIONAL ADAPTATION

Nutrition plays a major role in human adaptation. The fundamental challenge for Native Americans was to consume enough calories to meet their survival and energy needs—a question of quantity. More important for adaptation is the quality or the nutrition of these calories. There are essential nutrient components without which the human body cannot survive and reproduce. These include essential fatty acids, the amino acids that make up protein, vitamins, carbohydrates and minerals as well as trace components. The exact required amounts and proportions depend on numerous inherited, environmental and physiological factors, age, sex and reproductive status, such as whether a woman is menstruating, pregnant or lactating.

American Indians, quite unconsciously, developed nutritional adaptations, behaviors and biological traits that either reduced the impact of nutritional stress or improved the capacity of their primary foods. Rather than scientific nutrition, this process has been called the "evolution of indigenous American nutrition."[1] Culture played the most important role as an adaptive resource. At its simplest, a cultural nutritional adaptation might consist of making fire to roast food. A more complex example are the alkali processing techniques (described later in the chapter) used to enhance the nutritional value of maize.

How did Native Americans sense and regulate their intake level of nutrients when they had neither knowledge nor instruction? Were they perhaps satisfying innate unconscious nutrient-related cravings? Perhaps. Research has shown that rats can detect relative concentrations of different nutrients in their food and select proportionate amounts to balance their diet. Humans might have the capacity to do this as well. Hunger seems to be partly nutrient-specific. A taste for starchy food such as maize, for example, might have developed in response to physiological sensations of dietary needs and an evolving palate.

NATIVE AMERICAN DIETS

Broadly speaking, there were two distinct Native American diets: hunter-gatherer, more accurately referred to as gatherer-hunter because the bulk of the calories came from foraged materials, and agrarian, in which the majority of calories were provided by domesticated crops, specifically maize as the number-one staple, and to a lesser extent beans and squash. In general, the gatherer-hunter diet preceded the agrarian and gradually evolved into an agricultural approach to subsistence and settled existence. However, this was not always the case. The two also existed simultaneously within the same culture even as more and more tribes began to adopt farming. For geographic and cultural reasons, groups such as the tribes of the Northwest Coast simply never adopted agriculture. Other societies were primarily agrarian but supplemented crop food with gathering and hunting or fishing. Intense reliance on maize made the population nutritionally vulnerable to crop failure. Even after maize was introduced, the tribes in the Northeast and West Coast provided themselves with a nutritious and balanced diet by combining maize with nuts, berries, roots, tubers and other wild edible plants, wild game and fish.

Within each of these two categories of diet there was variation depending on regional environment. Those tribes that lived in the Southwest were all but vegetarian, consuming large quantities of maize supplemented by other vegetables, plants and fruits. Only fringe amounts of meat came from small game, including rodents, rabbits, hares, lizards, birds and in some places fish. The few large wild animals in the area were extremely difficult to hunt and kill, and there was precious little water for fishing. The cultures of the Northwest Coast consumed a high-flesh, high-fat diet that consisted almost exclusively of sea mammals, caribou and fish. The Plains Indians ate regimens high in meat, chiefly bison. Consequently, it is not accurate to speak of the Native American diet but rather diets.

Gatherer-Hunter Diet

The nomadic Native American tribes wandered in bands of twenty to eighty people from place to place according to season and the need to locate particular wild food. They moved every few weeks and stored little if any food. Feasting consisted of sharing meat and fat from large game animals. The most nutritionally significant portion of the diet (estimated at up to 80 percent of calories) came from foods gathered or foraged, an activity undertaken by women and children.[2]

Although foraging might seem a haphazard way to acquire food, humans have used this strategy for more than 95 percent of their existence, down to the beginnings of agriculture. The women in nomadic Native American tribes developed extensive botanical knowledge. More than anything, it was variety that characterized this diet. It is possible to survive without risking malnutriton on calorie requirements as low

California Pomo woman gathering seeds. Courtesy of Library of Congress, Prints & Photographs Division, Edward S. Curtis Collection (reproduction number: LC-USZ62-116525).

as 1,900 daily for men, and 1,000 for women and children. The mean life expectancy for neolithic adults was not high—between thirty-one and thirty-four for males, and twenty-eight to thirty-one for females.

One major cultural factor that gatherer-hunters had on their side was their small numbers. In groups of usually fewer than 100, everyone knew everyone else and members could all eat together. It is believed these Native Americans returned to camp with their gleanings, meat and fish and ate communally. This would have made it easy to exchange crucial food-related information, including where to find particular plants and roots, which ones were safe to eat, which to avoid, the best strategies for hunting and fishing, and gradually, how to prepare foods to make them edible and digestible. In this way, the younger generations as well as adults acquired critical nutritional information especially important for climates with tough winters. Behaviors that favored survival needed to be passed on to offspring.

Archaeological investigation of skeletons, dental remains and fossilized feces and analogy with contemporary groups of foragers have been used to determine more precisely what these bands ate. There are drawbacks, however, to these methods. Consequently, there is little precise information on amounts of particular foods consumed and nutritional values of those foods.

Archaeological excavation at two early Native American burial sites shows the vast differences among gatherer-hunter diets from different regions. Analysis of fossilized feces from a dig in the Chihuahuan Desert region of Southwestern Texas dating from AD 900 yielded evidence of prickly pear cactus (leaf bases, seeds, pads and fruits), onion bulbs and fiber, fish, rodents, birds, rabbits, flowers or seeds from mustard family plants, nuts, sagebrush and grass. This combination most likely provided sufficient nutrition.[3]

Around the same time from a site in Southeastern Alaska, excavation revealed a diet of seaweed and marine animals, both excellent sources of certain minerals and vitamins. Marine foods included leather chiton, dried sockeye salmon, cockles and oolichan, all high in iron (100 milligrams of smoked oolichan provides at least two-thirds of the adult recommended daily allowance [RDA] for iron). Leather chiton, seaweed and hard dried sockeye salmon are good sources of calcium; oolichan and leather chiton are high in vitamin A_1; 100 grams of leather chiton contains nearly one-quarter of the RDA for ribloflavin and niacin. With the exception of ascorbic acid (vitamin C) and thiamin, all nutrients were present in generous amounts in this Alaskan diet.

Gathering: The Lynchpin of the Diet. The wild plant kingdom offered a wide variety of nutritional foodstuffs for Native American nomads. Tens of thousands of undomesticated plants are edible. The nutrient content of most wild plant foods is high, especially when considering the ratio of nutrients to calories. Plant starches and sugars are the most quickly digested energy sources in the natural world and also high in fiber. Whereas items like berries might not have provided many calories, they were often rich in vitamins. Foraging is often more dependable for nutritional returns than hunting and burns less energy than tracking, pursuing and killing deer or antelope.

Although wild greens were the mainstay of the gleanings, gathering was not limited to plants. Once digging sticks were invented, it

Gathering seaweed. Courtesy of Library of Congress, Prints & Photographs Division, Edward S. Curtis Collection (reproduction number: LC-USZ62-115812).

became possible to forage for roots (lotus, asphodel and Solomon's seal, for example), bulbs, tubers and rhizomes of the canna lily. Willow and birch shoots, young nettles, ferns, seaweed, waterweeds and fungi were also popular items. A large proportion of gatherings were not plants at all. These included honey, insects, sap from various trees, shellfish such as snails, clams, crabs and mussels, frogs, lizards, turtles and eggs.

Gathering was not easy work. The women might have to walk several miles, dig in the hard ground for hours and then return to camp, carrying twenty-to-thirty-pound burdens. According to the theory of optimal foraging, gatherers maximized the time and energy they spent by selecting those foods that would return the greatest amount of calories or protein. This hypothesis is controversial. Other researchers have found cultural data that suggest gatherers allocated their time and energy to meet certain taste preferences for variety with foods that could provide flavor in an otherwise monotonous diet.

The Timbisha Shoshone tribe, located in what is today Death Valley National Park, California, followed a seasonal cycle. In the spring they collected mesquite pods, one of their staples, from the valley floors. In winter they moved to the high country of the mountains where they picked their second staple, pine nuts (pinyon). The Shoshone ground the starchy pulp from the massive collection of mesquite pods as well as other seed-producing plants into meal that was stored. Leafy greens, fleshy stalks and tubers were also common spring foods, as well as growth tips and fruits of the Joshua tree. In summer, berries, fruits and pads of cacti were collected.

Among the most nutritious gathered foods of early Native American groups were the following:

Wild Rice. Sometimes called the most nutritive food consumed by American Indians, wild rice, (actually an aquatic grass), is more nutritious than maize and richer in carbohydrates than any grain except white hominy. Before wild rice was gathered in central and northern Minnesota, the population was limited to the number of people who could be supported on food resources available in winter. As a result of intensive harvesting of the grass, the population of the early historic Dakota and later Ojibwa in northern and central Minnesota increased several-fold between AD 800 and 1000. One scholar has concluded, "It is therefore true that wild rice is the most nutritive single food which the Indians of North America consumed."[4]

Rose Hips. High in vitamin C.

Seeds. A good source of vitamin E; sunflower seeds high in protein.

Fiddlehead Ferns. A rich source of carbohydrates.

Pinyon (Pine Nuts). High-energy food containing 3,000 calories per pound; rich source of protein and fat; pinyon cakes were sometimes used as meat substitute.

Nuts. High in protein and fat.

Serviceberries. Sacred to the Cheyenne of the Great Lakes region; excellent source of iron.

Saguaro Fruit. Each contains about thirty-four calories, and is rich in protein, fat and vitamins.

Cholla Buds. Only two tablespoons contain forty-eight calories and more calcium than a glass of milk.

Agave. One-quarter of a cup contains thirty calories and more calcium than half a glass of milk.

Berries and Leaves Preserved in Seal Oil. Eaten by the Eskimo; these preserves were a great source of vitamin A.

Wild Persimmon. High in vitamin C—about 2,500 milligrams in each green fruit.

Trial and Error as Adaptation. Gathering was not as simple as collecting everything in sight, but rather a highly selective process. Perhaps the key nutritional adaptation for nomadic bands was establishing the difference between toxic and nontoxic plants. Some of this essential knowledge might have come from observing vegetarian animals eating plants, their selection and reactions. Each time an unfamiliar plant was encountered by foragers, the risk of ingesting a toxin needed to be weighed against the potential benefit of discovering a new source of nutrition. This has been called "the omnivore's dilemma." All plants contain toxins as part of their natural defense system. Few plants are actually lethal, but many are mildly toxic and produce undesirable effects when consumed. The distinction also had to be made in some cases between what stage of the plant was edible and which parts. Pokeweed, for example, grows in many southern states and was consumed by Native Americans. Its leaves and stems are edible when young but become toxic as the plant matures. The berries and root of pokeweed are always poisonous.

Along the road of trial and error, a number of tribal members would have become ill with vomiting or diarrhea, for example—typical immediate negative responses after ingestion of toxins. In these instances, there rapidly developed a self-protective conditioned response that would work to ensure avoidance. They would also have warned others not to eat these plants.

Another option would have been to devise a way to detoxify the substance. For example, boiling pokeweed in water—sometimes several times—overcomes its toxicity. These early groups were inventing a nourishing diet as they went along. This knowledge or information accumulated in traditional societies over time.

Gradually, these survival adaptations became incorporated genetically so that predispositions were determined at the genetic level that promoted adaptive food choice. The best documented of these is the innate preference for sweet over bitter. Bitter substances in plant foods often signal toxicity. Humans can detect bitterness at dilutions as tiny as one part in 2 million. That inborn sensitivity evolved from the risks and benefits of trying and rejecting new foods over many generations.

The Secondary Role of Hunting and Fishing. Although hunting and fishing were not as important in supplying calories as gathering (hunters might kill only a few large animals a year), they were crucial for providing fat, which was the real goal. Fatty acids are essential for proper metabolism and maintaining body temperatures during cold winters. Hunters and fishers sought species high in fat like bear and beaver, which store large amounts in preparation for winter hibernation, and oolichan and eel that are always high. In the Northwest, salmon were taken when they spawned, the time when they are heaviest and most loaded with nutrients. With those exceptions, wild animals in general are very lean during most of the year, averaging only about 4 percent fat versus 29 percent for domesticated animals. Lean muscle meat, however, was accompanied by fat from marrow, and there was fat in organs such as the brain and deposits in the thoracic and abdominal cavities.

The optimal hunting strategy was to slaughter the largest animals possible to obtain the maximum amount of edible calories for the

Native American man on horseback spearing bison. Courtesy of Library of Congress, Prints & Photographs Division (reproduction number: LC-USZ62-115188).

amount of energy expended. Once trapping and net hunting were invented, the efficiency of capturing small game was increased. Large animals like bison (the largest game animal available to the Indians), caribou and moose clearly offered advantages. The Blackfoot and other hunters on the North American Plains in Montana were extremely accomplished and efficient in hunting bison. They lured the animals into corrals, where they could kill anywhere from a few dozen to 200 at a time. The stomach contents and vitamin-filled innards and organs were eaten raw. Bison hump was highly prized for its fat content and other nutrients (although Native Americans did not consciously know this, of course); less than 0.1 pound of jerky made from the hump supplied the RDA for phosphorus, zinc and copper.

Meanwhile, in the Northwest, a single bull seal kill could have yielded as much as 318 pounds of meat and 231 of skin and blubber. Another reported slaughter produced ten meals and its blubber was used as cooking fat for about thirty.[5] The internal organs that the Inuit (Eskimo) of Alaska also consumed furnished a range of vitamins and minerals. When hunting was good, an adult might eat as much as twelve pounds of meat a day, a diet obviously high in fat and cholesterol, balanced by some plants, roots, berries and buds. Small amounts of vitamin C and other nutrients in meat were protected from oxidation because these Indians ate most of their meat raw or slightly roasted. Calcium is the only mineral necessary to survival that is lacking in meat. Yet the Inuit suffered from no nutritional diseases, most notably no heart disease. Nor did the Inuit seem to have developed cholesterol-lowering physiological adaptation. Instead, studies suggest that simultaneous consumption of marine mammals and fish, rich in omega-3 polyunsaturated fatty acids, was the dietary factor responsible for the protective effects against cholesterol and heart disease.

Among the Canadian subarctic Indians, moose hunting was considered most efficient, netting about 100,000 calories for human consumption per person-day of work compared to beaver at 15,000 to 24,000 calories per person-day; fishing at 10,000 calories per person-day; small game at 3,000 calories per person-day. The number of people who could be supported for one day by moose hunting was twenty-one; beaver hunting, three to four; fishing, a little more than two.

Food Processing for Greater Nutrition. A number of food processing and preparation methods, including cooking itself, evolved among the early nomadic bands to favor nutritional adaptation. None of these techniques was practiced intentionally to enhance the nutritional profile of foods. Most developed for culinary reasons.

Leaching. Leaching (also described in Chapter 3) is a processing technique, a complex behavior necessary to transform marginally nutritious and toxic foods, most often acorns and camas bulbs, into high-quality nutritious ones. The toxin tannic acid had to be removed from acorns to make them palatable and safe. Early on this was accomplished by burying whole acorns in mud or water for several weeks or even months before eating. This process sweetened the nuts but was inefficient because it often spoiled the food and eliminated only a small amount of tannin.

Later, the Indians developed a three-step leaching process: shell the nuts, pound and grind them into flour or meal, and spread the meal in a shallow depression made in porous soil or sand and flush it through with both cold and warm water. Pulverizing the acorns first made for better tannin removal. Although water warmed in baskets with hot stones increased the efficiency of leaching, particularly for those acorns containing greater amounts of tannin, more nutrients were lost. Moreover, leaching was a long, tedious process. White or blue acorns with low tannins required about two hours; black nuts took four to six.

Cooking. At first, gatherer-hunters ate all their food raw, but they soon discovered that this could produce illness. Once these wandering Native American bands discovered fire, probably accidentally when lightning struck and ignited, they could master reproducing and controlling it as a source of heat and light. Then it was probably a short step to sampling food that had fallen into the fire. It has been speculated that cooking evolved from religion because fire inspired great awe. The spirit capable of transforming meat from raw to cooked and endowing it with totally different flavor and texture (essentially converting it into a new food) clearly possessed supernatural powers—or so the thinking may have gone. It does not take much imagination to envision a piece of meat or other food accidentally slipping into the fire. Rather than being wasted, it was eaten to favorable response. The use of fire for roasting produced a major revolution among these nomadic peoples. Roasting was the first step in the development of cuisine. The process destroyed toxins, bacteria and parasites, and made protein in meat and fish easier to digest. A preference for roasted foods over raw would have developed culturally over a long period of time as advantages came to be recognized. Biologically, it altered the evolution of the digestive system. The gastrointestinal tract cannot process the cellulose walls of plant cells and raw starch that make up the bulk of most plant foods; heat, however, breaks down cellulose and chemically converts starches into more easily digested sugars.

Boiling came later than roasting. It was not until the end of the Paleolithic era (20,000 years ago) that there was archaeological evidence of boiling containers, such as fire-cracked heating rocks used to boil foods in liquids. (Bones were also boiled so that fat could be extracted.) Because cooking broth was consumed, nutrients that might otherwise have been lost were consumed.

Recognition of Nonnutritional States. Survival and nutritional adaptation depended on the development of acute observational powers— the ability to recognize symptoms of vitamin deficiency as well as excess. Total malnutrition from winter starvation or famine would have been obvious, of course, and might have resulted in death. Other nutritional vagaries, however, could have taken many generations to associate symptoms with the correct dietary cause, and then make alterations in eating behavior.

A case diagnosed retrospectively as hypervitaminosis of vitamin D was reported among a Northwest Coast tribe in the late "prehistoric" period where salmon was the staple. Tribal members were getting much more vitamin D than needed, especially the children. This excess state was debilitating and potentially acute, eventually destroying the kidneys. It produces visible symptoms including vomiting, constipation, weakness, nausea, confusion and disorientation. The Indians actually cut back on their consumption of salmon. Whether this was due to reduced availability of the fish or conscious reasons emanating from observing the short recovery time in people suffering from hypervitaminosis is not known. A researcher commented, "We believe that it is the result of the recognition by the aboriginal groups in the area of an obvious malnutrition state, hypervitaminosis D, and their correct association of this state with increasing dietary dependence on salmon."[6]

Nutrition of the Gatherer-Hunter Diet. Clearly, the gatherer-hunter diet favored survival and evolution. However, it did better than meet minimal requirements—it actually fostered growth and contained the appropriate amounts of nutrients. Somewhat surprisingly, foragers typically acquired from 1.5 to 5 times the RDA levels of vitamins and minerals each day. The nomadic process of what has been called "nutritional sampling and selection" eventually produced a sound diet, adequate for normal growth and development.[7] The consumption of a greater diversity of foods is presumed to be responsible for taking in a fairly complete mix of nutrients. Carbohydrates and sugars, vitamin C and fiber were supplied by tubers, roots, shoots, nuts, fruits, berries, leafy and starchy vegetables. Protein, fat, other vitamins, minerals, trace elements and amino acids were provided in quantities sufficient for healthy existence. The diet was low in sodium and included lean meats, as there is less fat and cholesterol in wild game than domesticated meat (venison steak, for example, derives 82 percent of its calories from protein and only 18 percent from fat). The diet was also richer in omega-3 fatty acids and higher in unsaturated versus saturated fats. Research has shown that gatherer-hunters experienced infrequent famine and were generally better nourished than comparable agricultural cultures due in part to the wider variety of foods consumed. Fewer carbohydrates were eaten due to the near-total absence of cereal grains.

Although preliterate people did not possess an innate sense of nutrition, they had hundreds, if not thousands, of years of practical experience in gleaning food from their environment. This experience eventually showed them, however unconsciously, what worked well and what did not.

The Agrarian Diet

As many early nomadic bands began to transition to raising crops and a settled life, significant cultural changes began to take place. The population of later groups known as "complex hunter-gatherers" rose dramatically. Storage of food became possible when people lived in one location, and large plant-roasting pits were invented to cook for a crowd. Competitive feasting was practiced for the first time.

In other Native American areas, cultivation of crops, chiefly maize, may have diffused northward from Mexico. The adoption of agriculture touched off a second major food revolution. Now the diet revolved around calorically rich, storable staples—primarily maize, beans and squash.

Archaeological evidence collected from the site of Pecos Pueblo close to Santa Fe, New Mexico, dated to around AD 1300 showed that the major constituents of the diet were maize (representing up to 100 percent of calories), beans (up to 20 percent), supplemented by wild amaranth seeds (up to 15 percent), wild pinyon seeds (up to 15 percent), mule deer (up to 10 percent), pronghorn antelope (up to 5 percent), and negligible amounts of other substances.[8] Meat still needed to be hunted, as the only domesticated animals raised for possible slaughter were dogs.

As agricultural practices were refined, crop yields became greater. The downside was that agriculture increased the population's reliance on a small handful of crops. Not only is it impossible for a single plant or even small group to meet all nutritional needs, but dependence on only a few makes a population extremely vulnerable in the event of crop failure.

However, a new type of social organization emerged to deal with this eventuality. Once the food yielded by agriculture allowed the population to increase, it became impossible for every tribal member to know every other and resolve conflicts face-to-face. It seems to be an anthropological truism that when cultural groups reach a population of about 500, a chief or leader emerges and in turn appoints a ruling elite to govern. This upper strata no longer farmed or hunted but instead managed the production of food, often collecting it all, deciding how much to store, and how much to redistribute among the community. The primary function of reallocation was to even out production inequities among different villages. Considerable redistribution took place within the context of festivals and ceremonial display. Settled life favored more elaborate religious practices partly because sites of ceremonies and rituals were fixed. Much ceremonial life centered around food and its growth.

Ritual, ceremony and myth were all used to perpetuate and transmit food-related practices necessary for greater nutrition. Sheer repetition reinforced memory and obligation. The impact of diet and foodways on maintaining and restoring order in the natural, social and spiritual realms was recognized.

Maize—The Nutritive Anchor. When maize became the staple of agricultural American Indians, their diet underwent a monumental change and conformed to many other cultures. It has been noted that "almost all human beings who have ever lived over a period of some 10 to 12,000 years have subsisted primarily on some one principal complex carbohydrate around which their lives are built." This "nutritive anchor" provided the underpinning for Native American civilization.[9]

However, maize was nutritionally deficient because it was low in specific essential amino acids, components of protein that our bodies cannot synthesize from other dietary sources. One is niacin, crucial to the metabolic processes of every cell to keep tissues from degenerating. Maize also lacks tryptophan, which can be used by the body to synthesize niacin. Continuous reliance on a high-maize diet leads to large-scale incidence of pellagra (niacin deficiency), which produces such symptoms as dermatitis (severe burning and itching of the skin), diarrhea and dementia, and can be deadly. Women have a 2.5 times higher rate of pellagra than men.[10]

Alkali Processing. Alkali processing is the single most important nutritional adaptation evolved by Native Americans. To make maize-grinding easier, the Indians needed an easy way to loosen the hard hulls on the kernels of ripe and stored dried maize. They discovered that by soaking the kernels in water and wood ashes (lye/potassium or sodium hydroxide), the hulls slipped right off. The reason: The combination of water and ashes produce an alkaline solution that works chemically to detach the hulls. It also worked serendipitously to increase the availability of niacin and tryptophan and improve the digestibility of the amino acids lysine and tryptophan. In other words, alkali processing, as the technique became known, corrected for the dangerous nutritional limitation of maize. One anthropologist noted, "It is possible to suggest that alkali treatment became the basis for optimizing the nutritional quality of maize. More specifically, this food processing technique was almost certainly involved in facilitating the intensification of maize agriculture."[11] The method may have migrated north from Mexico, where it was routinely practiced, or developed independently among Native Americans. Alkali processing became the traditional method of preparing maize among those cultures for whom maize was a primary food. For most, the practice was sanctified by the culture, ensuring that it would be carried on.

The Hopi of Arizona and New Mexico, who considered blue maize sacred and *piki*, tissue-thin blue maize bread, the ultimate food, made an important refinement in alkali processing. Rather than removing the hulls and then grinding the corn, they finely ground blue maize with its hulls intact into a gray-white dust. Then they mixed the flour with water and ashes from the salt bush, producing the alkali response as well as an intensification of the azure color as the meal was heated. Blue maize, rich in athocyanin dye that produces the color in the thin outer layer covering the endosperm, is highly sensitive to pH changes that occur as the ash solution moves from acid to alkaline. This trans-

Hopi women filling jugs with water. Courtesy of Library of Congress, Prints & Photographs Division, Edward S. Curtis Collection (reproduction number: LC-USZ62-094090).

forms the color from red to blue and beyond to gray and brownish yellow. At one point in the scale, there is an optimum level of alkalinity that produces the desired hue. If the pH was too high, the color would degrade and coincidentally, the essential amino acids as well. In other words, there was a visual pH indicator that guided the Hopi to optimum alkalinizing not only for cultural or sacred reasons, but coincidentally for the release of niacin. This "*piki* litmus test" showed, according to an anthropologist, how "a highly significant nutritional practice is so embedded in the cultural traditions of a society that the appropriate practice is carried on in a very carefully preserved and unbroken tradition from one generation to the next over time."[12]

Another critical cultural component was the importance attached to perfecting *piki*-making for female identity and marriage in Hopi society. The proper execution of this culinary task required great skill and was emphasized for females from childhood onward. It garnered future rewards in terms of betrothal and marriage (a potential bride could be rejected on the basis of her *piki*); played a prime role in the wedding ceremony itself, for which huge amounts were prepared; and gained kind regard from in-laws. The culture ensured that the behavior would be repeated many times over a lifetime so the younger generation learned how to precisely create the color blue and consequently enhance nutrition from maize. It is interesting to consider this cultural emphasis against the background of the heightened sensitivity of women to developing pellagra.

Green Corn Ceremonies. Most agricultural American Indian tribes practiced green corn ceremonialism (see Chapter 5), in which huge amounts of immature maize in the milky stage were harvested, honored with rites and prepared for feasts. These ceremonies celebrating an early developmental stage of a foodstuff were significantly different from the ubiquitous first food celebrations that welcomed other newly ripe foods of the season—berries, salmon, squash and beans, for example. Green maize provided greater nutrition than ripe because it contained more available niacin. As maize matures, this bioavailability decreases and eventually becomes biochemically bound, resulting in the nutritional limitation. The cultural significance, preparation and consumption of green maize provided an anti-pellagra factor by fortifying people early in the season with complete protein. Thus, eating maize at different points in its developmental cycle also helped overcome its nutritional limitations.

Nutritional Combos. The evolution of the human diet is marked more by synergistic combinations of foods rather than increments in the value of individual nutrient sources. One such combo was the cooking and eating of maize with beans. (Squash played a much more minor role.) Common beans in a number of forms are a significant source of the three amino acids lacking in maize—niacin, tryptophan and lysine. Bean seeds (which became larger as beans continued to be domesticated) are higher in protein than beans themselves; pods are rich in lysine and tryptophan. The two crops complemented each other and produced a reasonably balanced diet in the absence of meat. The addition of wild greens, particularly young, tender herbs that might also include flowers and stems, eaten raw or lightly cooked, provided sufficient calcium, vitamin A, thiamin and riboflavin. Lime from marine shells, sometimes used in maize alkali processing, also added some calcium.

Floodwater Field Irrigation. In the Southwest, the use of flood-water field irrigation of the tepary bean crop actually increased its protein content and seed yields. This was important because teparies were the staple rather than maize for the Pima and Tohono O'od-ham tribes in Arizona. In the desert there are typically no more than five or six rains a year, but they are sufficient to stimulate plant growth. The Southwest Indians planted their beans in sunken plots where the seasonal floods spread out. The plants would then be naturally irrigated by stormwaters flowing through watercourses called washes. On these floodplain fields, rain and runoff were concentrated and held at those times of year when storms were most probable—from July through August and December through January.[13]

Fermentation. Actually a form of spoilage, fermentation helps break down indigestibles and enhances nutrient value of food and safety by preservation. No doubt discovered accidentally, this process produced the growth of yeasts that increased protein content, including the amino acids niacin and lysine, and many B vitamins. Digestibility was enhanced by breaking down antinutritional factors such as bitter tannins and contributing intestinal microflora. Fermentation required relatively airtight spaces where pathogenic microorganisms would be reduced due to restricted oxygen, increased carbon dioxide, lowered pH and microbial competition. Ceramic vessels for fermentation were designed with narrow necks so carbon dioxide would concentrate. Storage pits with narrow openings, bottle or bell-shaped, were also ideal environments.

Maize was fermented by the Huron Indians of the Great Lakes. According to one early European observer, "*Leindohy*, or stinking corn, is a large quantity of corn, not yet dry and dead, in order to be more apt to spoil, that the women put in some pond or stinking water for the space of two or three months; at the end of this time they take it out, and it serves to make feasts of great importance; it is cooked like the *Neintahouy*, and they also eat it baked under the hot ashes, licking their fingers at handling these stinking ears, just as if they were sugar cane, although the taste and smell of it is very foul, and it stinks more than do sewers."[14]

Maize was also fermented in the Southwest. The meal was mixed with water and boiled to make fermented corn soup, called *sofki*. The Eskimo of Alaska who hunted caribou ate the fermented stomach contents of these plant-eating mammals in addition to the meat. These innards were rich in carbohydrates and vitamins synthesized by bacteria during fermentation. The Sioux of the Dakotas fermented their staple wild rice. Tribes of the northern Plains gathered camas root and fermented it in pits where it stayed for several days. When removed, it was dark brown in color and reportedly sweet like molasses. Indians of the Northwest Coast made lactic acid fermentations of fish-heads, whale, seal, walrus and reindeer in underground pits. Fermented beverages made by Native Americans, including saguaro wine, are discussed in Chapter 2.

Salt Adaptation. Salt (sodium chloride) is essential to humans for the functioning of the nervous system. It helps control osmotic pressure in body fluids which in turn determines the amount of water retained in the body. The salt requirement is not stable, but changes in conjunction with physiological state. The primary nutritional use of salt among "prehistoric" Indians was to balance the low sodium content of maize. Salt was obtained principally by evaporating salt water, which might come from a salt spring or ocean. Salt pans were left in the sun or boiled over fire. In the Great Basin, salt was gathered from the surface of land in and around dry lake beds. Salt was an important trade article in the Southeast, Southwest and California. In the Southwest, salt was gathered by those tribes living closest to the source who then traded it. It was widely exchanged in the Southeast on the Mississippi and in California from the east side of the Sierras, where there was plenty, to the west side, where it was less common.

Native Americans fell into two groups in regard to salt use: those who used salt except for occasional abstention (for example, Iroquois of New York State abstained if they had suffered an injury), and those who used no salt in addition to that naturally contained in foods. The salt-eaters were generally confined to the Southeast and were seldom found among those who relied primarily on fish and meat, which do contain salt. In the Southeast, after the maize supplies dwindled in late August, there was little danger of sodium deficiency since the diet then contained a greater percentage of meat. The hunting parties returned not only with meat but also with salt. Eating raw and roasted food furnished enough sodium chloride for physiological equilibrium without supplementation. Supplements were necessary in populations eating primarily boiled foods.

Salt played a prominent role in religion, mythology and ceremonies. Elaborate salt-gathering expeditions were undertaken in which every detail was prescribed by ritual. One way in which salt was regulated and adjusted in the diet was through taboos that applied to salt itself as well as salt-containing foods such as meat. These prohibitions were widely practiced throughout North America. It has been suggested that many American Indian food taboos served nutritional ends, and nowhere is this more clear than with salt. For many Southeast tribes, including the Cherokee of Tennessee and South Carolina, Creek of Georgia, Chickasaw and Choctaw of Mississippi and Alabama, salt taboos were in force during times of emotional and physical stress—menstruation, pregnancy, illness and mourning. It is thought that restrictions developed because they were found through many years to be advantageous for the population as a whole. For example, a high sodium intake during pregnancy can lead to edema, hypertension, pre-eclampsia and eclampsia, all high-risk situations at a time when a woman's body is already retaining high levels of sodium. The taboo might have evolved from observing that pregnant women who consumed too much salt suffered complications of pregnancy and birth such as spontaneous abortion or stillbirth. Because menstruation causes the body to retain both salt and water, the taboo during this time, which included not eating fish or meat, decreased chances of edema or bloating.

Recognition of Vitamin C Deficiency (Scurvy). Vitamin C (ascorbic acid) works with iron to make red blood and collagen and holds tissue together. The body cannot make or store C, so it must be consumed every day. Fresh meat, fruits, plants, buds, berries and some vegetables would have supplied enough vitamin C for the Indians. It is not known whether Native Americans ever suffered from deficiency. If so, they would have been unlikely to forget it. Scurvy, vitamin C deficiency, is characterized by fatigue and muscle weakness, festering wounds, bleeding under the skin and spongy and bleeding gums; it can eventually lead to death. Some proof that Indians had knowledge of vitamin C deficiency comes from the contact period. In 1535, French explorer Jacques Cartier lost twenty-five men to scurvy when his ship was icebound in the St. Lawrence River in Canada. He appealed to the Indians for help. Cartier recorded in his journal that an Indian chief sent two women to gather some bark and needles, "and therewithall shewed the way how to use it, and that is thus, to take the barke and leaves of the sayd tree, and boile them togither, then to drinke of the sayd decoction every other day, and to put the dregs of it upon his legs that is sicke."[15] It is not clear exactly what tree supplied the bark and needles—most likely black spruce, but possibly white pine or hemlock. Clearly, some Native Americans were experienced with this deficiency.

Optimal Food Preparation and Drying. Cooking can enhance nutritional properties. The common practice of roasting sweet (ripe) maize caused the conversion of bound niacin into a free bioavailable form, overcoming the limitations of maize. Methods of drying also influenced nutritional content. The Hopi, for instance, dried maize by baking it on the cob, a technique that retains more nitrogen, potassium and trace minerals than air- or fire-drying. Drying fish actually concentrates more calories and protein per unit of weight than can be acquired from fresh whole fish.

Trade and Exchange. Nutritional variety and substitution were enhanced by trading with other tribes for complementary or supplemental nutrients. The foragers may have exchanged with other bands to accommodate permanent, seasonal or unpredicatable shortages. The Comanche who ranged from Wyoming to Texas and the Crow of Montana who did not grow maize traded for it with the Eastern tribes. The Northwest Coast Niska traded oolichan for such items as dried fish, meat and soapberries. The Paiute of Nevada made salt cakes that they carried across the Sierra to trade with the California tribes for acorns.

The Agrarian Diet: How Nutritious? Clearly, the agrarian diet favored survival and evolution. However, its nutritional advantages over the forager diet are often questioned. Some research shows that agricultural products actually provide less nourishment than those that are gathered and hunted, and that growing crops does not extend the lifespan. Some experts maintain that cultivators suffered more often from starvation than wandering nomads partly because the agriculturalists had increased workloads and their numbers were greater. The agrarian diet actually introduced some nutritional deficiencies (pellagra, for example), an increase in some infectious diseases and general decrease in quality of health. The intensive exploitation of calorically high starches eliminated some marginal foods and resulted in a loss of variety as well as some nutrients. Storage destroyed some vitamins like C and B-complex.

Agriculture did provide a more dependable food supply, but it was not foolproof. Crop failure, flooding, drought, pests and war could compromise the amount of available food. Maize cultivation and yield in particular were more sensitive to drought than many other crops. Famine was a real possibility in a settled society with many more mouths to feed.

Culturally developed customs and behaviors helped solve some nutritional problems. It is difficult to pinpoint the biological and cultural mechanisms by which nutritional advantage became translated into cultural food preferences and practices. A favorable nutritional combination might have been physiologically experienced as superior, and once "discovered," transmitted and preserved in the cuisine so that each generation would not have to rediscover it.

Maize, green corn, *piki*, the combination of maize and beans as well as alkali processing—all these became important symbols of cultural identity that were perpetuated, broadcast and sustained by culture. According to an anthropologist, "Specifically, any change in behavior that can be regularly and reliably transmitted by learning can be more rapidly established as part of the cultural information pool than a change that is genetically based. Of course, the latter is only true when the learning is deemed important . . . by the people doing the teaching and if the successful behavior is transferred from one generation to the next."[16]

FOOD AS MEDICINE

Native Americans typically attributed illness to supernatural causes. Someone might have offended a spirit or the soul of an animal he had slain. Certain foods, however, were believed to contain magic healing properties if they were consumed in prescribed ways. The major use of over 150 species of wild plant foods among the Plains Indians was as medicine. Some tribes combined roots with herbs to cure rattlesnake bites. The Navajo roasted locusts in ashes to cure stomachache and prevent various contagious diseases; they cured sore throat by administering a cold infusion both internally and externally, twice a day with an interval of three hours. They believed blue maize mush or gruel would cure an invalid. The Pima gave a tablespoon or more of a bitter decoction of sunflower leaves for high fever. Tea made of the green bark of oak in the Southwest was supposed to be a powerful astringent and antidiarrhetic. Beans were used as medicine by a number of tribes. For a dermatological remedy, the Iroquois used wild bean, and the Pawnee spider bean. The Omaha had bush clover or rabbit food as an analgesic; the Cherokee chewed tickseed or trefoil roots for sore gums and mouths. The Mohegan of Connecticut made a blood purifier from rattle box root. The Iroquois made ball player pudding, boiled parched corn meal mixed with maple syrup and bits of meat, as a charm. A woman afflicted with disease made the pudding and presented it to the ball player, who, eating it, was supposed to charm away the disorder.

Tribal medicine-men served as physicians, prophets, shamans and priests all in one, and occupied a separate elite caste. The medicine societies of the Iroquois were invoked in certain ailments and prepared ceremonial maize foods. Meat was prohibited when they were being administered. The medicine men in Sioux village were required to be members of the "medicine mystery." An early traveler wrote in his diary, "The medicine mystery or college is a secret society composed of the principal men of the tribe who are initiated into the mystery with great ceremonies & bound to secrecy; . . . The dance & medicine feast take place at the same time and are the principal festival of the order."[17]

NUTRITIONAL STRESS

Whether permanent, seasonal or unpredicatable, nutritional stress affected food choices and social relations surrounding food. Rationing was practiced in many tribes during lean times—typically cutting back from two meals a day to one—sometimes to the detriment of the elderly. In one tribe, old people ate only once every three days in times of stress in order to leave more food for children. Food sharing could not be taken for granted and nutritional status over an annual cycle was compromised.

Food scarcity was a seasonal certainty for many tribes as a result of both environmental cold and heat. Wild animals, leaner than domesticated ones, became more so during winter. For example, samples of ham and loin from mule deer in the Southwest in August contained 4.5 grams of fat per 100 grams of meat, whereas this ratio dropped to 0.9 grams of fat per 100 grams of meat in January. Similar seasonal fluctuations have been recorded for antelope. A diet consisting primarily of extra-lean meat available in winter can result in protein poisoning, which induces people to eat three to four times the normal amount because they do not feel full. This condition may result in diarrhea, sickness and eventually death. To efficiently use food energy provided by meat, fats or carbohydrates must be consumed along with the protein. Many Indians hunted for fat-rich raccoon and beaver (specifically the tail), although these animals also lost some fat in winter.

Throughout the writings of early Europeans and tribal descendants, the severity of seasonal deprivation becomes evident. A member of the 'Ksan of the Northwest noted, "If the winter was longer or colder than usual, or if the salmon run was late, or the winter supply of stored food was destroyed by fire, or raiders came from the Nass, or some other calamity occurred, then things could be tough—very tough."[18] John Tanner, a white man taken captive by Plains Indians, wrote often about the extreme hunger and weakness suffered by the family who adopted him. "After we had supped, for when we were in want of provisions we commonly ate only at evening, all the food we had remaining, was a quart or more of bear's grease in a kettle. It was now frozen hard."[19] "Wa-me-gon-a-biew [his Indian older brother] could not walk at all, and every one of the family had failed more than the old woman."[20] Even the capture of a bear, an event foreseen by his Indian mother, did not go far to alleviate hunger. "He [the bear] was large and fat, but Wa-me-gon-a-biew, who accompanied them, received only a small piece for the portion of our family. The old woman was angry, and not without just cause."[21]

Some populations, it has been suggested, might have become physiologically "famine adapted," gradually developing smaller body size and consequently, decreased caloric needs. The Eskimo in Alaska were said to be "physiologically adapted to seasonal and selective food scarcities, which put them at risk for nutrition-related health disorders in new environments with more abundant and carbohydrate-rich foods."[22]

On the other hand, nutritional stress might have spurred development of some unique survival mechanisms. As one anthropologist observed, "A society may survive because of the accumulation of information that codes for survival under extreme nutritional conditions. Just as there are genes that are only expressed in extremes, there may be cultural behaviors that are transmitted from one generation to the next but are only expressed when the society runs out of food."[23]

Famine Food

All eating rules seem to have been suspended in times of crisis. Famine or emergency nutrition required special knowledge, behaviors and suspension of social conventions, which most often meant taboos. There were few prohibitions among the tribes against eating plant foods. This may have been intentional to ensure that people were always permitted greens, berries, nuts, fruits whether fresh or dried. Normally tabooed foods, like seed stock allocated for next season's planting, might be a resource of last resort.

Seasonal hunger and periods of low food availability could, of course, be anticipated and might require a recurring "winter diet." In Minnesota, for example, before wild rice was gathered, food was generally available only between mid-March and the end of November. For the remaining three-and-a-half months of the year, there were only a few mammals, some birds, lichen and bark.

The need for emergency nutrition ranged from hunger seasons to full-scale famine. When lack of food was severe, Native Americans could not be choosy. Survival foods had to meet certain characteristics: edible (nontoxic), available even when more frequently eaten foods were not and drought-resistant (cacti, for example) if drought was the problem.

Residents of the desert borderlands in the Southwest had become familiar with shortages over thousands of years and developed a repertoire of coping strategies. Famine provisions might include low-preference foods, foods normally consumed in small amounts (mesquite fruits, hearts and liquid from charred leaves of the century plant) and foods located in hostile territory (for example, under normal conditions, the Pima of southern Arizona would not collect century plant in areas frequented by warring Apache).

As winter lengthened in western Alaska, members of the Ten'a culture were apt to run out of fresh meat and fish, sometimes producing starvation. One observer of tribe members noted, "Some people like to talk about themselves and say they never eat dried fish as a regular diet in the winter, this is just talk, to put on a big front and to give the impression that they always have some fresh fish or meat on hand. . . . There come times to all of them when they have to eat the dried fish which they stored up during the summer or else starve."[24]

The Canalino Indians of California, under environmental pressure from dwindling forest and game, moved toward the coast and they came to rely almost exclusively on shellfish as their staple, a switch that proved as nourishing as a meat-centered diet when rounded out with plants. The abundance of shellfish was greater than any other food animal in the area, although labor required for collecting, shelling and discarding refuse was considerable.

It is interesting to consider how Native Americans kept track of famine plant resources consumed so infrequently that they might be relevant only once in a generation. Where plants were concerned, the process of "ethnobotanical information transfer" relied on oral tradition, myth and ritual that might perpetuate stories of prior food shortages and the "magic" foods that helped people survive. These cultural devices made it possible to pass on knowledge of famine food to subsequent generations; otherwise, it would have quickly and easily become lost.

In times of stark famine, such as periods of drought, even tiny differences in food preparation that favored greater nutrition could mean the difference between life and death. Therefore, the performance of these practices in a ritual, prescribed way became indelibly associated with survival and magic, a supernatural ability to sustain life. No one in the tribe would want to risk losing that power. Whereas wild berries and nuts in normal years were stored as a pleasant addition to the diet, they became indispensable in lean years. Among the Zuni of New Mexico, the chant known as "Sayataca's night chant" required repetition of a great many edible plants, including, "the seeds of the pinyon tree, the seeds of the juniper tree, the seeds of the oak tree . . . the seeds of the black wood shrub," and on and on, making it difficult for people to forget these sources.[25] Because seeds were incorporated into Zuni ritual, they had to be gathered each year. This maintained knowledge of their location.

In the desert lands of the Southwest, seven categories of famine foods have been proposed:

Inner bark from pinyon, juniper and aspen trees—low nutritional value and much effort to collect;

Cacti, including sagauro and prickly pear fruit, stem pulp and stems, and cholla buds;

Agave and agave-like plants, including the century, which provided hearts and liquid from charred leaves, and stems from yucca;

Perennials, like pigweed, bitter fruit of coyote melon, fleshy berries of wolfberry, squaw currants and dried fruits of native rose (both Hopi famine foods), mesquite and screwbean seeds, acorns, mangrove and jojoba fruits, and ricegrass, which had a relatively high protein content;

Roots and tubers;

Annuals—seasonal foods that became famine foods;

Others including eelgrass, and pith of the desert fan palm.[26]

In the Northwest Coast societies, Native Americans used more than 100 species of plants to relieve hunger. In addition to the types of foods mentioned already, these included "true famine foods," items eaten only in times of extreme hunger. These were most likely to be consumed raw, increasing chances of toxicity. Many were bitter, unpalatable and hard to digest. Skunk cabbage rhizomes, for example, are toxic in their raw state. Lupine roots contain potent alkaloids that act negatively on the nervous system. Other foods in this category contained enzyme inhibitors and additional toxins that could cause headaches, nausea and dizziness.

Many types of lichen that survived under extreme conditions of heat and cold were eaten in emergencies, scraped from rocks or trees and devoured raw or boiled with fat (if there was any) to remove the bitter taste. Reindeer moss was a famine food among the Northern tribes, and Iceland moss and rock tripe boiled to jelly consumed elsewhere.

An interesting category of famine treatment used on the Northwest Coast were temporary hunger suppressants and thirst quenchers. These items, such as licorice fern rhizome, were usually used during short times of low food and water supply—for example, when traveling, hunting, berry picking or lost in the woods.

Cannibalism and Dog-Eating

Sometimes threat of starvation drove tribes to break the ultimate taboo against eating another human being. Famine cannibalism, meaning eating those who had starved to death, was rare. One observer remarked, "Cannibalism was resorted to by the Cree only in cases where actual starvation threatened. Driven to desperation by prolonged famine and often suffering from mental breakdown as a result thereof, the Cree would sometimes eat the bodies of those who had perished, or, more rarely, would even kill the living and partake of the flesh."[27]

An Indian captive describes another desperate measure. "We so killed our last dog, who was getting too weak to keep up with us; but the flesh of this animal, for some reason, the old woman [his Indian mother] would not eat."[28]

NOTES

1. Lawrence Kaplan, "Ethnobotanical and Nutritional Factors in the Domestication of American Beans," in *Man and His Foods: Studies in the*

Ethnobotany of Nutrition; Contemporary, Primitive and Prehistoric Non-European Diets, ed. Earle C. Smith, Jr. (Birmingham: University of Alabama Press, 1973), 77.

2. Peter Farb, *Man's Rise to Civilization as Shown by the Indians of North America from Primeval Times to the Coming of the Industrial State* (New York: E. P. Dutton & Co., 1968), 47.

3. Kristin D. Sobolik, "Prehistoric Diet from the Lower Pecos Region of Texas," *The Plains Anthropologist* 36, no. 135 (1991): 139.

4. Albert Jenks, *The Wild Rice Gatherers of the Upper Lakes: A Study in American Primitive Economics* (Lincoln, NE: J&L Reprint Co., 1977), 1083.

5. Jeff Rubin, "Train Oil and Snotters: Eating Antarctic Wild Foods," *Gastronomica: The Journal of Food and Culture* 3, no. 1 (Winter 2003): 40.

6. Richard A. Lazenby and Peter McCormack, "Salmon and Malnutrition on the Northwest Coast," *Current Anthropology* 26 (1985): 379.

7. Kaplan, 77.

8. M. J. Schoeninger, "Reconstructing the Prehistoric Human Diet," *Homo* 39 (1989), 78.

9. Sidney W. Mintz, *Sweetness and Power: The Place of Sugar in Modern History* (New York: Penguin Books, 1986), 9.

10. Solomon H. Katz, "Cultural Evolution and Biology: The Biocultural Evolution of Nutriculture," in *The Epic of Evolution: Science and Religion in Dialogue,* ed. James B. Miller (Upper Saddle River, NJ: Pearson Prentice Hall, 2004), 133.

11. Solomon H. Katz, "Food and Biocultural Evolution: A Model for the Investigation of Modern Nutritional Problems," in *Nutritional Anthropology,* ed. F. E. Johnston (New York: Allen Liss, 1987), 46.

12. Solomon H. Katz, "Biocultural Evolution of Cuisine: The Hopi Indian Blue Corn Tradition," in *Handbook of the Psychophysiology of Human Eating,* ed. R. Shepherd (New York: John Wiley & Sons, 1989), 129.

13. Gary Nabhan, "Papago Indian Floodwater Fields and Tepary Bean Protein Yields," *Ecology of Food and Nutrition* 10 (1980): 71–78.

14. W. Vernon Kinietz, *The Indians of the Western Great Lakes, 1615–1760* (Ann Arbor: University of Michigan Press, 1940), 34–35.

15. Michael Weiner, *Earth Medicine—Earth Food: Plant Remedies, Drugs, and Natural Foods of the North American Indians* (New York: Macmillan, 1980), 119.

16. Katz, "Biocultural Evolution of Cuisine," 122.

17. Frank Blackwell Mayer, *With Pen and Pencil on the Frontier in 1851: The Diary and Sketches of Frank Blackwell Mayer* (St. Paul: Minnesota Historical Society, 1932), 118.

18. People of 'Ksan, *Gathering What the Great Nature Provided: Food Traditions of the Gitksan* (Seattle: University of Washington Press, 1980), 13–14.

19. John Tanner, *A Narrative of the Captivity and Adventures of John Tanner During Thirty Years Residence Among the Indians in the Interior of North America, Pt. 1* (1830; reprint Ann Arbor, MI: Xerox University Microfilms, 1975), 67.

20. Ibid., 76.

21. Ibid., 67.

22. Ellen Messer, "Anthropological Perspectives on Diet," *Annual Review of Anthropology* 13 (1984): 214.

23. Katz, "Cultural Evolution and Biology," 133.

24. Robert J. Sullivan, *The Ten'a Food Quest* (Washington, DC: Catholic University of America Press, 1942), 136.

25. Paul E. Minnis, "Famine Foods of the Northern American Desert Borderland in Historical Context," *Journal of Ethnobiology* 11, no. 2 (Winter 1991): 250.

26. Ibid., 238–241.

27. John M. Cooper, "The Cree Witiko Psychosis," *Anthropological Quarterly* 6 (1933): 21.

28. Tanner, 75.

GLOSSARY

Adistsiin. Navajo for the bundle of thin stirring sticks made of sage, salt-bush or greasewood used exclusively for maize dishes.

Ak chin **farming, also called dry farming.** Method used by the Tohono O'odham and Pima of Arizona to grow crops in the floodplain during the seasonal rainstorms.

Alkali processing. In this technique, discovered serendiptiously, maize kernels are soaked in water and wood ashes (which produce lye), chemically loosening the hulls. This process has the nutritional benefit of increasing the availability of niacin and tryptophan, enhancing the niacin-deficient profile of maize.

Atole. Spanish name for a hot drink made of maize and water and drunk in the Southwest.

Biscuitroot (*cous* **or** *cowas***).** Fleshy roots that were an important food of the western Indians.

Broadswords. Name for dish of green maize dumplings prepared by the Cherokee of the Southeast.

Chamisa. Culinary ashes made by the Hopi of Arizona by burning branches of the four-wing saltbush. Mixed with water, the ashes produced lye, which intensified the azure color of blue maize.

Clambake. The name given to a technique of steaming shellfish and cobs of maize, alternated with layers of seaweed, in a pit. Although widely attributed to New England Indians, it has now been found that they made their clambakes above ground.

Corn smut fungus. An edible fungus that grows on the corn ear.

Earth oven. A pit oven covered with earth in which food was steamed, often overnight.

Fry bread (*Ban ik' aha*). Puffed circles of white wheat flour dough, deep-fried in lard, that have become an American Indian icon even though ingredients (wheat and lard), process (deep-frying) and cooking vessel (metal fry pan) are not of Native origin but rather Spanish introductions.

Green corn. Immature, unripe corn, said to be "in the milk" because of the milky substance that can be extracted from the young kernels by scraping with a shell or jawbone of an animal.

Heap oven. A method of steaming mussels (usually freshwater ones) in which a heap of mussels are covered over with clay.

Hominy. Maize that has the hard outer coatings of the kernels removed (hulled). Word taken from the Algonquian *rockahommic.*

Horno. An above-ground dome-shaped communal adobe oven introduced by the Spanish and built on the roof of each story of a pueblo.

Hull. The hard external shell of a kernel of maize (corn).

Indian bread (*Tuckahoe*). An edible tuber that grew on roots of large trees in fields and marshes throughout a wide area of the Northeast and Southeast.

Jerky. Meat slowly smoke-dried on racks during the day, taken off at night and laid on the ground, covered with a bison robe and trampled to squeeze out the blood. The following day, it is smoke-dried on the racks again.

Kachinas. Spirits of the religion of the Hopi of Arizona. The *kachinas* are believed to have influence both in bringing rain and fostering cooperation among the villagers; also, the dancers who represent the *kachinas* in traditional ceremonies.

Ka-nuh:sioka. Hopi term for those foods that may not be eaten, as opposed to *nuh:sioka,* those that may be eaten.

Kiva. An underground ceremonial chamber used in the Southwest.

Leaching. The process of repeatedly washing a food (specifically acorns) to rid them of the toxin tannic acid.

Leindohy. Maize fermented in a pond for some months; a delicacy of the Huron Indians.

Lolensh. The fermented seeds of the yellow pond water lily.

Mano. Spanish word for the stone roller used by the Pueblo Indians of the Southwest to grind maize.

Mastication. The process of pre-chewing food before combining it with other ingredients and cooking. This introduces the enzyme salivary amylase, which converts carbohydrates into simple sugar, sweetening the food.

Metate. Spanish word for the grinding trough used by the Pueblo Indians of the Southwest to grind maize.

Muller. A short wooden or stone pestle or pounder with a flat rounded base, used for pounding in small mortars.

Nasaump. A thickened broth of boiled clams used to flavor bread among New England Indians.

Navai't. Saguaro wine made in the Southwest by the Arizona Tohono O'odham and Pima Indians.

Navajo taco. Fry bread, topped with layers of fried ground beef or lamb, beans, cheddar cheese, chiles, shredded lettuce, onion and diced tomato that is served as a contemporary snack or meal substitute.

Nokechick. Narragansett word for parched cornmeal; this word was re-spelled as "no cake" by the colonists.

Nuh:sioka. A term given by the Hopi to those food that may be eaten, as opposed to *ka-nuh:sioka*, those that may not be eaten.

Numayms. Ranked kinship groups in the Northwest Coast cultures. Membership was assigned at the huge feasts known as potlatches.

Oolichan (candlefish). Much-prized fish caught by the Northwest Coast tribes for its oil and grease.

Parching. A technique of extreme drying of maize by placing already air- or sun-dried kernels in containers above the fire.

Patshatl. A word of the Nootka from Washington State that later was an-glicized as potlatch. The patshatl was a ceremonial feast on a grand scale held by Northwest Coast tribes at which huge amounts of food were consumed, material goods given away, and rank and/or status conferred on the honoree.

Pellagra. Niacin deficiency. It produces symptoms such as diarrhea, dermatitis and dementia, sometimes leading to death.

Pemmican. Dried meat, berries and tallow pounded together so that it becomes portable.

Piki. Wafer-thin blue maize bread; the sacred food of the Hopi of Arizona.

Pinyon. The name of a tree (pinyon pine) and its seeds that were gathered in Arizona, California, Colorado, Idaho, Nevada, New Mexico and Utah.

Pit roasting. Roasting in a stone-lined pit in the ground.

Pone. The anglicized version of the Algonquian word *apan*, meaning baked; refers to a flat baked maize bread.

Potlatch. See *Patshatl.*

Powcohiccora. The milky liquor that results from mashing pecans in water. It was made and consumed where pecans grew in the alluvial soils of the

Mississippi and its tributaries from Illinois and Iowa south to the Gulf Coast of Louisiana and west to part of Texas.

Quahog. A word derived from the Narragansett, referring to the hard-shelled round clam gathered in New England.

Rockweed. Brown seaweed gathered in the Northwest.

Sagamite. Name given by the French to a boiled maize dish made by Indians in the Southeast; also called *samp* by the English.

Saguaro. A very tall cactus, sometimes with arms, that grows throughout the Southwest.

Shaman. Medicine man or priest.

Shnaps. Parched fermented seeds of the yellow pond water lily, often eaten dry but usually moistened with water.

Sofki. A mixture of a maize gruel, water, crushed flint corn and ashes, simmered for several hours until thick, then allowed to sour for three days to make a symbolically important food to the Creek of the Southeast.

Someviki. A traditional Hopi dish made of parched blue maize meal, placed in dried husks and boiled, then served as wedding cake.

Spokwas. The most prized seeds of the yellow pond water lily that grew in Oregon and were gathered by the Klamath Indians.

Stone boiling. The earliest method of boiling, in which heated stones were placed in a vessel, removed as they cooled and replaced with hot stones; especially favored in those cultures in which water was scarce.

Sukquttahash. A Narragansett word later anglicized to succotash, meaning a mixture of boiled maize and beans, a dish adopted by the early colonists.

Tallow. Animal fat.

Tuna. The edible fruits of the prickly pear cactus.

Wapatoo. Nutritious, starchy bulbs of the Arrowhead plant, harvested most by the Northwest tribes.

Winnowing. The process in which kernels of maize (corn) are tossed in the air in a basket to separate the lighter kernels to the top from the heavier hulls concentrated at the bottom. After winnowing, the hulled kernels can easily be picked off the upper layer.

Wokas. The roasted acorn-sized seeds of the pods of the yellow pond water lily that grew in Oregon and were roasted by the Klamath Indians.

Xnois. The fruit of the submerged, saltwater vegetation called eelgrass that was gathered by the Northwest Coast Indians, principally the Seri of California.

SELECTED BIBLIOGRAPHY

GENERAL

The Cambridge History of the Native Peoples of the Americas. 3 vols. New York: Cambridge University Press, 1996–2000.

Driver, Harold E. *Indians of North America.* Chicago: University of Chicago Press, 1961.

Fussell, Betty. *The Story of Corn.* New York: Knopf, 1992.

Hoxie, Frederick E., ed. *Encylopedia of North American Indians: Native American History, Culture and Life from Paleo-Indians to the Present.* Boston: Houghton Mifflin, 1996.

Index of Native American Resources. http://www.hanksville.org/NAresources.

Kimball, Yeffe, and Jean Anderson. *The Art of American Indian Cooking.* Garden City, NY: Doubleday, 1965.

Maxwell, James A., ed. *America's Fascinating Indian Heritage.* Reissue ed. Pleasantville, NY: Reader's Digest Association, 1990.

Native American Technology and Art. http://www.nativetech.org/food.

Native Web. http://www.nativeweb.org.

Niethammer, Carolyn. *American Indian Food and Lore.* New York: Macmillan, 1974.

The Smithsonian Institution. http://www.si.edu.

Sturtevant, William C., general ed. *Handbook of North American Indians.* 13 vols. Washington, DC: Smithsonian Institution, 1978–2001.

Washburn, Wilcomb E., comp. *The American Indian and the United States: A Documentary History.* 4 vols. Westport, CT: Greenwood Press, 1979.

Weatherwax, Paul. *Indian Corn in Old America.* New York: Macmillan, 1954.

World Food Habits Bibliography. http://www.lilt.ilstu.edu/rtdirks/content_frame.htm.

REGIONAL

The American Indian Library Association. http://www.nativeculture.com/lisamitten/aila.html.

Cushing, Frank Hamilton. *Cushing at Zuni: The Correspondence and Journals of Frank Hamilton Cushing, 1879–1884.* Ed. Jesse Green. Albuquerque: University of New Mexico Press, 1990.

Edaakie, Rita, comp. *Idonapshe = Let's Eat: Traditional Zuni Foods: Stories and Recipes.* Albuquerque: University of New Mexico Press, 1999.

Fontana, Bernard I. *A Guide to Contemporary Southwest Indians.* Tucson, AZ: Southwest Parks and Monuments Association, 1999.

Frank, Lois Ellen. *Foods of the Southwest Indian Nations: Traditional & Contemporary Native American Recipes.* Berkeley, CA: Ten Speed Press, 2002.

Hudson, Charles M., ed. *Black Drink: A Native American Tea.* Athens: University of Georgia Press, 1979.

Kavena, Juanita Tiger. *Hopi Cookery.* Tucson: University of Arizona Press, 1980.

Keegan, Marcia. *Southwest Indian Cookbook.* Santa Fe, NM: Clear Light, 1990.

Jenks, Albert Ernest. *The Wild Rice Gatherers of the Upper Lakes: A Study in American Primitive Economics.* Lincoln, NE: J&L Reprint Co., 1977.

Mills, Earl, Sr., and Betty Breen. *Cape Cod Wampanoag Cookbook: Wampanoag Indian Recipes, Images & Lore.* Santa Fe, NM: Clear Light, 2001.

People of 'Ksan. *Gathering What the Great Nature Provided: Food Traditions of the Gitksan.* Seattle: University of Washington Press, 1980.

Russell, Howard S. *Indian New England Before the Mayflower.* Hanover, NH: University Press of New England, 1980.

Ulmer, Mary, and Samuel E. Beck, eds. *Cherokee Cooklore: Preparing Cherokee Foods.* Cherokee, NC: Museum of the Cherokee Indian, 1951.

INDEX

About the Author

LINDA MURRAY BERZOK is a food writer and historian who has contributed articles and essays to *Encyclopedia of Food and Drink in America* and *Encyclopedia of Food and Culture*, among others.

Edwards Brothers Malloy
Thorofare, NJ USA
April 6, 2012